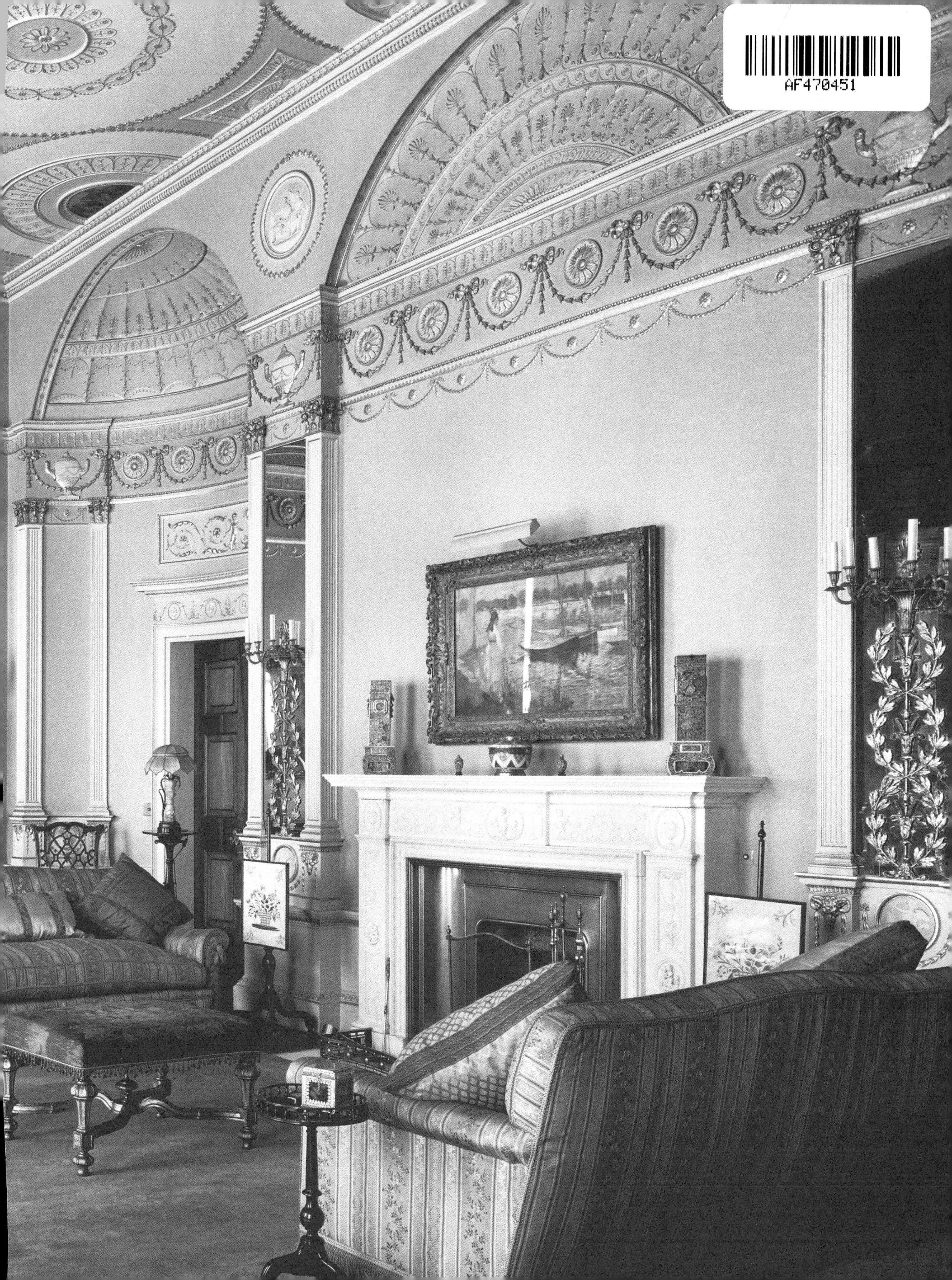
AF470451

Courtauld Impressionists

From Manet to Cézanne

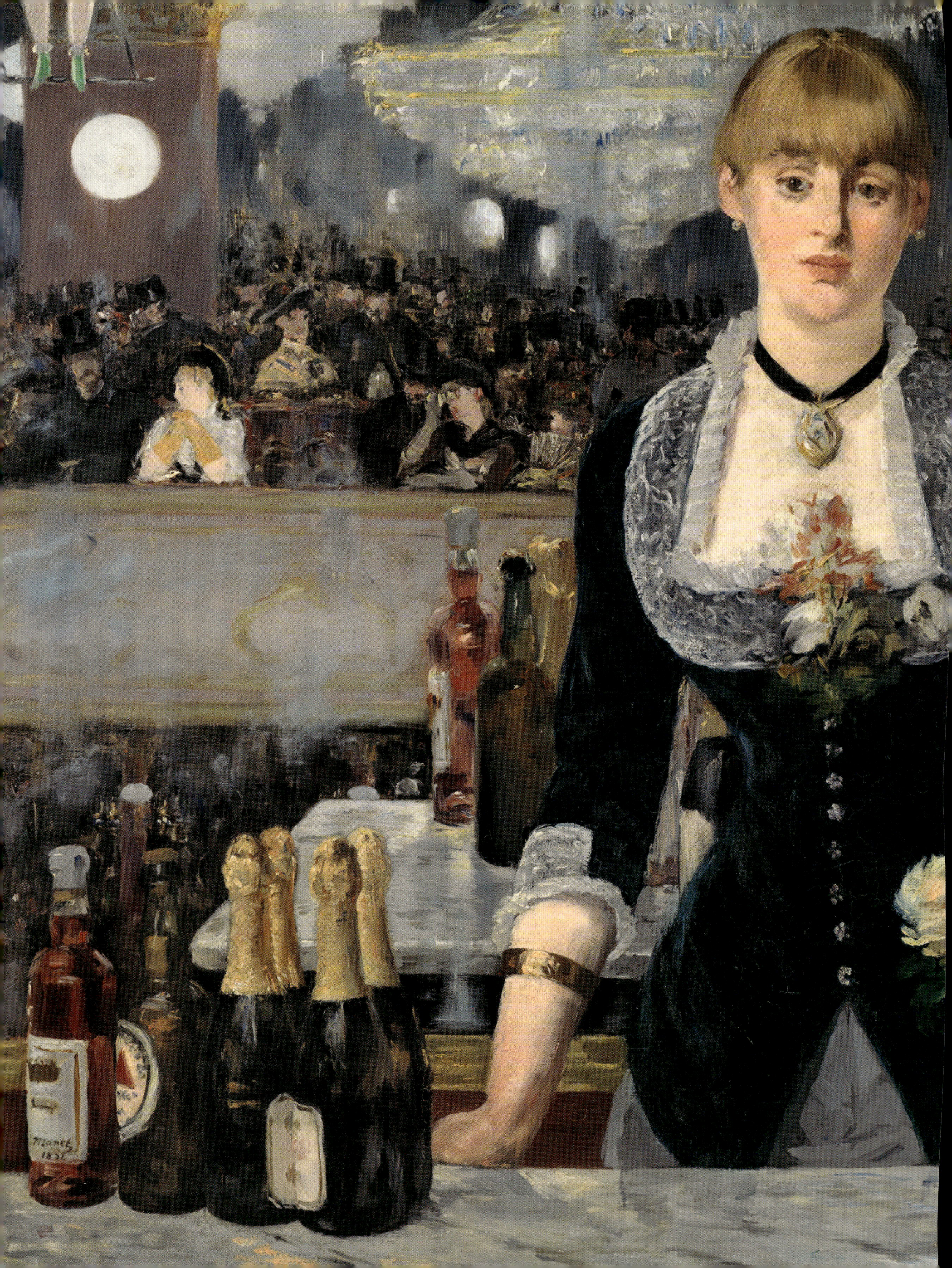

Manet
1882

Courtauld Impressionists

From Manet to Cézanne

Anne Robbins

With an essay by Caroline Campbell and contributions
by Christopher Riopelle, Sarah Herring, Rosalind McKever
and Julien Domercq

National Gallery Company, London
Distributed by Yale University Press

Published to accompany the exhibition
Courtauld Impressionists: From Manet to Cézanne
17 September 2018 – 20 January 2019

Exhibition sponsored by
BNP Paribas Real Estate

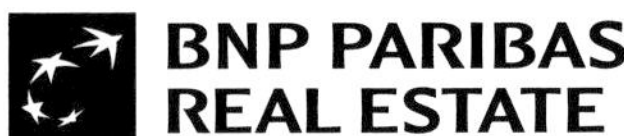

This exhibition has been made possible
by the provision of insurance through the
Government Indemnity Scheme.
The National Gallery would like to thank
HM Government for providing Government
Indemnity and the Department for Digital,
Culture, Media and Sport and Arts Council
England for arranging the indemnity.

First published in Great Britain in 2018 by
National Gallery Company Limited
St Vincent House
30 Orange Street
London WC2H 7HH
www.nationalgallery.co.uk

ISBN: 9781857096385
1046414

British Library Cataloguing-in-Publication
Data. A catalogue record is available from
the British Library.
Library of Congress Control Number:
2018947032

Publisher: Jan Green
Project Editor: Sophie Kullmann
Editor: Linda Schofield
Picture Researcher: Suzanne Bosman
Production: Jane Hyne

Designed by Mark Thomson
Printed in Italy by Printer Trento

All measurements give height before width

Front cover: Detail of Pierre-Auguste Renoir,
La Loge (Theatre Box), 1874
Back cover: Detail of Paul Cézanne,
Lac d'Annecy, 1896
Frontispiece: Detail of Edouard Manet, *A Bar
at the Folies-Bergère*, 1882

Endpapers (front): Home House, the Front
Drawing-Room, originally designed as the
Music-Room, photographed in 1932
Endpaper (back): Home House, the Front
Parlour looking west, photographed in 1932

KEY TO AUTHORS
JD   Julien Domercq
SH   Sarah Herring
RMcK   Rosalind McKever
CR   Christopher Riopelle
AR   Anne Robbins

Exhibition curated by Anne Robbins

Contents

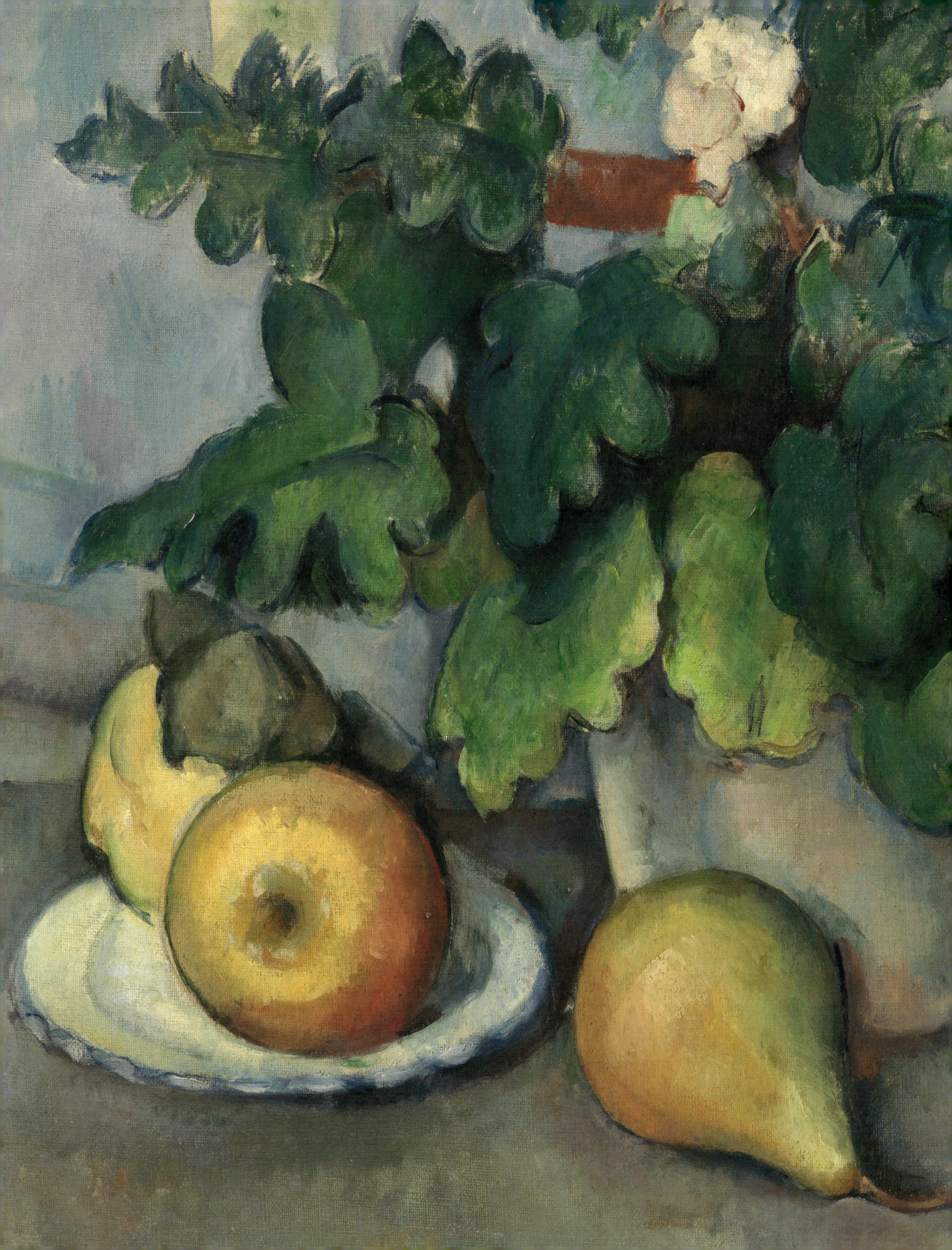

Director's Preface

The room at the National Gallery that attracts most visitors is invariably the one with paintings by Vincent van Gogh, Paul Gauguin and Georges Seurat. But there was a time when these artists, together with the French Impressionists, were not welcome. In 1905, more than 30 years after the first Impressionist exhibition, a proposed gift of a work by Claude Monet to the Gallery, to be paid for by public subscription, was turned down before it had progressed very far. A decade later a Gallery trustee responded to the offer from the dealer and collector, Hugh Lane, to show a group of modern French masters at the National Gallery by declaring that 'I should as soon expect to hear of a Mormon service being conducted in St Paul's Cathedral, as to see an exhibition of the modern French Art-rebels in the sacred precincts of Trafalgar Square'.

Samuel Courtauld (1876–1947), textile industry magnate, collector and philanthropist, did perhaps more than anyone to change these attitudes. Passionate about modern French painting, he established the Courtauld Fund in 1923 so that works by the most significant artists, including certain living painters, could be acquired for the nation. It is thanks to his vision and his munificence that Van Gogh's *Chair* and *Sunflowers*, Seurat's *Bathers at Asnières* and Paul Cézanne's *Self Portrait* came to form part of the Gallery's collection. The paintings he purchased for himself, among them Edouard Manet's *A Bar at the Folies-Bergère* and Gauguin's *Nevermore*, were to become the basis of the collection of the prestigious Courtauld Institute of Art, which he co-founded in 1932.

As the Institute embarks on 'Courtauld Connects', a major refurbishment project in 2018, this exhibition brings together a superb group of paintings that celebrate Samuel Courtauld's collecting and his public beneficence. It has been possible thanks to the extraordinary generosity of the Courtauld Gallery and we are enormously indebted to Lord Browne of Madingley, Chair of the Courtauld Institute of Art, and Andrew Adcock, Chair of the Samuel Courtauld Trust, Deborah Swallow, the Märit Rausing Director of the Courtauld Institute of Art, and to the Head of the Courtauld Gallery, Ernst Vegelin van Claerbergen, and his curator colleagues, Barnaby Wright and Karen Serres. We are also grateful to Maria Balshaw, Director of Tate, for her support of the exhibition. BNP Paribas Real Estate has sponsored *Courtauld Impressionists* and to them we want to say thank you.

Gabriele Finaldi

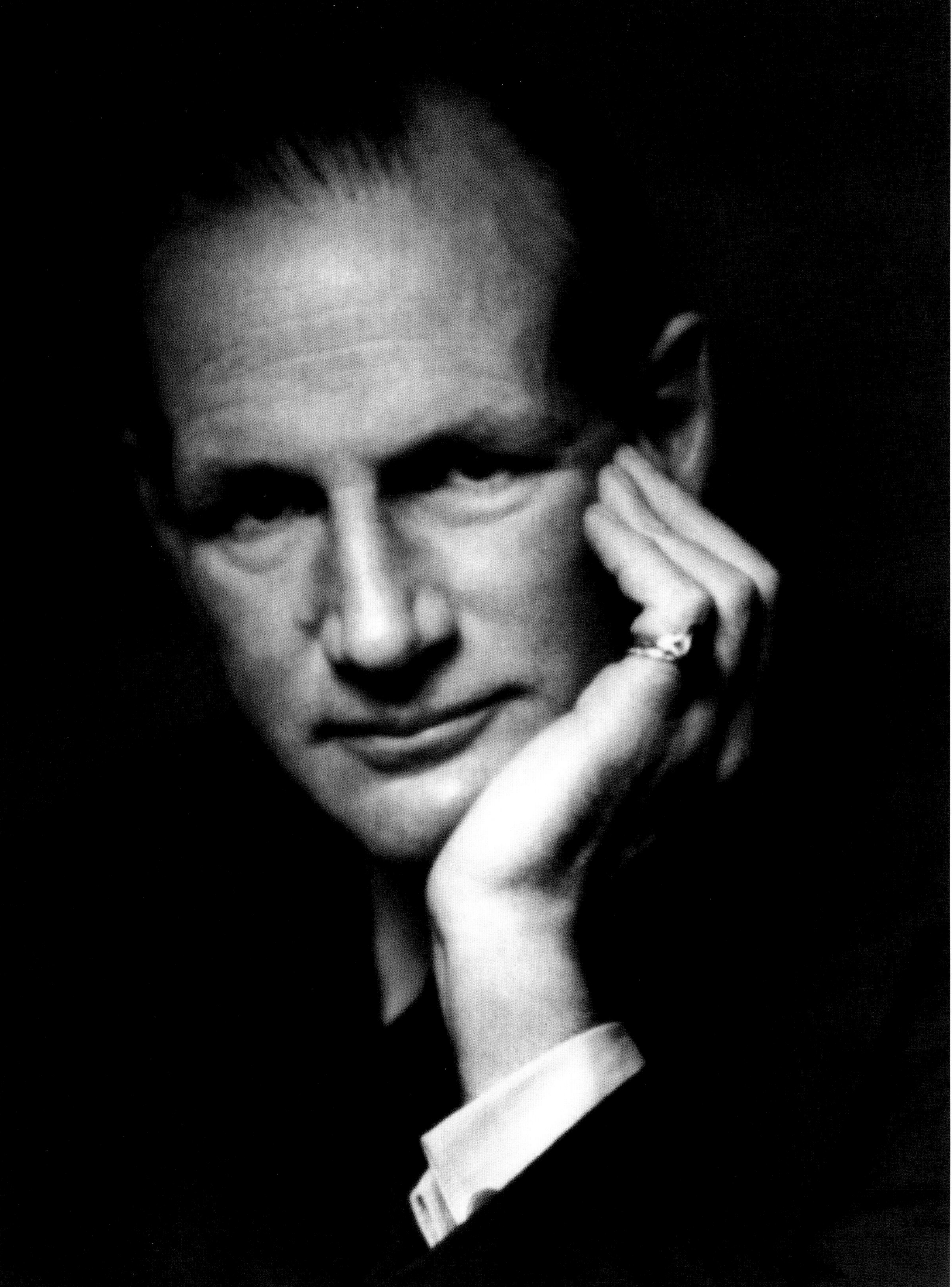

Caroline Campbell

Samuel Courtauld: Man and Collector

Paul Nash (1889–1946)
Samuel Courtauld's bookplate, 1930
The Samuel Courtauld Trust, The Courtauld
Gallery, London

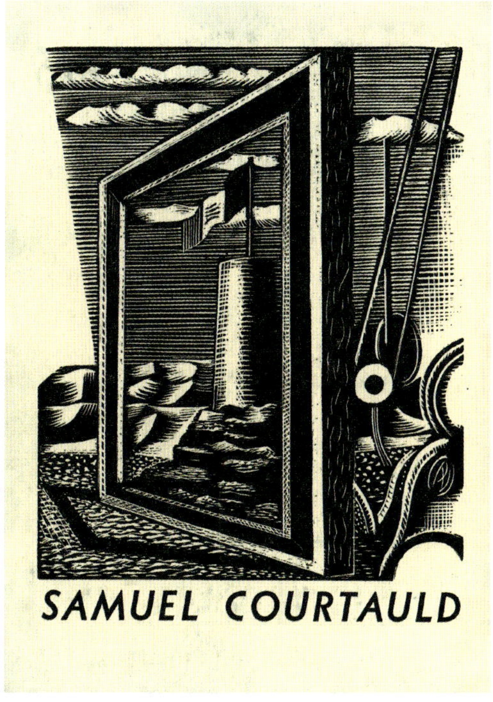

Who was Samuel Courtauld, and why did he, in a short time span, form two of the greatest collections of French Impressionist paintings in the world? Courtauld (1876–1947) was at once a conventional and a surprising man. He spent most of his life as an industrialist, turning his family's textile firm into a successful multinational business. But he is best known today for the two groups of French Impressionist paintings – one assembled for his own private enjoyment, and the other for the public good (see the essay by Anne Robbins, pp. 18–35) – that he amassed between 1922 and 1931, and for the Institute devoted to the study of art history and conservation that bears his name.

We can divine a certain amount about Courtauld, how he saw himself and how he wanted to be seen, from his bookplate, designed by Paul Nash in 1930.[1] Wood-engraved bookplates were *de rigueur* for members of the British cultured and wealthy elite of the late 1920s and early 1930s, and they are often illuminating about their commissioners' senses of identity. Courtauld's is composed of familiar objects, but arranged in a surprising fashion (even taking into account Nash's interest in Surrealism). A wooden frame is placed at an angle on what might be a floor or a table. Does this allude to Courtauld's collecting and his belief in the transcendental powers of art? Through it, we see a tower, topped with a French flag, standing against a seascape, which, bizarrely, continues behind the frame. The tower, although it looks to be made of sand rather than of stone, is probably a Martello tower, one of many dotted along the East Anglian coast, built in the early nineteenth century to protect the English coastline from Napoléon Bonaparte's forces; it could also refer to La Rochelle, the French port near the Courtaulds' ancestral home on the French island of Oléron. This motif combines the Courtauld family's French origins, their proud British identity, and the concentration of their family and business life in Essex. To the right of the frame, a bobbin and two threads refer to Courtauld's public position, as managing director and subsequently chairman of his family's fabric company. Taken together, these suggest a captain

Left: Portrait of Samuel Courtauld, 1935
The Samuel Courtauld Trust, The Courtauld
Gallery, London

of industry who enjoyed an inner intellectual and spiritual life, which was based
on the powers of seeing.

Samuel Courtauld was perhaps the most illustrious member of a family who
together have made a significant impact on British economic, social and cultural
life. He was born in the Essex town of Bocking in 1876. His father, Sydney, was
employed in the family's textile business, centred in Bocking and the neighbouring
towns of Braintree and Halstead, and his mother, Sarah, was the daughter of a
north London solicitor. Both families were Unitarians,[2] and Samuel's parents had
married at the celebrated dissenting chapel at Newington Green in Islington.
Samuel's childhood was comfortable and moneyed, but unlike many comparable
late Victorian childhoods it was not isolated from the world in a cosy cocoon. Like
many Unitarians, Sydney and Sarah Courtauld had a strong sense of the social
responsibility that money and business gave, and of the importance of education.
They put these beliefs into action, with a paternalistic care for those who depended
on them financially, which was typical of many Unitarian industrialists. In 1888,
during a period of decline in the textile trade, they gave their garden to the people
of Bocking 'whither the tired mechanic could resort, with his wife and children and
where the industrious tradesman could escape for a brief spell from his cares and
worries of business'[3] (we can only imagine how the Courtaulds' young children felt
about this). Sarah was part of the first generation of women to take a sanctioned –
if limited – role in British public life. In 1872 she joined the School Board of
Braintree, two years after W. E. Forster's Education Act, which had established
elected school boards to provide non-denominational education, funded by local
rates. These were among the first state entities in Britain in which women were
allowed to vote on the same terms as men, and could stand for election.

It is perhaps not surprising that Sydney and Sarah's six children – to a greater
or lesser extent – used their privileges and financial resources for the common good.
The girls, Sydney Renée (1873–1962) and Catherine (1878–1972), were given the same
educational chances as their brothers and, together with many members of the
wider Courtauld clan and other affluent Unitarian families, were actively involved
in the women's suffrage movement.[4] William Julien (1870–1940), who like Samuel
entered the family business straight after school, was High Sherriff of Essex, and
his gifts to his local community included Braintree Town Hall and Registry Office,
and the local hospital.[5] John (1880–1942) sat as Conservative MP for Chichester
from 1924 until his death.[6] He and Stephen (1883–1967), the youngest Courtauld
child, were both awarded the Military Cross for their active service during the First
World War. Stephen – who is perhaps best known today for his jet-set lifestyle and
the reconstruction of Eltham Palace as an Art Deco mansion – should instead be
celebrated for the significant difference that he and his wife Virginia made to the life

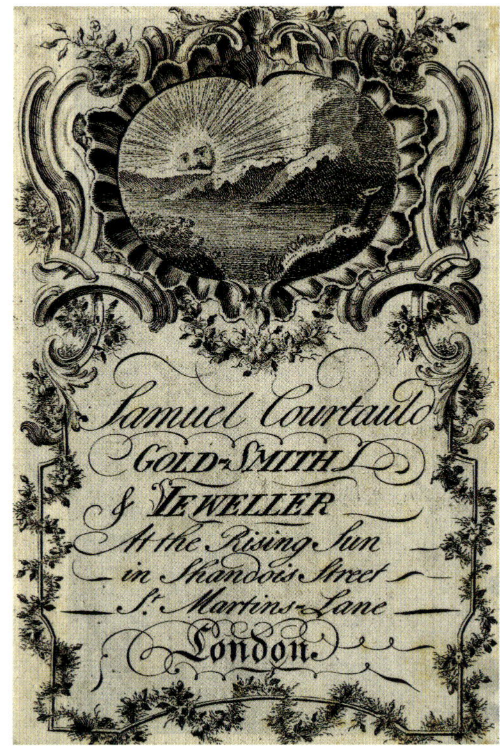

Trade card of Samuel Courtauld, Goldsmith &
Jeweller at the Rising Sun, 1740–50s
British Museum, London, Heal, 67.94

of Southern Rhodesia (now Zimbabwe), where they settled in 1951.[7]

The moral compass that guided Samuel and his siblings was shaped by their faith, their ancestry and their business interests. The Courtauld family had come to England in the late seventeenth century, fleeing religious persecution. They were among the 50,000 or so French Protestants (called Huguenots) who left France after Louis XIV revoked the Edict of Nantes in 1685, cancelling the civic rights of non-Catholics in his domains. These refugees were France's loss, but England's gain. If one were to characterise the Huguenots, it would be as model citizens and intensely hard-working: examples of the so-called 'Protestant work ethic' identified by Samuel Courtauld's contemporary, Max Weber.[8] The Courtaulds settled in London, part of a community of French refugees that was centred in Soho, or in Spitalfields. Most Huguenots were employed in either silk weaving or gold and silver smithery. Samuel's ancestors started in the latter – between 1708 and 1780, three generations of the family were registered with the Goldsmiths' Company[9] – and moved to the former. In 1780, Samuel Courtauld I (1752–1821), the family's last metalworker, left a partnership with his mother, Louisa,[10] in order to emigrate to the USA, where he began a career as an 'itinerant merchant', according to the account of his brother George.[11]

George (1761–1823) was a radical, who had been apprenticed as a silk weaver, and he experimented with various means of mechanising this trade.[12] He was a talented entrepreneur, but a somewhat inept businessman. It was his son, Samuel III (1793–1881), who became an important silk manufacturer. Courtauld and Taylor – created by Samuel with his partner and brother-in-law Peter Taylor (1819–1891) and his

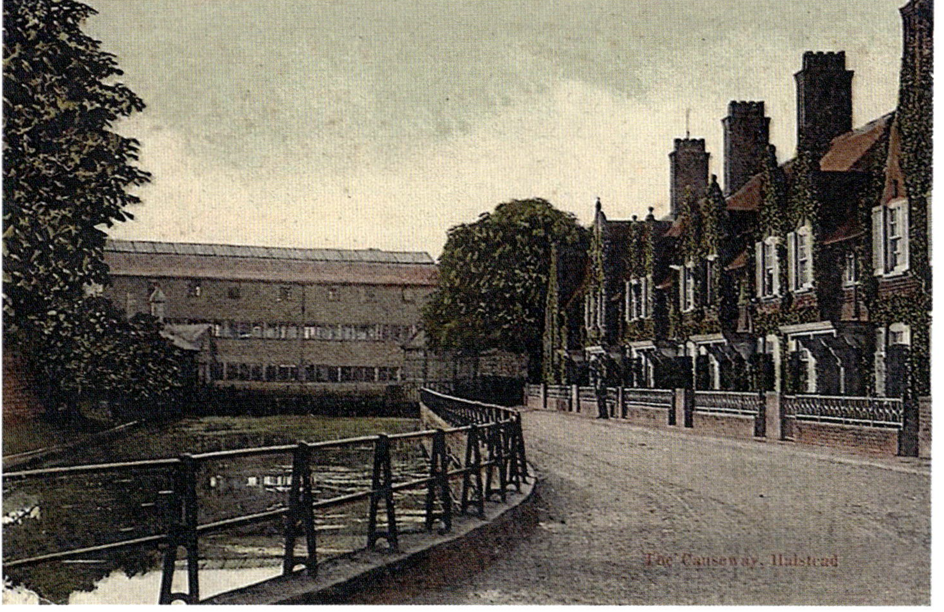

Postcard of Halstead silk mill and workers'
cottages, about 1900
Private collection

brother George (1802–1861) – used steam power to produce silk yarns in the Essex towns of Braintree, Bocking and Halstead. By the middle years of the nineteenth century it was a considerable enterprise, which prospered through the Victorian obsession with death. The firm's principal production was silk crape, in which widows were supposed to swathe themselves for two years after their spouse's demise. In a society in which respectable citizens were required to enter mourning for relatives on both sides of the family, and where it was thought unacceptable to recycle 'widow's weeds', the opportunities for profit were considerable. By the early 1870s, the return on the surviving partners' capital was more than 48 per cent.[13]

Under the leadership of Samuel Courtauld IV, and his predecessor as chairman, Henry Greenwood Tetley (1851–1921), the Courtauld business was transformed from an Essex concern into one of the world's leading textile and chemical companies, but which – despite its scale – aspired to care for its workers' well-being. Courtauld's factories were substantial enterprises, employing large percentages of the population in each locality. They made a significant impact on the social and economic make-up of these towns and cities, as did their decline and fall. In particular, their large female workforce transformed many communities.[14] Thanks to Tetley, the Courtaulds were able to diversify out of crape and embrace the great opportunities provided by synthetic fabrics. By 1905, the firm had opened a massive operation producing artificial silk at Coventry in the West Midlands, far from its East Anglia heartland. And in 1909 it had acquired the monopoly of the highly lucrative North American market. Meanwhile Samuel, who had gone straight from Rugby School to study the silk industry in Germany and France, was running the silk mill at Halstead, and from 1908 was the general manager of all the firm's textile's operations. In 1917 he was appointed joint managing director, and in 1921 on Tetley's death, chairman. The next nine years were ones of extraordinary financial success, although (in retrospect) they were dangerously dependent on rayon, in the form of viscose (ranging from women's stockings to tyre cords) and cellulose acetate.[15] Over £2 million per annum was paid out in shareholders' dividends between 1924 and 1928. The company weathered the economic crash of 1929, and its conservative financial management and advantages of scale enabled it not just to survive, but to prosper. By the 1930s Courtauld PLC was an international brand, with factories across Britain (for instance in Flintshire, Wolverhampton and Preston), France, Italy, Germany and North America.[16] In the postwar period it would expand further across Britain and the world, including in the Far East. But never again would the company, or its profits, match the heady days of the 1920s.

It was at this point of Courtauld PLC's greatest prosperity that Samuel Courtauld began, with little apparent warning, to purchase art on a grand scale.

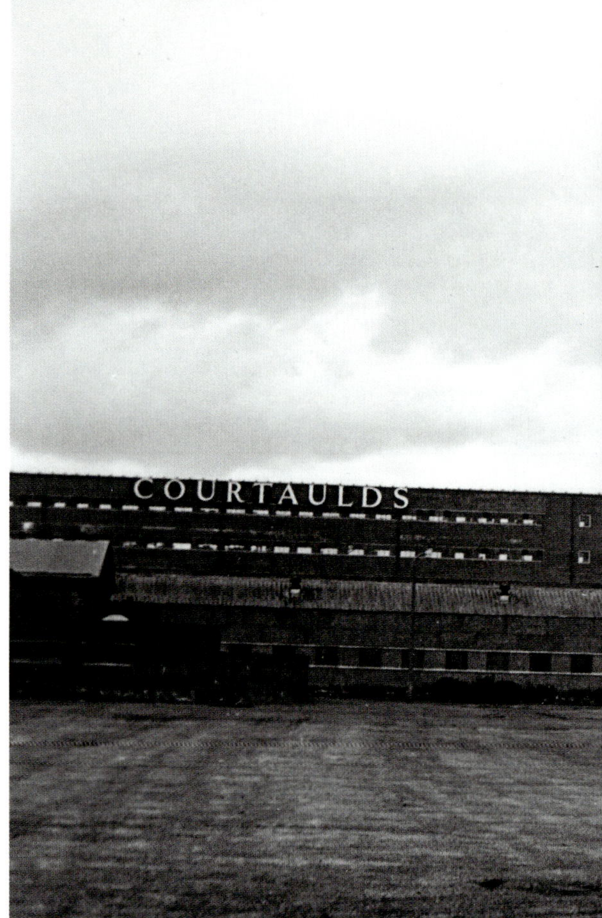

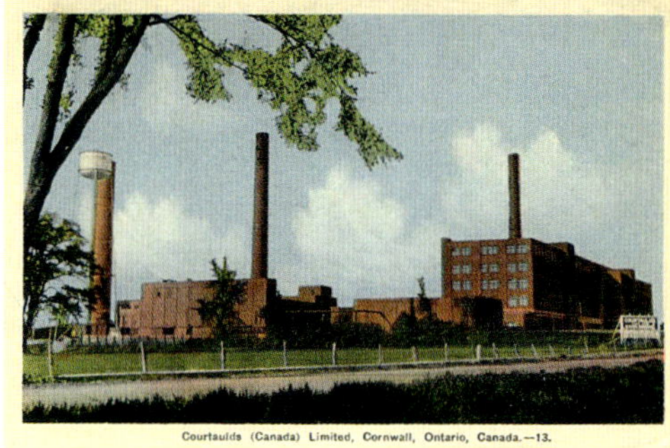

The Courtauld factory in Carrickfergus, County Antrim, about 1950
National Museums Northern Ireland

Postcard of Courtaulds (Canada) Limited, Cornwall, Ontario, Canada, 1950s
Courtesy Lily Worrall

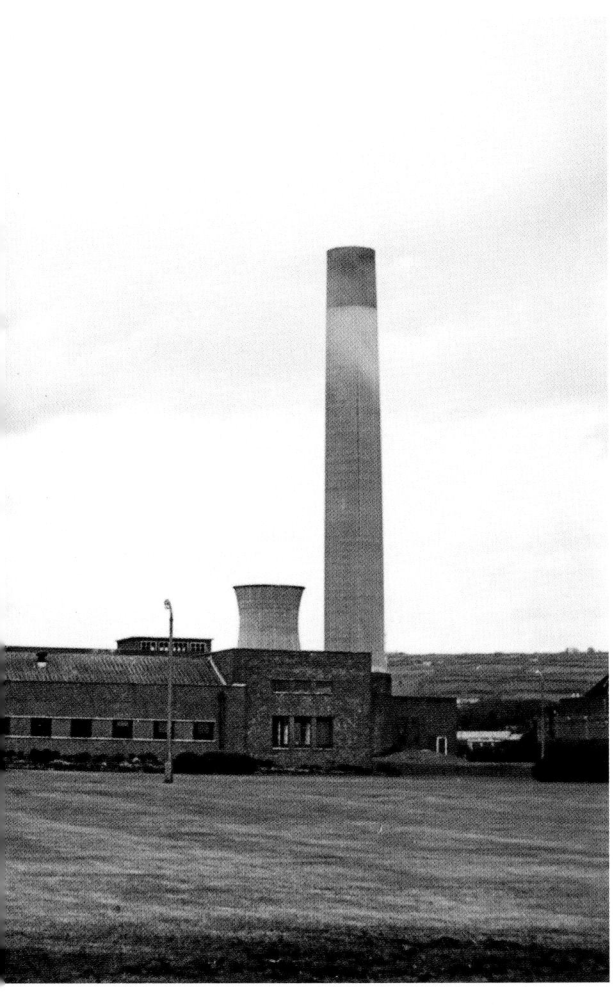

This seems to have been a joint enterprise undertaken with his beloved wife Elizabeth.[17] Courtauld had not grown up in a consciously 'artistic' family, for all that Bocking Place had contained some pictures and antiquities inherited by his mother from the collection formed by the early nineteenth-century poet and National Gallery trustee Samuel Rogers (1762–1855),[18] and he had not enjoyed his early visits to the National Gallery (see the essay by Anne Robbins, pp. 18–35). The transformation, as for so many of his generation, happened in Florence, under the impact of the great paintings of the Italian Renaissance, even if this change was not as emphatic or as quick as it was for Lucy Honeychurch, the heroine of E.M. Forster's 1908 novel *A Room with a View*. As Courtauld himself was to later write of this trip:

> The old masters had come alive to me, and British academic art died. In the former I now perceived a wonderful mastery allied with strong emotion and with life itself; I felt strong and exciting currents still flowing beneath the surface of the paint. In the latter I felt nothing but artificiality and convention, and could detect no progress in technique.[19]

This holiday seems to have alerted Courtauld to what was lacking in the paintings of his contemporaries.[20] The call to action, however, was slow, and in the medium term Elizabeth and he found solace in music.[21] Everything changed with two exhibitions in London – in Courtauld's own words: 'My second real "eye-opener" was the Hugh Lane collection which was exhibited in London at the National Gallery in 1917.'[22] The great works of Edouard Manet, Hilaire-Germain-Edgar Degas and Pierre-Auguste Renoir shown there made a deep impression on him, as did subsequently the paintings of Paul Cézanne. On seeing *The François Zola Dam*, then owned by Gwendoline Davies (now National Museum of Wales), in London in the summer of 1922, Courtauld recalled: 'At that moment I felt the magic, and I have felt it in Cézanne's work ever since'.[23] These were the great modern works for which he had been looking. Now roused, Courtauld began almost immediately to purchase modern French paintings: the first two pictures, acquired in September of this year, had been painted between 1918 and 1921.[24]

As his collection developed, however, it followed the enthusiasm of Roger Fry for Georges Seurat and Cézanne, as well as concentrating on 'High Impressionist' paintings by Claude Monet, Renoir and Manet of the 1870s and early 1880s.[25] But no one other than Courtauld himself, and Elizabeth, was responsible for the formation of the collection. Although he trusted the dealer Percy Moore Turner[26] – through whom he made many purchases for his private collection, and some for the Courtauld Fund, and whom he asked to hang his pictures in Home House

Overleaf: The Front Parlour looking east, Home House, 1932
Photograph
Country Life

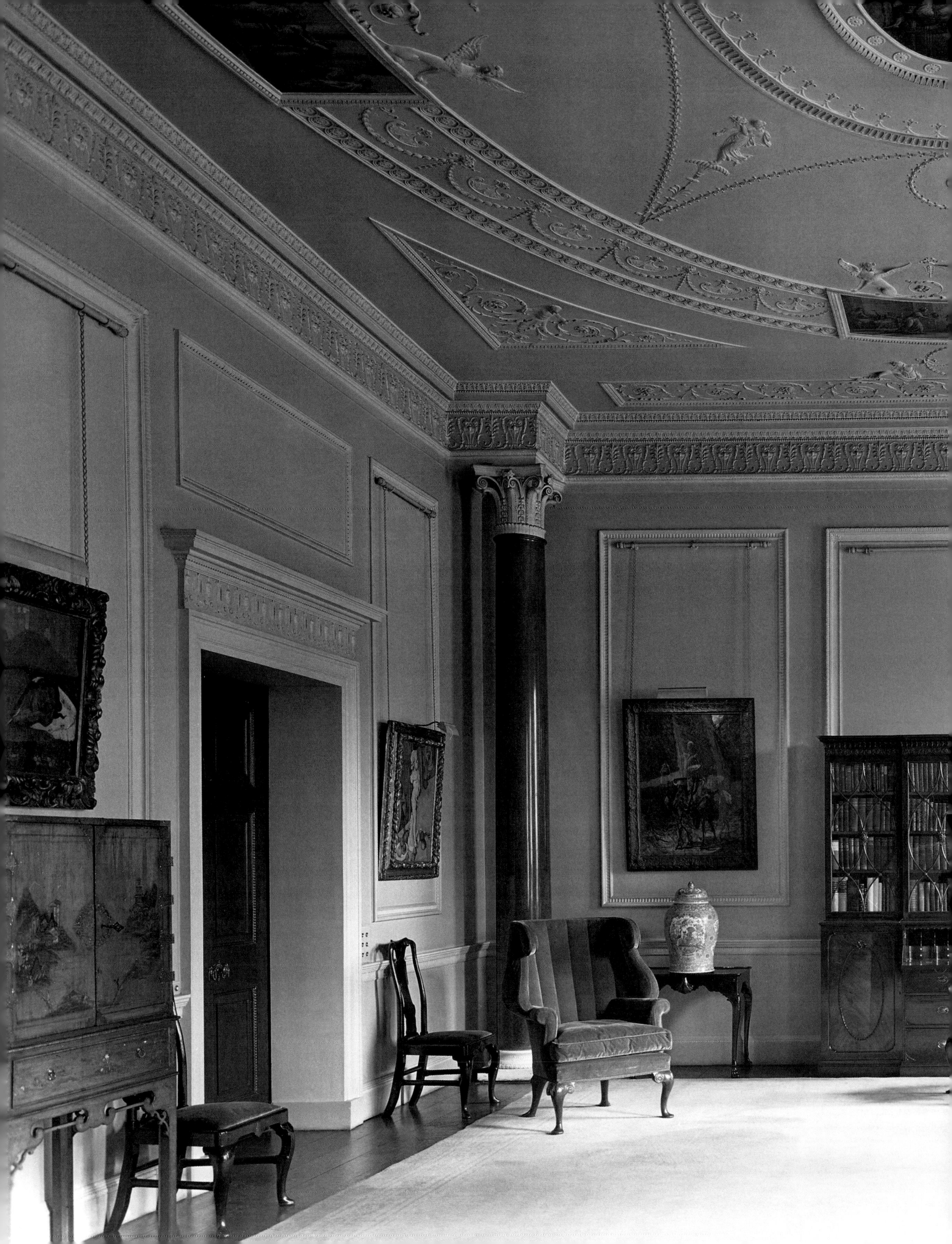

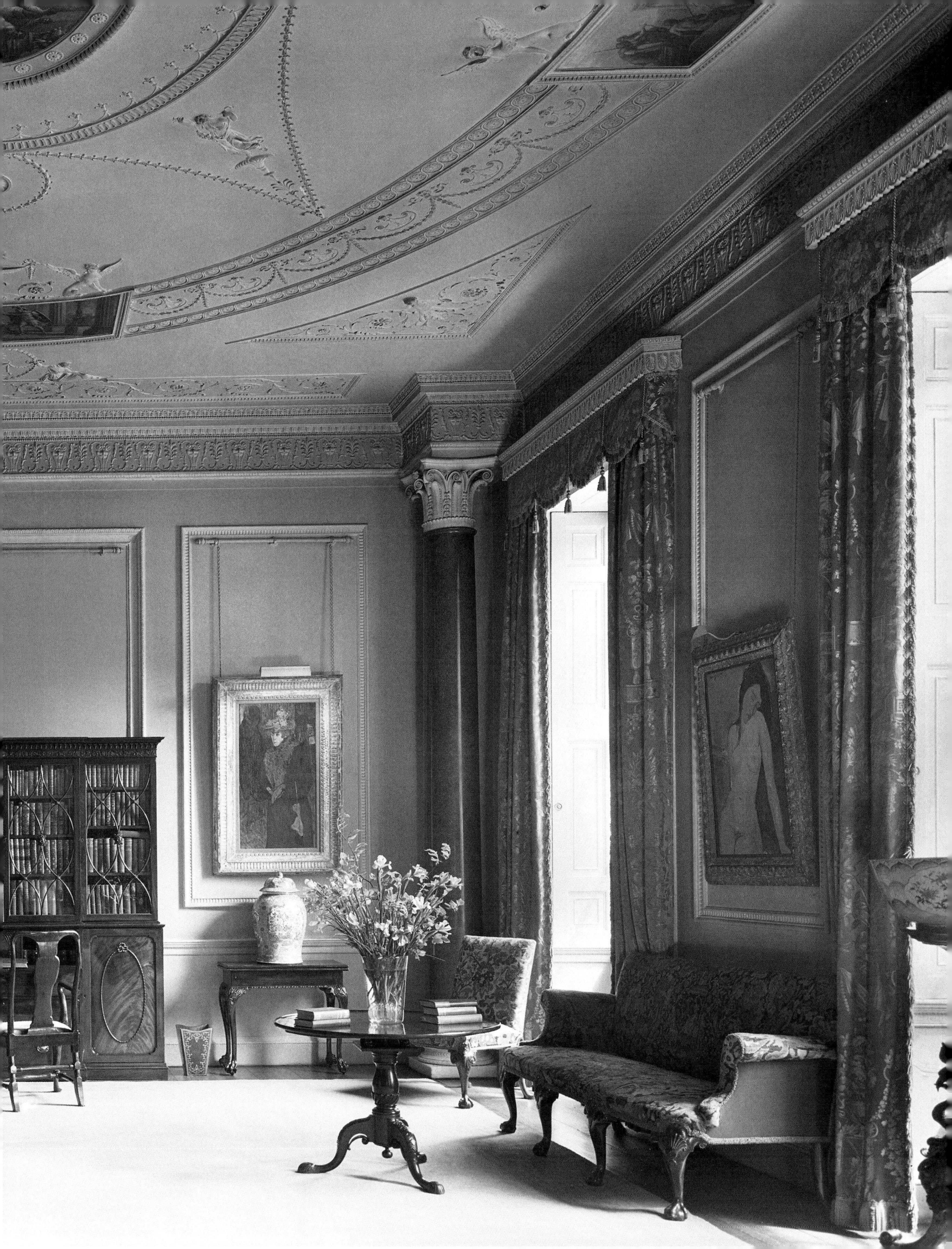

(the great Robert Adam mansion to which the Courtaulds moved in 1926) – he ultimately depended on his and his wife's judgement.

Owning pictures, and looking at them, was evidently a very personal matter for Courtauld. He wished to see almost all the many works that were offered to him in the flesh, never buying on hearsay, and always – if at all practicable – living with the piece in his own home before reaching a decision to purchase it.[27] Photographs taken of Home House in the early 1930s (pp. 14–15 and endpapers) show the special ahistorical synergy that existed between Adam's architecture and Courtauld's collection. His reactions to paintings were instinctive, highly personal, based on their 'spiritual and emotional significance' to him,[28] and how they fired his 'insight and imagination'.[29] He was endlessly inspired and rejuvenated by looking at outstanding art, because 'unfettered imagination, human emotion and spiritual aspiration go into the creation of all great works, and a share of the same qualities is needed for the reading of them.'[30]

It is telling that Courtauld's picture buying ceased abruptly as a result of Elizabeth's sudden illness and death in 1931. This tragic event offered the ever-opportunistic Arthur Lee an ideal hook on which to persuade Courtauld to back the Institute of Art History and Conservation, which they were ultimately to found the following year, with Sir Robert Witt. The Courtauld Institute, in training those art experts who would themselves educate a wide public, would be a living memorial to the ideas that had inspired Elizabeth and Samuel Courtauld: that art had the power to change lives. Courtauld's hope for the institute that bore his name, and for the pictures that he and his Fund had acquired, was that they could enable others to be inspired by great art. The true love of art, he wrote, came from being an 'unadultered amateur' and responding spontaneously to the power of the visual.[31]

Courtauld was an idealist, who viewed art as: 'universal and eternal, it ties race to race, and epoch to epoch. It overleaps divisions and unites men in one all-embracing and disinterested and living pursuit.'[32] In his only public musings on the benefits of culture, published in 1949, two years after his death, Courtauld argued that the public needed to be educated against a 'barbarous taste', and a 'vulgar' culture of popular entertainment that had 'nothing whatever to do with art and beauty',[33] to enable them 'to envisage something – if only a little – beyond the bare necessities of existence'.[34] He was gratified by the mass audiences for classical music concerts and art exhibitions during the Second World War. For him these were evidence, at a moment of national crisis, 'of a new and almost universal groping after those spiritual values of which art rightly claims a share'.[35] This must have given Samuel Courtauld a sense of pride, although (typically for a modest man) he did not express it. For it was precisely as a practical means of 'raising the general level of public taste' that he had established the Courtauld Fund, and endowed the one and only British institute of art history and conservation with his three most prized possessions: his name, his income and his private collection.

I would like to acknowledge Ernst Vegelin van Claerbergen's very helpful comments on this essay.

1 'Sam Courtauld and Paul met at a dinner party I gave at Number 15 The Street, and Courtauld persuaded Paul to design a bookplate for him. The result was one of the most charming he ever made.' See Sieveking 1957.

2 As a creed Unitarianism was bedevilled by dissent, precisely because Unitarians held that religion should not be trammelled by fixed doctrine. However, most Unitarians were consistent in their denial of the Trinity and original sin, and their belief that rational education could change everything. George Courtauld (1761–1823), Samuel's great-grandfather, introduced the family to Unitarianism.

3 Bardell 2012.

4 Sydney Renée Courtauld was educated at Roedean School and Newnham College, Cambridge. She worked as a social worker, including at the Women's University Settlement (which placed university-educated women in deprived parts of London, where she met Octavia Hill, founder of the National Trust), and was an active member of suffrage societies in London and Essex. After the female vote was partially achieved, in 1918, she lobbied her MP to support women's membership to the University of Cambridge. She was a champion of the National Trust, and in particular of women in education. In her will, she left bequests to promote female access to education. Her younger sister Catherine worked as an artist, and used her artistic production in the cause of women's suffrage, being a member of the Suffrage Atelier. Several of her suffrage designs were produced as posters and postcards. See https://courtauld.ac.uk/celebrating-courtauld-suffragette-centenary-representation-people-act-1918 for Catherine's art in the cause of the vote. For more on both sisters and the wider Courtauld family involvement in suffrage, see Crawford 1999, pp. 142–3.

5 The William Julien Courtauld Hospital was sold by Mid-Essex Hospitals NHS Trust to a housing development firm in 2013.

6 www.theyworkforyou.com/mp/21374/john_courtauld/chichester (accessed May 2018).

7 In 1951 Stephen and Virginia Courtauld settled in the Eastern Rhodesian highlands, where they built an estate at La Rochelle, outside Mutare. Stephen died there, and in accordance with both their wishes, Virginia bequeathed the property to the National Trust of Zimbabwe in 1972. They supported the local people and their workers by establishing an agricultural training farm, a school, and a theatre and multiracial club in Mutare. On a national level, they were major champions of Zimbabwe's National Gallery, the College of Music and the University of Rhodesia, and they financially backed the Capricorn Society, a body that sought to improve relations between the different peoples of the British-administered sub-Sahara.

8 Weber (1904–5) 1932.

9 For the fullest account of the Courtaulds as silversmiths, see Braham 2003.

10 Murdoch 1994, p. 49; Stephen T. Clarke, Harley Preston and Tim Barton, 'The Courtauld Family', *Oxford Art* online: www.doi.org/10.1093/gao/97818846054.article.t019923 (accessed July 2018).

11 Murdoch 1994, p. 49.

12 Ibid.

13 Ibid., p. 50.

14 For the fullest account of Courtaulds as a company, see Coleman 1969–80. This account is indebted to Professor Coleman's magnum opus. Coleman notes that some contemporary commentators were critical of the company's attitude to its workers.

15 Murdoch 1994, p. 52.

16 In 1909, Courtaulds had moved to the American market, with the purchase of J. R. Pettit's viscose process patents. An American company, AUC, was formed under the aegis of Courtaulds. In 1941, Courtaulds was forced to sell AUC to the Americans as part of the UK-American deal that led to the ratification of Lend-Lease.

17 Samuel Courtauld and Elizabeth Kelsey ('Lil', 1875–1931) had married in 1901. Their only child, Sydney Elizabeth (1902–1951), was born the following year. She was to marry the Conservative politician 'Rab' Butler.

18 Blunt 1954, p. 2. Among the paintings that Rogers bequeathed the National Gallery was Titian's *Noli me Tangere* (NG270).

19 Quoted in Blunt 1954, p. 3.

20 His efforts to develop this in Britain are shown by the financial support he gave the London Artists' Association from 1925, the Contemporary Art Society and the East London Art Group. See Stephenson 1994, pp. 41–2.

21 Music was Elizabeth's true love. In 1925–7, the Courtaulds directed the Covent Garden Opera, and after Elizabeth's death Samuel continued the Sargent-Courtauld concerts that she had founded with Sir Malcolm Sargent. These were intended to give everyone access to good classical music, regardless of their income.

22 Quoted in Blunt 1954, p. 3.

23 Ibid., p. 4.

24 Courtauld's first acquisitions were *Saint Paul, Côte d'Azur* by Jean-Hippolyte Marchand, and Renoir's *Woman Tying her Shoe*, cats. 28 and 43 in London 1994, pp. 22, 112, 142, 221.

25 House 1994, pp. 22–3.

26 For the fullest account of Percy Moore Turner, see Turner 2018.

27 House 1994, p. 23.

28 Quoted in Blunt 1954, p. 8.

29 Ibid., p. 7.

30 Ibid.

31 Ibid., p. 6.

32 Courtauld 1949, p. 45.

33 Ibid., p. 49.

34 Ibid., p. 48

35 Ibid., p. 52.

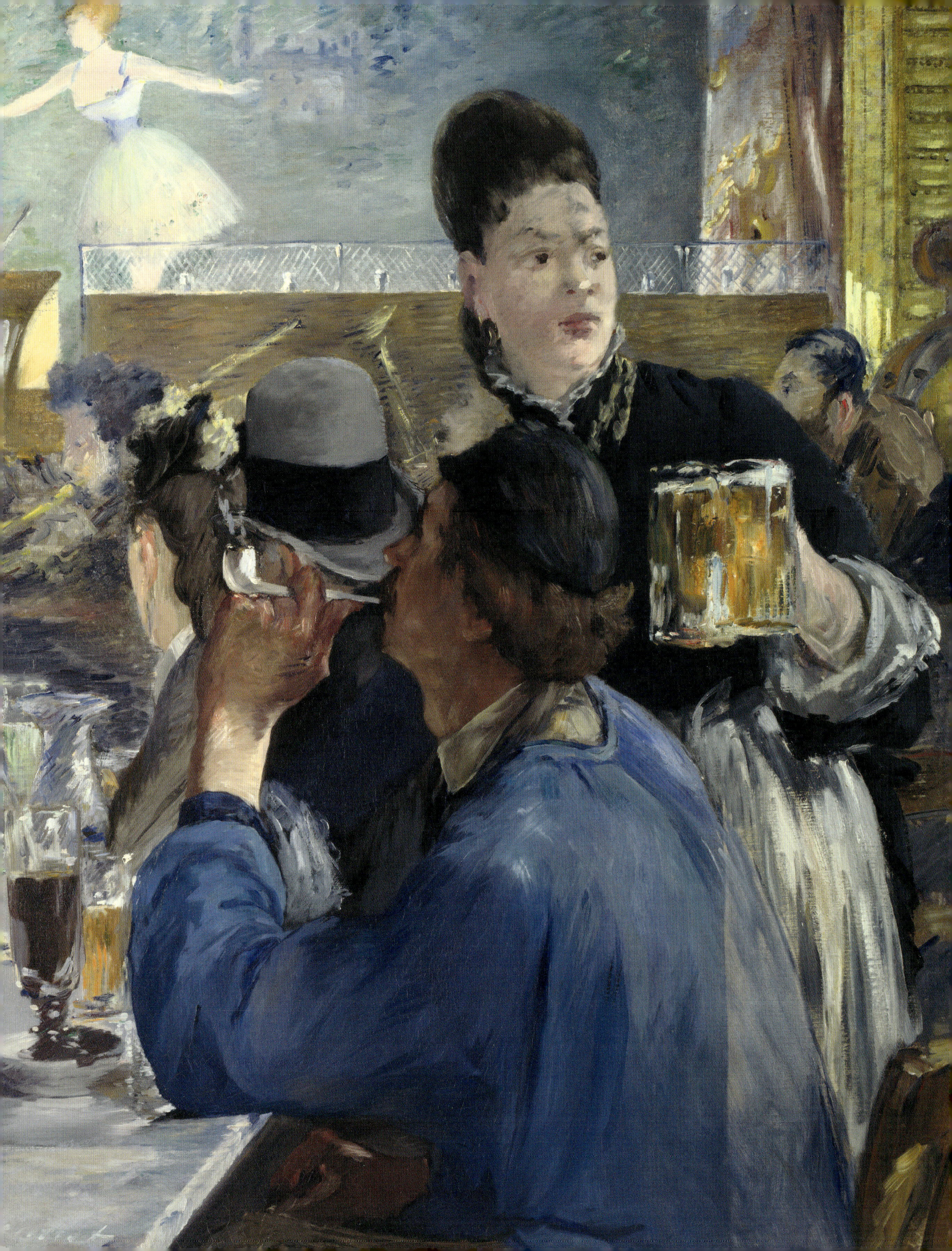

Anne Robbins

Courtauld and the National Gallery: 'An assault on a big scale'

Samuel Courtauld, July 1936
The Samuel Courtauld Trust, The Courtauld
Gallery, London

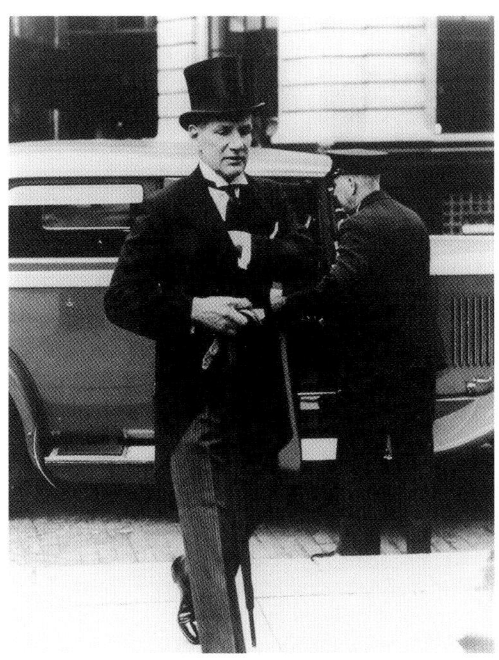

The remarkable achievements of Samuel Courtauld as a collector, his extraordinary public-spirited benefactions and firm commitment to fostering the knowledge and appreciation of modern art have long been celebrated, not least at the National Gallery, where his legacy is profoundly felt.[1] His first act of generosity was towards the national collection, in the form of a munificent gift of £50,000 for the purchase of recent French pictures in the 1920s. These were then still considered contentious in Britain, and hardly represented on the walls of its museums and public art galleries. Courtauld's gesture had a far-reaching effect: in less than three years, starting in 1923, the paintings acquired from this special fund transformed the national collection by introducing artists like Georges Seurat, Vincent van Gogh and Paul Cézanne, whose reputation in Britain had until then mostly been negative; it was immediately recognised as 'an assault on a scale big enough to overwhelm… obstinacy and ignorance'.[2] Today these paintings form the core of the Post-1800 holdings at the National Gallery in Trafalgar Square, a collection Courtauld not only funded but brought together on his own terms, while at the same time building a first-rank collection of paintings for himself. They reflect his personal taste, his hesitations and dilemmas, and above all his absolute faith in the educational power of art.

Courtauld was born into a cultivated Unitarian family in which the arts were taken seriously. His early introduction to painting involved childhood trips to the National Gallery, which he recalled with mixed feelings, daunted by the 'rarefied atmosphere of education and sanctity which damped [his] spirits as [he] approached its portals.'[3] Courtauld would later develop an intense interest in the Old Masters while spending time in France for his family's artificial silk business and during a holiday in Italy in 1901. At the National Gallery he was impressed by more recent pictures, 'enjoy[ing] the rich colours of Turner's *Fighting Temeraire* and *Ulysses deriding Polyphemus.*'[4] These, then, were among the National Gallery's most 'modern' paintings. It was not in its remit to collect contemporary painting, let alone recent

Edouard Manet (1832–1883)
Corner of a Café-Concert, probably 1878–80
Oil on canvas, 97.1 × 77.5 cm
The National Gallery, London
NG3858

foreign art; the rare examples on the Gallery's walls resulted from isolated gifts and bequests. In 1897 the Tate Gallery, located at Millbank, had been created as the National Gallery of British Art. However, until 1917 it was neither in the National Gallery's nor the Tate's mandate (both then part of the same institution) to collect modern foreign paintings. Crucially, this coincided with or possibly resulted from an entrenched resistance towards the latest developments in Continental painting. In 1905 an attempt to 'force the gates' of the National Gallery with the gift of a landscape by Claude Monet, offered by public subscription, was dramatically unsuccessful. Yet for all its reticence to such art, the Gallery triggered what Courtauld later described as his conversion to Impressionism: in 1917 the exhibition of paintings from the bequest of Irish dealer and collector Sir Hugh Lane proved for him an 'eye opener'.[5] The show featured major works by such 'advanced' painters as Edouard Manet and the Impressionists, and Courtauld remembered especially Renoir's *Umbrellas*, Manet's *Music in the Tuileries Gardens* (p. 89) and Degas's *Beach Scene*.[6] The pictures formed a small nucleus, supplemented the following year by 13 French paintings purchased at the posthumous auction of Degas's collection in Paris, including a still life by Paul Gauguin and important works by Manet, marking the first sign of the Gallery's active commitment to the cause of representing modern French painting. Also in 1918, the dealer and patron of the arts Sir Joseph Duveen announced he would finance the construction of a building to house this burgeoning group of Impressionist and Post-Impressionist paintings: a gift gratefully accepted. The new national gallery of modern foreign painting would be erected on a vacant site at the back of the Tate.

While the start of the actual construction of the new gallery was much delayed by the First World War, attitudes were slowly changing; exhibitions and publications were widening the knowledge of Impressionism and Post-Impressionism in Britain. A regular visitor to galleries, Courtauld's artistic sensibility was developing as fast as his financial means. The family company was turning into a major textile multinational, expanding rapidly. Already an accomplished businessman, in 1921 he was elected chairman of Courtauld PLC. He and his wife, Elizabeth Kelsey, soon embarked on occasional purchases of modern French art: first a drawing by Henri de Toulouse-Lautrec,[7] then two paintings – a late work by the recently deceased Pierre-Auguste Renoir (p. 119) and a landscape by the contemporary painter Jean-Hippolyte Marchand, bought a few months after its completion from the newly opened Independent Gallery in London.[8] The excitement of these first acquisitions, the realisation that good pictures could still be obtained on the market, and the alarming lateness of museums in their endorsement of Impressionism prompted Courtauld to act. 'I have been turning a scheme over in my mind for some time, & not knowing whom to

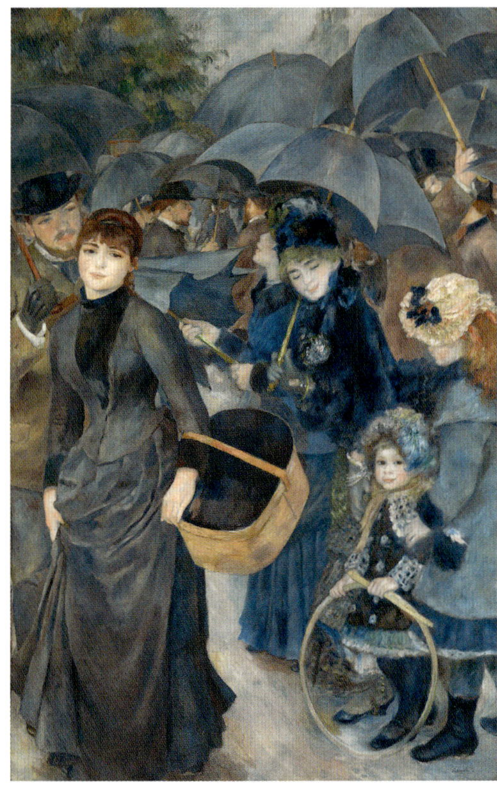

Pierre-Auguste Renoir (1841–1919)
The Umbrellas, about 1881–6
Oil on canvas, 180.3 × 114.9 cm
The National Gallery, London
NG3268

address, nor where such works could be placed, I turned to Sir Charles Holmes [director of the National Gallery] for advice'.[9] A newcomer on the artistic scene, Courtauld does not appear to have been aware of the advanced plans for new galleries at Millbank destined precisely for that purpose.

Likewise Courtauld does not seem to have known how much his scheme would entail, or what sum would be necessary to bring the collection to a decent standard. The dealer Percy Moore Turner, from the Independent Gallery, recalled Courtauld's first visit, a few days after his initial sale of the Renoir and Marchand paintings to his wife. Turner alerted him to 'the British authorities' [neglect] of the vital French movement of the 19th Century' and 'its absorption by European countries and America', to such a point that, if the situation were to persist, 'nothing worthwhile would be available for the education of our own people.'[10] Courtauld asked Turner 'how much money it would take to right the situation' in Britain, and whether '£40,000 [would] be adequate'.[11] In the end, Courtauld gave £50,000, which he established as a trust fund for the purchase of modern French art: a considerable amount, equivalent to twice the cost of the building funded by Duveen. This reflected the strength of Courtauld's resolution to fill this gap in the collection, the extent of his public-spiritedness, and his firm belief in the educational purpose of art, its universal appeal and power to transcend anyone's life: ideas that echoed the progressive principles he fostered in his business activities.[12]

While fast expanding his private collection with two important works by Cézanne (one illustrated on p. 56), just as many by Gauguin (p. 78 and left), as well as a flower piece by Monet and a painting by Daumier (p. 65), Courtauld was hatching his plan and by June 1923 had established the founding principles of the fund that was to bear his name.[13] The trust would be managed collegially, with its own separate committee administering it, entirely distinct and free from the influence of the still largely conservative National Gallery Board. Five Courtauld Fund trustees were appointed: in addition to himself, and the directors of the Tate and the National Gallery, Charles Aitken and Charles Holmes respectively, Courtauld proposed Michael Sadler, an educational theorist, recently appointed Master of University College and pioneer collector of major Post-Impressionist paintings, and Lord Henry Bentinck, 'whose well-known sympathy for the school of painting in question would be... of great service in giving the scheme a good start.'[14]

Crucially a list of the artists to be acquired was drafted, featuring 35 names, all of them French with the exception of Pablo Picasso, and with an extremely broad scope, from Jean-Siméon Chardin to Henri Matisse.[15] Courtauld was conscious that 'the fund won't be large enough to secure them all', but he thought them 'well-connected together' as 'the main artists of the modern movement from its inception to the present time'.[16] He also stated that 'in [his] own mind the central

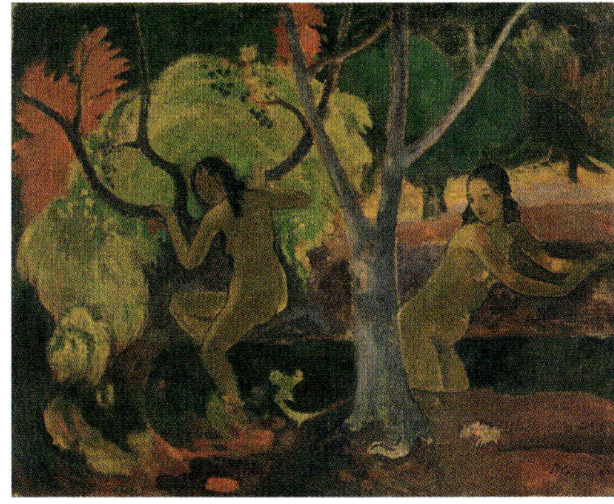

Paul Gauguin (1848–1903)
Bathers at Tahiti, 1897
Oil on sacking, 73.3 × 91.8 cm
The Trustees of the Barber Institute of Fine Arts,
University of Birmingham
49.9

men of the movement [were] Manet, Renoir, Degas, Cézanne, Monet, Gauguin and Van Gogh.'[17] The list included some nineteenth-century masters such as Jean-Auguste-Dominique Ingres, Eugène Delacroix, Gustave Courbet and Jean-Baptiste-Camille Corot, as well as the names of 10 living artists, asserting the contemporary orientation of the collection to be formed, although in the end only three paintings by living artists were bought.[18] Whenever possible contacts were made with the artists themselves; a letter reveals that in 1924 Courtauld may have envisaged a visit to the elderly Monet.[19] As the sole backer of the Courtauld Fund, and naturally its most committed trustee, Courtauld often went abroad to meet prospective sellers, dealers and intermediaries: to Paris on a regular basis, and to Amsterdam in 1924, to see Madame van Gogh-Bonger, the artist's sister-in-law, who held the paintings that remained in the family.[20] Thoroughly researching his potential purchases, Courtauld also visited the sites of Impressionist paintings – for instance Aix-en-Provence in March 1926, in the footsteps of Cézanne – to deepen his knowledge and further develop his sensibility and expertise.[21] He had purchased *Montagne Sainte-Victoire*, his most expensive Cézanne, in April 1925.

In this search for great pictures for the nation, Courtauld and his fellow trustees benefited from the advice of astute advisers and mentors. These included Roger Fry, the prominent art critic, theorist and organiser of two groundbreaking exhibitions of Post-Impressionist paintings in London 10 years earlier.[22] His views differed slightly from Courtauld's, whose taste did not stretch further than Post-Impressionism (a term coined by Fry himself), never extending to Fauvism or Cubism. Yet Courtauld saw the point of enrolling Fry's help, writing to Aitken: 'I like your idea of making a kind of "left wing" and asking Roger Fry to scout for us. We might get some 20th Century masterpieces for a tenth part of the money.'[23]

On a more regular basis advice was sought from dealers such as Percy Moore Turner of the Independent Gallery in London,[24] Charles Carstairs at the Knoedler Gallery, or from Duveen himself, in his capacity as a dealer. Courtauld asked Duveen for his opinion when considering the two first purchases – and the most expensive ones – out of the Courtauld Fund: Manet's *Corner of a Café-Concert* (probably 1878–80) and Renoir's *At the Theatre* (*La Première Sortie*) (1876–7) (p. 115): '[Duveen] is very much impressed with "La servant des bocks" [*sic*], but says he is sure we can get it for £10,000 if we stick to it & offer cash. He would secure this first, then negotiate for the Renoir.'[25]

Dealers brought their connoisseurship as well as their knowledge of the market and its opportunities. They often suggested acquisitions or acted as go-betweens, willing to offer optimal conditions, such as waiving fees: a key factor, as Courtauld was determined to make the best use of the Fund. As an important Van Gogh exhibition was about to open in London, at the Leicester Galleries in December

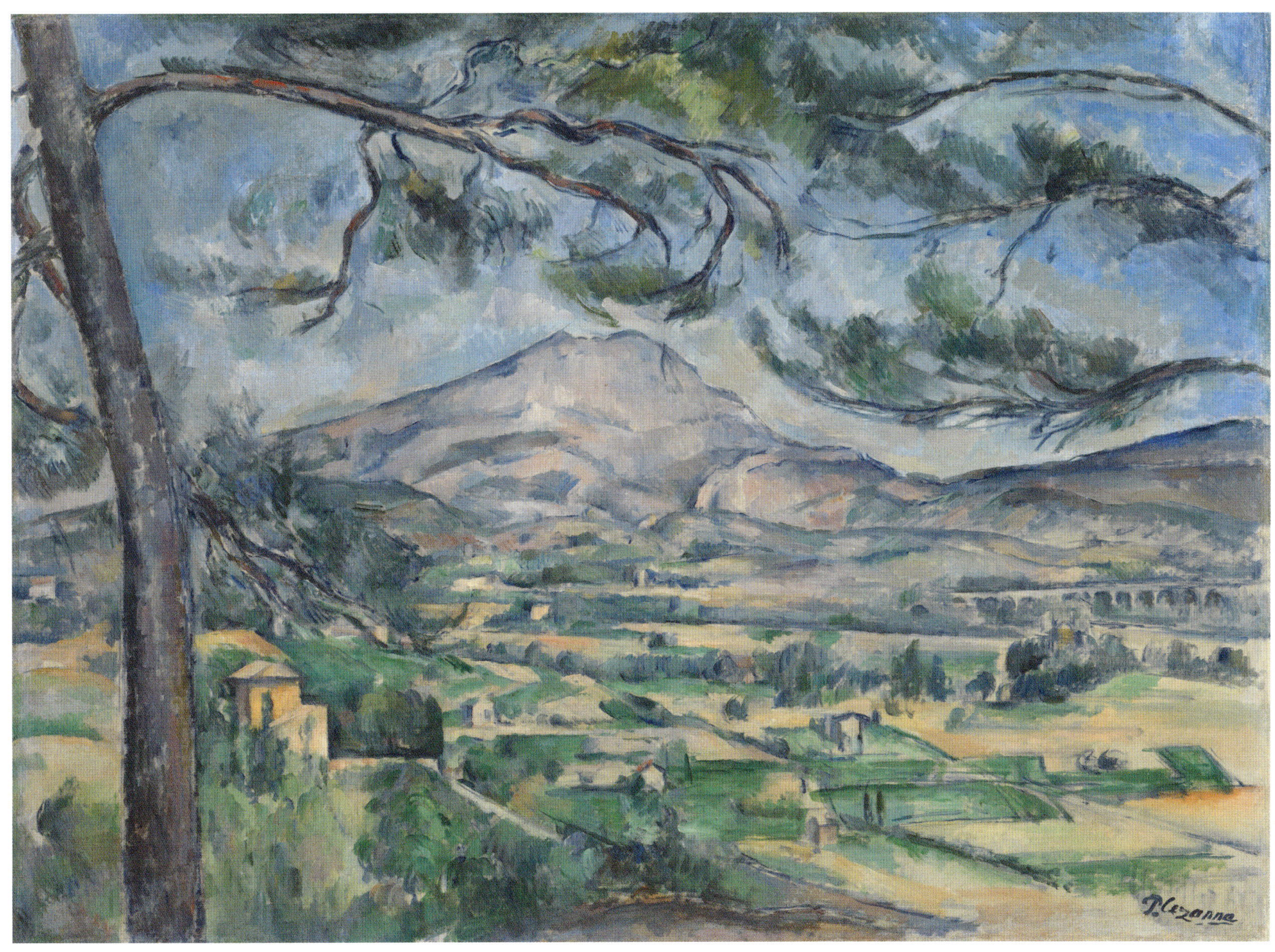

Paul Cézanne (1839–1906)
Montagne Sainte-Victoire with Large Pine, about 1887
Oil on canvas, 66.8 × 92.3 cm
The Samuel Courtauld Trust, The Courtauld
Gallery, London
P.1934.SC.55

1923 – the first solo show of the artist in Britain, with works coming directly from
the family's holdings in Amsterdam – its organisers offered the Fund trustees first
option, and lowered the prices for them. Dealers were drawn to the prestige of
having 'any pictures purchased for the Foreign Section of the National Gallery.'[26]

The French dealer and critic Félix Fénéon, owner of Seurat's *Bathers at Asnières*
(1884) (p. 121) until its sale to the Courtauld Fund, felt the same pride: 'The entrance
of *Bathers* into an illustrious gallery will consecrate Seurat's glory'.[27] *Bathers* remains
one of the Fund's most remarkable acquisitions on account of its size and art-
historical significance; it was also one of Courtauld's most personal choices. Soon
after his initial sale to the Fund trustees in October 1923 – Van Gogh's *Wheatfield with
Cypresses* (p. 137), the first of the artist's works to join a public collection in Britain
– Percy Moore Turner offered Courtauld further advice. Having 'suggested Seurat,
and, if possible, one of his two masterpieces "La Grande Jatte" ou "La Baignade"',
he 'ran them both to earth…had the offer of both pictures and telephoned to
Courtauld from Paris, advising him to buy both. But he would only buy one and
left the choice to me', Turner recalled.[28] Courtauld may simply have been deterred
by the price tags, 'which for Seurat were then almost fantastic'.[29] In any case, the
offer had to be seized promptly as the seller, Fénéon, 'would not wait any longer'
and 'a decision had to be made at once, by wire'.[30] With Turner unable to 'hold' the
painting for a few weeks, which would have allowed Courtauld to go and see it and
consult his fellow trustees, Courtauld took it upon himself to purchase it from the
Fund. He immediately informed Aitken: 'I hope you will not mind my having taken
this decision. I am prepared to accept full responsibility – but please support me if
you think I did the right thing. I am writing to the other trustees explaining what
I have done.'[31]

The flexibility of the terms of the Courtauld Fund allowed purchases to be
made with a certain degree of speed and informality, but the Seurat remains an
exceptional case. Typically, potential acquisitions were debated between trustees,
and decisions made collectively; a majority seems to have been needed for a deal
to go ahead.[32] When Degas's *Young Spartans Exercising* (about 1860) came to the
consideration of the Fund, Courtauld could 'not quite make up his mind' about it:

> It is attractive to me on account of its original character & showing something of
> the ultimate Degas even at that early date….Do you know what Sir Charles Holmes
> thinks of it? And has Lord Henry Bentinck seen it?…Personally I should be inclined
> to recommend it if all the Trustees are really agreed.[33]

Judgements were made on quality as well as price, and the merits of each picture
weighed with rigour and enthusiasm in exchanges where individual opinions had

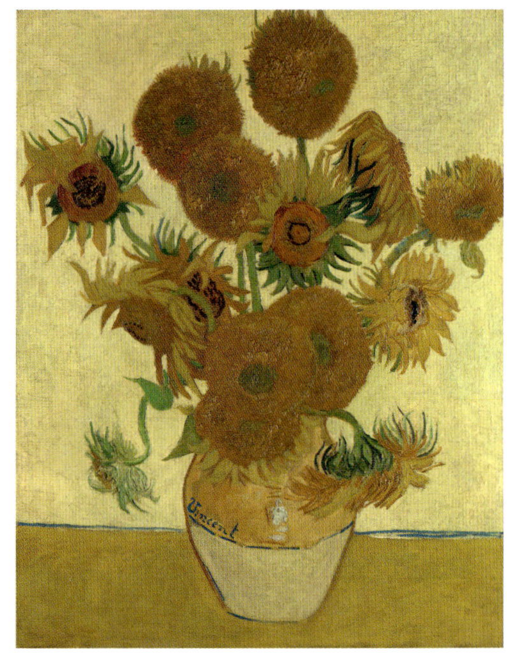

Vincent van Gogh (1853–1890)
Sunflowers, 1888
Oil on canvas, 92.1 × 73 cm
The National Gallery, London
NG3863

to be balanced out against the general consensus, with some paintings garnering only half-praise. 'I certainly think that you might do worse than acquire the Pissarro Boulevard' (p. 109), Holmes wrote. 'As you say, it is much more lively than the majority of his works'.[34] As for Maurice Utrillo, one of the 10 contemporary painters on the Fund's list, he was deemed 'not a first-rate man, Aitken reckoned, but in some [works] he has a charm…and Courtauld wished to get one, the price not being, for French pictures, exorbitant'.[35] Courtauld had first settled on a view of the church of St Etienne du Mont in Paris, sold by the Lefevre Gallery. Aitken was 'never enthusiastic' about the painting, 'as the sky in it is so bad'; it was immediately exchanged for another view of Paris, from the same gallery, *La Place du Tertre* (about 1910), showing a 'luminous, hazy sky and street effect', which was thought to represent Utrillo 'almost at his best'.[36]

The provision for such exchanges or resales actually formed a constituent part of the Courtauld Fund's conditions, and one of its most important clauses: the building of a collection depended on what was available on the market, with the risk of finer pictures coming up for sale at a later stage. This possibility of swapping and selling pictures to acquire better examples was exercised on many occasions, starting in January 1924. The Van Gogh exhibition organised by the Leicester Galleries in 1923 bore the promise of many exciting prospects of purchases from the Fund, as it featured a number of the artist's signature paintings, including one of his *Sunflowers* still lifes from the family's collection. Madame van Gogh-Bonger

Maurice Utrillo (1883–1955)
La Place du Tertre, about 1910
Oil on canvas, 50 × 73 cm
Tate, London
N04139

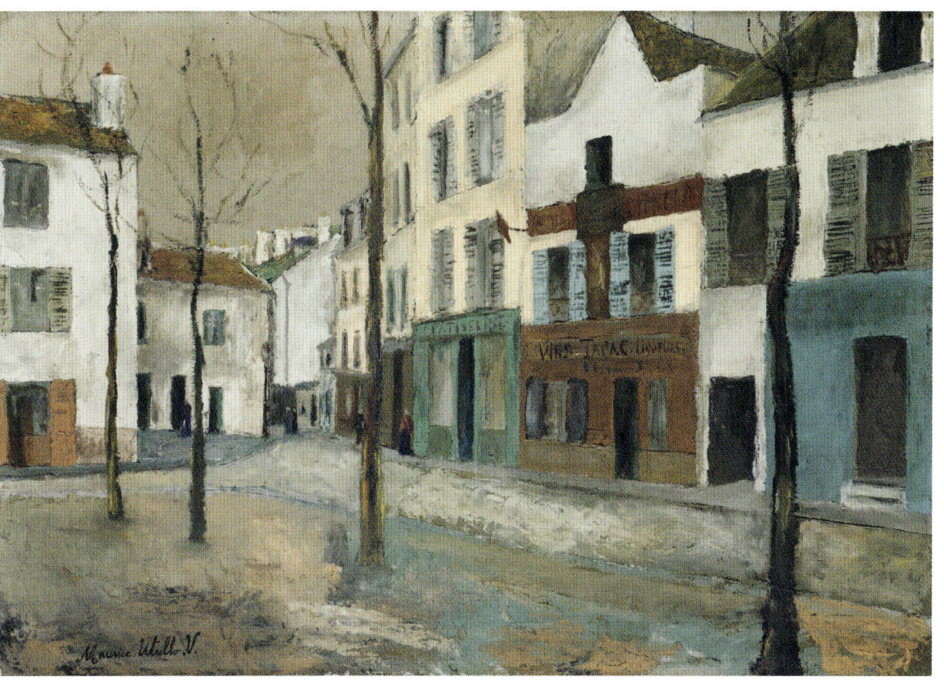

had warned: 'the sunflowers are not for sale, never; they belong in our family, like Vincent's *Bedroom* and his *House at Arles*.'[37] The trustees selected Van Gogh's *Chair* (1888) and a portrait of postman Joseph Roulin, settling the deal on 27 December. Yet barely two weeks later Courtauld started to 'feel a little bit doubtful about "the postman". I do not like it so well as I thought at first,…I should welcome the opportunity of exchanging it for a better picture'.[38] Courtauld's second thoughts were heard and Madame van Gogh was persuaded to sell *Sunflowers* (1888) instead, famously confiding: 'I felt as if I could not bear to separate from the picture…It is a sacrifice for the sake of Vincent's glory.'[39] Similarly a landscape by Alfred Sisley bought in October 1925 was returned less than two years later to the gallery that had sold it, and Monet's *Water-Lily Pond* (1899) was acquired instead, entailing an extra payment of £1,000 from Courtauld.[40] When the collection of paintings bought from the Courtauld Fund was first put on display at the Tate in January 1926, this scheme of possible resales was praised by reviewers as a welcome practicality. It was suggested that *Young Spartans Exercising* (p. 67) and *Miss La La at the Cirque Fernando* (1879) by Degas should be eventually sold, as they lacked the artist's 'rich inventiveness, the daring flash of colour, the brusque, emotional linework';[41] as for Camille Pissarro's *The Boulevard Montmartre at Night* (1897), 'one can so much as conceive [it] being one day exchanged', the same critic wrote.[42] In the end, thankfully, they were not; but Renoir's *Young Woman Bathing* (1888), purchased just a month earlier and also exhibited, while highly acclaimed by the same reviewer,[43] was ultimately sold by the Tate 19 years later – arguably with Courtauld's consent.[44] It was replaced after the latter's death by a view of Notre-Dame de Paris by Matisse of around 1900, as well as a 1910 Cubist nude by Picasso.[45] These were acquired by the Tate in 1949, and in 1954 the balance (resulting from the sale of Renoir's nude in 1944) went towards the purchase of another Renoir: a small Guernsey landscape of about 1883.[46] Although these painters featured on the list of artists to be acquired from the Courtauld Fund, this soon caused a great outcry: the Picasso, while a major work, did not comply with Courtauld's taste, which never embraced Cubism;[47] and in the middle of a wider controversy about the Tate Gallery's administration of its trust funds, the Renoir landscape was criticised as a minor work in comparison with the dismissed nude sold in 1944.[48]

This provision for replacement and exchanges almost caused the loss to the national collection of another one of its great works by Van Gogh: the *Chair*, which Courtauld briefly considered swapping for the *Long Grass with Butterflies* (1890). Concerned about over-representing the artist, he was 'not inclined to get the landscape unless we will part with the Chair.'[49] Courtauld and his fellow trustees clearly aimed for an even representation of each artist. This accounts for the way in which the purchases evolved and this collection developed. No painting by

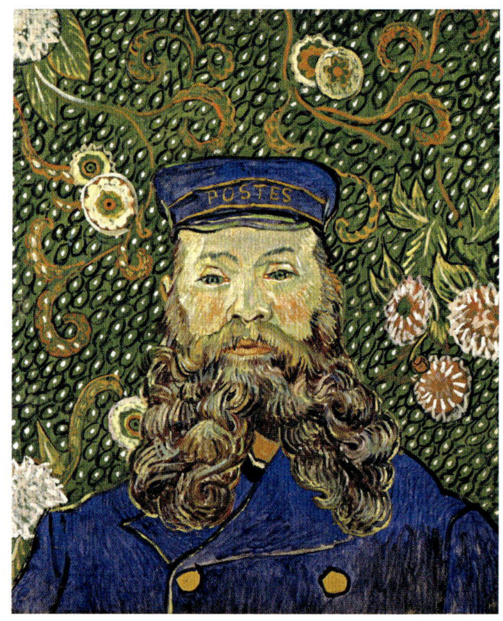

Vincent van Gogh (1853–1890)
Portrait of Joseph Roulin, 1889
Oil on canvas, 64.4 × 55.2 cm
The Museum of Modern Art, New York
196.1989

Pierre-Auguste Renoir (1841–1919)
Young Woman Bathing, 1888
Oil on canvas, 81.3 × 65.4 cm
Pola Museum of Art, Hakone

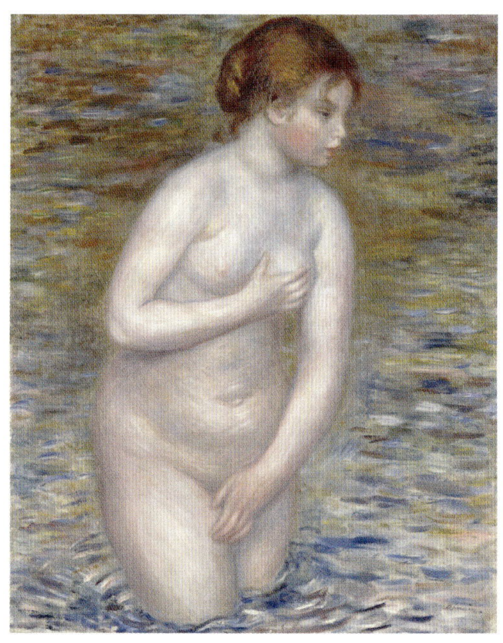

Right: Hilaire-Germain-Edgar Degas (1834–1917)
Miss La La at the Cirque Fernando, 1879
Oil on canvas, 117.2 × 77.5 cm
The National Gallery, London
NG4121

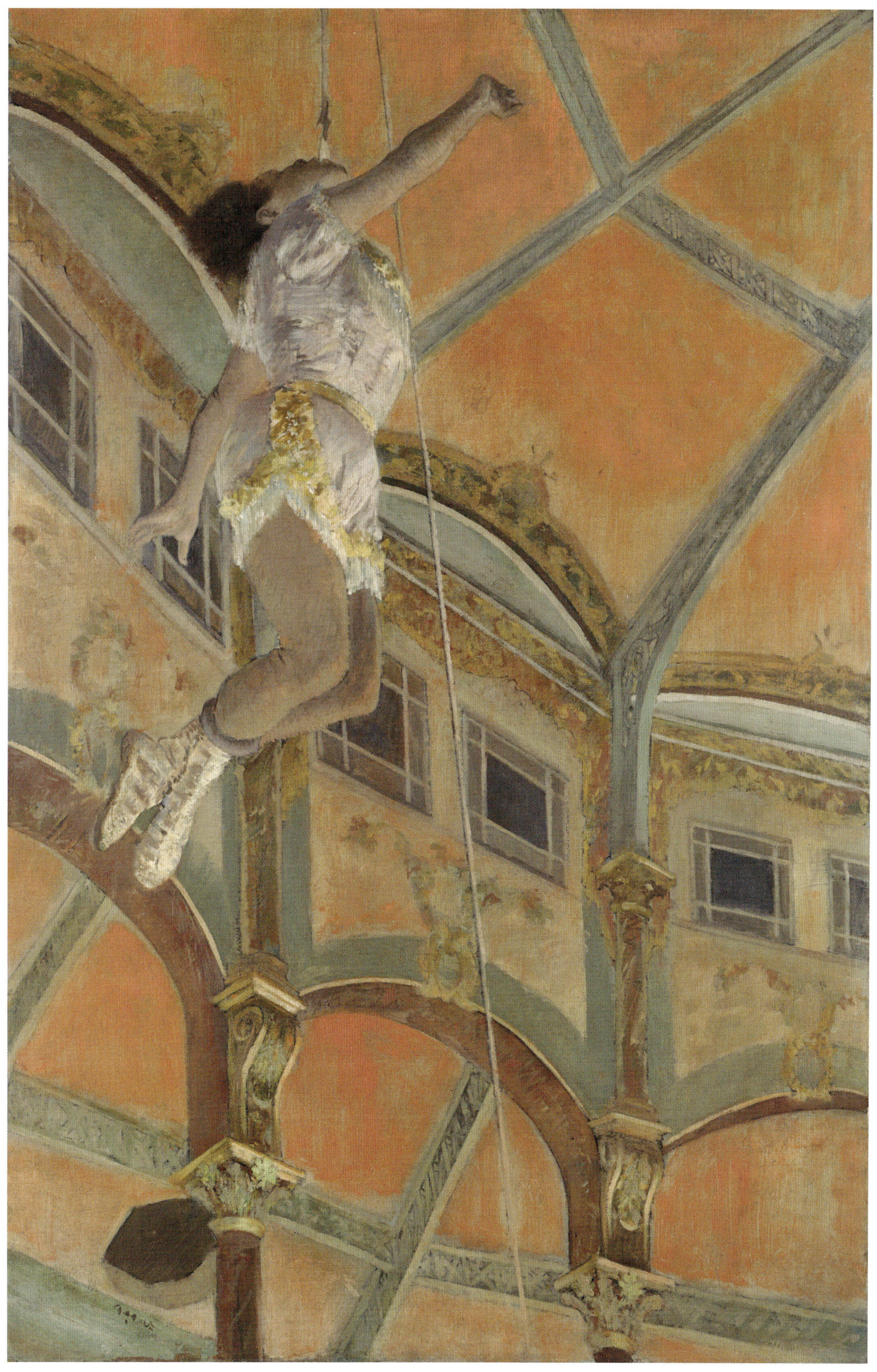

		£	s	d
1924	Manet: Servante de Bocks.	10.000	.	.
	Renoir: Première Sortie	7.500	.	.
	Van Gogh: Landscape Cypress Pines	3.300	.	.
	Degas: Jeunes Spartiates	1.200	.	.
	Van Gogh: Sunflowers ⎱ 75.000 garden			
	do : The Yellow Chair ⎰ 8.000 Julien	2.005	.	.
	G.P. Seurat: Baignade 3560·16·7 + 356·1·8 =	3916	18	3
Apl.	Neal & Wilkinson: Carriage Seurat — Ca Book	15	13	10
	Brown & Phillips: Freight & Insce. Van Gogh	10	15	.
May	Independent Gallery: Seurat ⎱ Frame 31·6·— ; Packing 1·13·3 ⎰ Carriage 1·8·5	34	7	8
1925 July 26	Lefevre: Monet: Plage de Trouville	**650**	.	.
Sep Oct 6	Wallis & Son: "Lola" by Degas	3350	.	.
	Lefevre: "Moret" by Sisley	1200	.	.
Nov.	C. Aitken.	13	1	5
"	Wallis: Boul.ᵈ des Italiens: Effet de Nuit by Pissarro	15 75	.	.
"	Coates Son & Co.	89	7	10
Dec	Independent Gallery: Renoir £6.000 Nu dans l'Eau / P.M. Turner Portrait: Cézanne £6000	12.000	—	.
"	Insurance of Renoir & Cézanne	15	—	.
	Lefevre: Rue du Tertre, Paris	350	.	.
" 28	Independent Gallery: La Table: Bonnard	750	.	.
	do L'Abreuvoir: Sisley	1150	.	.
	Boulot Frames.	41	.	6
		49 125	8	—

List of Courtauld Fund purchases for 1924–5,
manuscript
Tate Archive, London
TG17/3/4

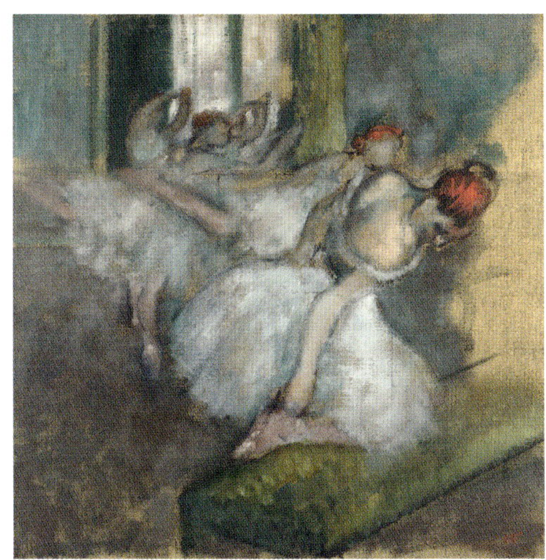

Hilaire-Germain-Edgar Degas (1834–1917)
Ballet Dancers, about 1890–1900
Oil on canvas, 72.5 × 73 cm
The National Gallery, London
NG4168

Gauguin was acquired, probably because good examples of his work were already part of the national collection, including *Faa Iheihe* (1898), presented by Duveen a few years earlier.[50] Works by Cézanne – an artist who featured prominently in Courtauld's private collection – were not hunted with particular urgency. Paintings were considered in October 1923 and July 1924, and declined;[51] prices were high and his paintings still far from consensual, as indicated by the debates surrounding the offer by Welsh collector Gwendoline Davies of the loan of two Cézanne paintings she owned.[52] Besides, Aitken presumed – erroneously – that this work, as well as Courtauld's own, would eventually join the national collection, and he supported with only limited enthusiasm the idea of buying *Hillside in Provence* (about 1890–2) (p. 51): 'Courtauld seems keen and if he insists, we get it for very little of the Fund money'.[53] In the end the painting was purchased, reflecting Courtauld's authority as the leading voice among the trustees.

The two collections Courtauld built simultaneously – one with the guidance of his wife, and the other with the advice of his fellow trustees – were kept watertight at all times. No artwork ever featured in both, and only Manet's *Luncheon* (p. 99) – 'said to be the original, although of course the composition isn't so carefully thought out'[54] – seems to have been considered for one, maybe declined for that very reason, and eventually bought for the other three years later.[55] Inevitably works were acquired from the same dealers, not least the indefatigable Percy Moore Turner, also responsible for hanging Courtauld's pictures in his new home, Home House, a grand eighteenth-century house on Portman Square, London, into which the Courtaulds moved in March 1926. But transactions of pictures intended for one or the other collection were kept strictly separate. In June of that year, Courtauld's double purchase of Sisley's *Snow at Louveciennes* for him and his wife and Degas's *Ballet Dancers* (about 1890–1900) for the national collection appear on the same bill,[56] although in this instance the work by Degas was entirely paid for by Courtauld – out of his own account – and given to the nation, as by then the Fund was nearly exhausted.

The timeframe of the two collections differed entirely, one stretching over a decade, the other barely three years; nor were the sums spent on each comparable. The combined cost of Renoir's *La Loge (Theatre Box)* (1874) and Manet's *A Bar at the Folies-Bergère* (*Un bar aux Folies-Bergère*) (1882) was equivalent to the entire Courtauld Fund.[57] In both cases budgets were kept completely secret; Courtauld did not want any figures to be published alongside Courtauld Fund announcements or press releases.[58] He also refused publicity for his extraordinary private purchases, only occasionally letting journalists or art critics into his house, probably to avoid comparisons between the 'private' and the 'public' paintings; for that very reason he declined to lend anything – apart from his Marchand landscape[59] – to the first

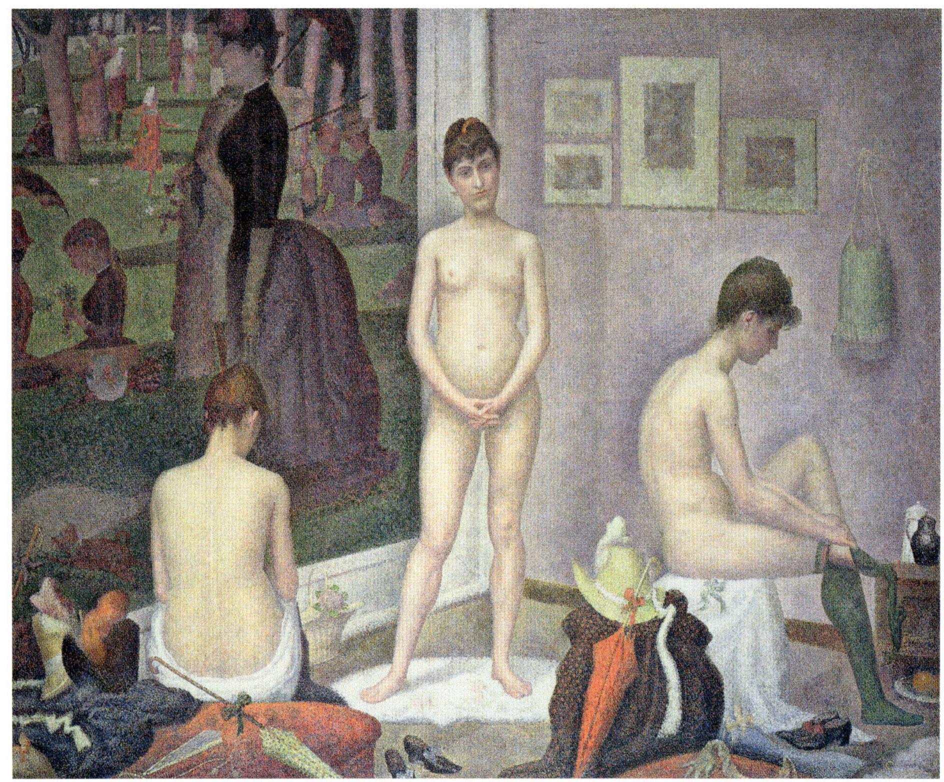

Georges Seurat (1859–1891)
Models (Poseuses), 1886–8
Oil on canvas, 200 × 249.9 cm
The Barnes Foundation, Philadelphia
BF811

showing of the Courtauld Fund pictures in the newly built Duveen Galleries.[60] Quite understandably, Courtauld also wished to enjoy his pictures in his new home.[61]

In fact, by the time the Courtaulds settled into Home House, the Fund had almost entirely dried up,[62] the national collection of modern paintings it had enabled had been formed and the new gallery was about to open, bringing to a close three years of fast-paced activity. The Courtauld Fund was time-limited, with an implicit deadline: the opening of the new Modern Foreign Galleries in June 1926. It started in high gear with the two most costly purchases made in August 1923 (p. 115),[63] five months before the Deed of Trust was actually signed and approved, prompting Courtauld to warn: 'Now we must go a bit slow, or the Fund will not last half as long as I intended'.[64] Its rhythm quickened again in the autumn of 1925, as the completion of the building was imminent, with the trustees pondering what to buy as the 'concluding "big bang"'.[65] In January 1926 the first 16 paintings acquired were shown for the first time, as a unit, in Gallery X at the Tate, Millbank. Six months later, 20 works featured prominently – alongside Lane's pictures and paintings on loan from private collections – in the initial hang of the new Duveen Galleries, formally opened on 26 June 1926 by King George V and Queen Mary.[66] Once these new galleries were inaugurated, the Courtaulds focused on building their own collection, with a peak in 1926–8 corresponding to a period of spectacular levels of profit for the company.[67]

Differing in scale, timing and purpose, the two collections shared a common mission – filling the empty shell of the new Duveen Galleries for one, the grand Home House interiors for the other – and a focus on largely the same artists. They evolved alongside each other, honed by Courtauld's developing expertise. Learning from one to test or enrich the other, sharpening his artistic judgement along the way, in 1923 Courtauld dismissed a work by Daumier offered to the Fund trustees, which he thought compared unfavourably to the one he had acquired five months earlier.[68] Similarly, when Seurat's other great masterwork, *Models* (*Poseuses*) (1886–8), became available in Paris in the spring of 1926,[69] Courtauld pondered the merits of this 'most remarkable work', measuring them against those of *Bathers*, bought for the nation two years earlier. 'Though not so strong nor carried so far, the colour [in *Bathers*] pleases me better, I find the design more harmonious & certainly more restful'; at the same time he settled for the purchase of *Young Woman Powdering Herself* (p. 127) for himself.[70]

With a scholarly approach to collecting, Courtauld also enjoyed building connections between 'his' two collections, acquiring for himself works directly related to major paintings secured for the nation from the Courtauld Fund. In June 1925 he purchased a small study for Seurat's *Bathers*,[71] possibly as a memento of one of the most crucial acquisitions he had enabled a year earlier; he also bought a preparatory pastel for Degas's *Miss La La* only a few months after the painting joined the national collection.[72] No doubt wishing to see the two works reunited, Courtauld presented the pastel to the Tate in 1933.[73]

From Courtauld's early exchanges with museum officials it appears that he initially envisaged that the collection developed for the nation, although first displayed at Millbank, should ultimately join the National Gallery, where it could be seen close to Old Master paintings.[74] It is just as clear that he intended these works to be joined by his own private collection, and that the two would form one unit. Meanwhile the project for an institute of art in Britain, designed by the politician Lord Lee of Fareham and lawyer Sir Robert Witt, was taking shape. They enrolled Courtauld's support, and by the time of his wife's death in 1931, his plans had changed; he made over not just their house on Portman Square, but also his art collection for the use of the newly founded Courtauld Institute. Yet it is not impossible to surmise that Courtauld imagined and built these two groups of pictures as the two parts of what was to form, in due course, a single magnificent collection, under the same roof. Even once the Institute was founded, Courtauld made sure that pictures from his collection, now in the care of the Home House Trustees, could be regularly placed on loan to the National Gallery and the Tate.[75] Rather than bequeathing them to the national collection, Courtauld favoured the idea of long-term loans, so that future museum directors or trustees could not decide 'they should no longer want to exhibit them, or mishandle them in any way'.[76]

The first and most important of these loans Courtauld generously granted
was to the National Gallery, when in 1934 he facilitated the display 'for an indefinite
period' of Manet's *Bar* and of Cézanne's *Montagne Sainte-Victoire with Large Pine*
(p. 23).[77] The latter was the first painting by this artist to be shown on the walls at
Trafalgar Square. Thus Courtauld enabled the introduction of great Impressionist
and Post-Impressionist pictures to the Gallery, since that part of the collection
was then on view at Millbank.[78] Given the past resistance to showing Cézanne's
paintings, this marked 'a sign of change in official artistic opinion', as one critic
wrote, and 'perhaps the most sensational incident in the whole history of the
National Gallery'.[79] As for Courtauld he avowed himself 'pleased to help in getting
official recognition for Cézanne in England'.[80] Conscious of the heightened feelings that the paintings might still arouse, the Gallery's newly appointed director,
Kenneth Clark, insisted on Courtauld's paintings being glazed, judging this
measure 'especially necessary with the Cézanne, as it is just possible that some
enraged die-hard might assault it'.[81] Trying to further boost this nucleus of modern
French paintings at the National Gallery, Clark asked Courtauld whether he would
also lend some of his works by Renoir, to which Courtauld answered that *The Skiff
(La Yole)* (p. 113) (1875) 'could not be removed without utterly ruining [his] dining
room',[82] and that *La Loge* 'may go there, but I can't spare it yet'.[83] The latter did,
eventually, join the displays at the Gallery in 1937, in its recently opened 'French
Room', alongside other loans from the Courtauld Institute and Courtauld's own
home, including Cézanne's *Pot of Primroses and Fruit* (p. 49).[84]

The tight relationship between Courtauld, the Institute that bore his name
and the National Gallery was further strengthened by his role as a trustee on the
National Gallery Board, for two mandates in the 1930s and 40s, twice holding
the office of chairman, as well as serving on the Tate Gallery Board.[85] This placed
him at the heart of the National Gallery's functioning and allowed him to make
decisions influencing directly its position regarding modern foreign paintings at
a moment when the remits of the Tate and the National Gallery were being
rethought – a debate in which his voice was dominant.[86]

Indeed the story of Courtauld's involvement with the National Gallery did not
stop with the opening of the new Modern Foreign Galleries at the Tate, nor with
the exhaustion of the Courtauld Fund. His name remains closely interwoven with
the history of the National Gallery and its collection, in contributions that took a
great many forms: in 1926 Courtauld backed the commission of three mosaics from
the artist Boris Anrep, to decorate the entrance hall of the Gallery;[87] two years later
he covered a significant part of the costs of two outstanding acquisitions of Old
Master paintings for the collection: *The Wilton Diptych* (about 1395–9) and Titian's
The Vendramin Family (about 1540–5).[88] As war loomed he advised Clark in his

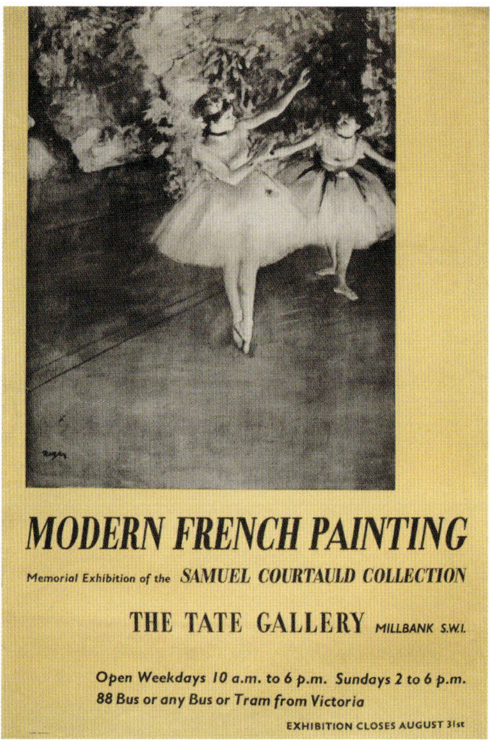

Poster for *Modern French Painting*, Courtauld
memorial exhibition at the Tate, 1948
Tate, London

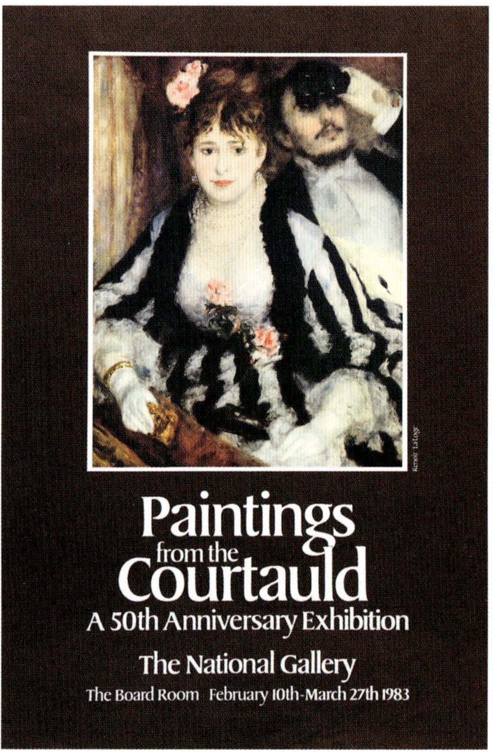

Poster for *Paintings from the Courtauld*,
50th anniversary exhibition at the National
Gallery, 1983
The National Gallery, London

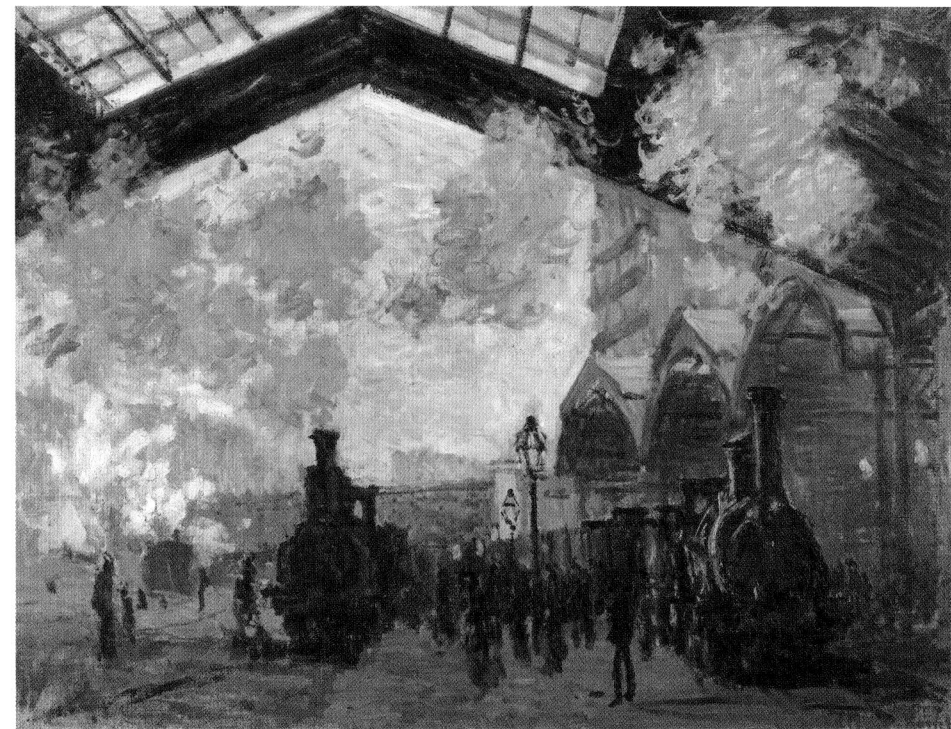

Claude Monet (1840–1926)
The Gare St-Lazare, 1877
Oil on canvas, 54.3 × 73.6 cm
The National Gallery, London
NG6479

search for secure storage for the Gallery's pictures; as a recently re-elected trustee his opinion was particularly valued.[89] The Welsh cave where the nation's pictures were transferred also served as a safe haven for Courtauld's own paintings, such as *The Skiff* (p. 113) and *La Loge* (p. 111), demonstrating the indissoluble ties between Courtauld and his paintings through the many vicissitudes of their history in the twentieth century.[90]

After Courtauld's death in 1947, a memorial exhibition was held at the Tate in 1948. His influence on the National Gallery was prolonged through his pictures: new developments and legal decisions regarding the distribution of modern foreign paintings between the Tate and the National Gallery meant that most of the Courtauld Fund artworks were transferred permanently from Millbank to Trafalgar Square.[91] They were joined by a regular stream of loans from Courtauld's own collection, left to his descendants or inheritors, three of which the Gallery was able to acquire in the 1980s and 90s: Monet's *The Gare St-Lazare* (1877),[92] Seurat's *The Channel of Gravelines, Grand Fort-Philippe* (1890) and Renoir's *The Skiff*, which Courtauld had particularly treasured. These paintings, with which he had felt an emotional connection, could now be enjoyed close to the Gallery's great collection of Old Masters, triggering fertile art-historical comparisons, and next to the works resulting from his far-sighted benefaction. The name of Samuel Courtauld, the most private and discreet of collectors, yet driven by the highest sense of public purpose, still resonates there today.

1 Samuel Courtauld's memorial exhibition, which brought together all of the paintings he had collected for himself as well as those purchased from the Courtauld Fund, was held at the Tate (where the latter were then housed) in 1948, a few months after his death. Subsequently the National Gallery organised two exhibitions marking Courtauld's achievements as a collector, in 1976 and 1983, with respectively nine and 16 loans from the Courtauld Gallery; on both occasions these were shown as a group, separately from the Courtauld Fund paintings, even though these, by then, had been transferred to Trafalgar Square. In the 1950s, agreements had been made for the distribution of these works between the Tate and the National Gallery.

2 John Maynard Keynes, comment on the Courtauld Trust, Nation and Athenaeum, 18 August 1923, p. 633. Quoted in House 1994, p. 238.

3 Samuel Courtauld, quoted in Blunt 1954, p. 2. On the essays written by Samuel Courtauld at the end of his life (which remain unpublished) and quoted by Blunt 1954, see also Wright 2008, p. 24.

4 Samuel Courtauld, quoted in Blunt 1954, p. 2.

5 Ibid., p. 3. The paintings bequeathed by Sir Hugh Lane were put on display at the National Gallery, Trafalgar Square. Spalding 1998, p. 39. See also National Gallery Board Minutes for 1917.

6 Ibid. There Courtauld had the revelation of modern French art, the absence of which he had noted on the walls of museums. With rare exceptions these artists had not yet been seen on the walls of public galleries in Britain; Lane's paintings attracted controversy, heightened by the political dispute surrounding the final destination of his bequest.

7 Henri de Toulouse-Lautrec, *In Bed*, about 1896, Courtauld Gallery. The drawing was acquired by the Courtaulds in February 1922.

8 Jean-Hippolyte Marchand, *Saint Paul, Côte d'Azur*, 1921, Courtauld Gallery.

9 Courtauld to Charles Aitken, Director of the Tate Gallery, 25 June 1923, Tate Archives, Courtauld Fund Papers, TG17/3/4. The Courtauld Fund Papers now form part of the Tate Gallery Archives. The correspondence for the period July 1924–August 1925 is missing.

10 Percy Moore Turner, 1948. Quoted in Salmon 2016, p. 65. Dealer Percy Moore Turner had just visited his friend and client Albert C. Barnes in Pennsylvania – businessman and insatiable collector of Renoirs and Cézanne's; Turner may have informed Courtauld of Barnes's venture, The Barnes Foundation, an educational institution for the appreciation of art, established in December 1922. This would have certainly struck a chord with Courtauld.

11 Ibid.

12 See Stephenson 1994, pp. 35–6.

13 Gauguin, *Bathers at Tahiti*, 1897, Barber Institute of Fine Arts, Birmingham, acquired by Courtauld in January 1923; Monet, *Vase of Flowers*, The Courtauld Gallery, bought by Courtauld in May 1923; Cézanne, *The Etang des Sœurs, Osny,* about 1875, The Courtauld Gallery, bought by Courtauld in July 1923.

14 Courtauld to Aitken, 15 June 1923, Tate Archives, Courtauld Fund Papers, TG17/3/4.

15 Korn 1996, p. 256.

16 Courtauld to Aitken, 25 June 1923, quoted in Korn 1996, p. 256.

17 Courtauld to Aitken, 25 June 1923, Tate Archives, Courtauld Fund Papers, TG17/3/4.

18 Monet, *The Beach at Trouville*, 1870, The National Gallery; Utrillo, *La Place du Tertre*, about 1910, Tate; Pierre Bonnard, *The Table*, 1925, Tate. Monet had died by the time his *Water-Lily Pond* was acquired (Monet, *The Water-Lily Pond*, 1899, The National Gallery). In addition, in 1939 a large watercolour by Dunoyer de Segonzac was purchased (partly) using the remainder of the Courtauld Fund, with the aid of the Contemporary Art Society: André Dunoyer de Segonzac, *The Road from Grimaud (La Route de Grimaud)*, 1937, Tate. Tate Archives, TG4/2/294/1 Acquisitions: 1939–1940.

19 '[Lucien] Pissarro is going to write to Monet about Courtauld's visit'. Manson to Aitken, 1924 [date incomplete], Tate Archives, Courtauld Fund Papers, TG17/3/4.

20 'I had a most delightful visit from Mr & Mrs Courtauld, it was a great pleasure to meet them.' Johanna van Gogh-Bonger to Aitken, 13 May 1924, Tate Archives, Courtauld Fund Papers, TG17/3/4.

21 'I am going to Provence on Sunday next & hope to visit Aix', Courtauld to Manson, 21 March 1926, Tate Archives, 806.1.216.

22 *Manet and the Post-Impressionists*, London, Grafton Galleries, 8 November 1910–15 January 1911; *Second Post-Impressionist Exhibition*, London, Grafton Galleries, 5 October–31 December 1912.

23 Courtauld to Aitken, 12 August 1923, Tate Archives, Courtauld Fund Papers, TG17/3/4.

24 Percy Moore Turner was simultaneously helping the Courtaulds shape their private collection; Douglas Cooper credited the dealer for "firing [the Courtaulds'] enthusiasm" for modern French painting. See Cooper 1948, p. 170.

25 Courtauld to Aitken, 24 July 1923, Tate Archives, Courtauld Fund Papers, TG17/3/4.

26 Ernst Brown & Phillips, Leicester Galleries, to Aitken, 16 September 1923, Tate Archives, Courtauld Fund Papers, TG17/3/4.

27 'L'entrée de la Baignade dans une galerie illustre consacrera la gloire de Seurat'. Félix Fénéon to Percy Moore Turner, 29 February 1924 [29 February crossed out], Tate Archives, Courtauld Fund Papers, TG17/3/4.

28 Percy Moore Turner, 1948, quoted in Salmon 2016, p. 65.

29 Ibid.

30 Courtauld to Aitken, 2 March 1924, Tate Archives, Courtauld Fund Papers, TG17/3/4.

31 Ibid.

32 Courtauld to Aitken, 16 November 1923, Tate Archives, Courtauld Fund Papers, TG17/3/4.

33 Ibid.

34 Holmes to Aitken, 30 October 1925, Tate Archives, Courtauld Fund Papers, TG17/3/4.

35 Aitken to Holmes, 9 December 1925, National Gallery Archives, 215.3 Tate Gallery 1923–5.

36 Ibid.

37 J. van Gogh-Bonger to H.S. Ede, 18 October 1923, Tate Archives, Courtauld Fund Papers, TG17/3/4.

38 Courtauld to Aitken, 9 January 1924, Tate Archives, Courtauld Fund Papers, TG17/3/4.

39 J. van Gogh-Bonger to H.S. Ede, 24 January 1924, Tate Archives, Courtauld Fund Papers, TG17/3/4.

40 See receipt, September 1927, in the Tate Archives, Courtauld Fund Papers, TG17/3/4 (24 February to 3 April 1928, Purchases, Receipts).

41 Tatlock 1926, p. 57.

42 Ibid.

43 Ibid., p. 58.

44 Renoir's *Young Woman Bathing* of 1888, featuring in the *Tate Gallery Catalogue, Modern Foreign School*, 1934, was sold to Messrs Arthur Tooth & Sons Ltd, London, in 1944, for £5,300. Cooper 1954B, p. 121.

45 Matisse, *Notre-Dame*, about 1900, Tate (see Tate Gallery Archives, TG4/2/694/1; 15 September 1949, sold to the Tate for 1,300,000 francs) and Picasso, *Seated Female Nude (Femme nue assise)*, 1909–10, Tate (Tate Gallery Archives, TG4/2/829/2). D. Cooper argued that the two latter works, acquired by the Tate Gallery in 1949, were 'deemed to have been acquired through the Courtauld Fund' a posteriori, 'by a way of replacement', 'by a transfer of funds decided upon in 1952 or 1953'. Cooper 1954B, p. 121.

46 Renoir, *Moulin Huet Bay, Guernsey*, about 1883, The National Gallery. This painting was brought to the Tate's attention in July 1952 and the Gallery's intention was originally to buy it from the Chantrey Bequest. As this proved impossible, it was decided to use the remainder of the Courtauld Fund (proceeds from the sale of the Renoir's *Young Woman Bathing* in 1944) towards this purchase: around £742, a little less than one third of the total cost of the picture. See Tate Gallery Archives TG4/2/865/2.

47 'The acquisitions seem, and are, out of character with the rest of the Collection, but then it should be remembered that Mr Courtauld had no hand in their choosing, for the arrangement was done after his death.' Cooper 1954B, p. 119. Also, quoting Cooper: 'It is true to say that as far as the Fauves, and even more the Cubists, were concerned, Courtauld never became a convert.'

48 '…some of the money for its purchase [of Renoir's *Moulin Huet Bay, Guernsey*] has come from the Courtauld Fund, but it is in no way a replacement of the *Young Woman Bathing* which was sold in 1944 for £6,000, since it is in every way a much less important even if an exceptionally charming picture." See 'Another Renoir for the Tate [...] Courtauld Fund used', *The Times*, 4 February 1954.

49 'Courtauld rang up [...] In regard to the Van Gogh – he wants to know whether the Trustees would care to sell "The Yellow Chair" and get the "Landscape" at the French Gallery".' Note, unsigned [February–March 1926], in Tate Archives, Courtauld Fund Papers, TG17/3/4.

50 Gauguin, *Faa Iheihe*, 1898, Tate, presented by Duveen in 1919. Sir Joseph Duveen, whose father had helped finance the 1910 Turner Wing at the Tate Gallery, was director of the Duveen Galleries in New York, and provided funding for the purchase of artworks, such as Degas's portrait of *Carlo Pellegrini* (p. 77). In 1914 he made an offer to pay for the construction of new Modern Foreign Galleries. The offer was ratified the following year, and formally announced in 1918. The new building cost £30,000. Spalding 1998, p. 45.

51 Courtauld to Aitken, 25 October 1923 and 28 July 1924, Tate Archives, Courtauld Fund Papers, TG17/3/4.

52 Cézanne, *The François Zola Dam*, 1877–8, and *Still Life with Tea Pot*, 1902–6, both Cardiff, National Museum of Wales. See Korn 2004, p. 204.

53 Aitken to Holmes, 12 December 1925, National Gallery Archives, 215.3 Tate Gallery 1923–5.

54 H.S. Ede [to Holmes], 23 May 1925, National Gallery Archives, 215.3 Tate Gallery 1923–5.

55 The painting was purchased by Courtauld in June 1928 from the Independent Gallery.

56 'Mr Courtauld rang up. He will be responsible for paying for the Degas [Degas, *Ballet Dancers*, about 1890–1900, The National Gallery]'. See manuscript note, 26 March 1926, Tate Archives, Courtauld Fund Papers, TG17/3/4. The Sisley in question is *Snow at Louveciennes*, 1874, Courtauld Gallery.

57 Renoir's *La Loge* and Manet's *A Bar at the Folies-Bergère* were purchased by Courtauld in May 1925 and March 1926 respectively, for the same amount: approx. £22,600 plus a commission of £1,500 to Percy Turner. House 1994, p. 222.

58 'I would like you to omit the "generous", & [...] omit the amount', Courtauld to Aitken, 15 December 1925, sending his comments on the draft press release for the January 1926 exhibition of the Courtauld Fund purchases, Tate Archives, Courtauld Fund Papers, TG17/3/4.

59 Jean-Hippolyte Marchand, *Saint Paul, Côte d'Azur*, 1921, Courtauld Gallery.

60 'I don't think I can spare "the Bar". The publicity it got was quite unwelcome to me, in spite of a written understanding that the purchase should be kept secret!', Courtauld, 20 Portman Square, to Aitken, 5 May 1926, Tate Archives, Courtauld Fund Papers, TG17/3/4.

61 'We shall be in our new house & probably entertaining good deal this summer, & I am very unwilling to let the pictures go.' Courtauld, Connaught Hotel, Mayfair, to Aitken, 27 March 1926, Tate Archives, Courtauld Fund Papers, TG17/3/4.

62 In 1932 a painting by Pissarro, *The Louvre under Snow*, 1902, The National Gallery, was bought through the aid of the Courtauld Fund, and in 1939 a watercolour by Dunoyer de Segonzac – a painter featuring among the 35 names of artists to be acquired from the Courtauld Fund (Korn 1996, p. 256) – could be purchased by using the remainder of the Fund, with the aid of the Contemporary Art Society: André Dunoyer de Segonzac, *The Road from Grimaud (La Route de Grimaud)*, 1937, Tate. Courtauld does not seem to have played any role in the selection of this work. Tate Archives, TG4/2/294/1 Acquisitions: 1939–1940.

63 Manet, *Corner of a Café-Concert*, probably 1878–80, The National Gallery, acquired in August 1923 for £10,000; Renoir, *At the Theatre (La Première Sortie)*, 1876–7, also bought in August 1923, for £7,500.

64 Courtauld to Aitken, 12 August 1923, Tate Archives, Courtauld Fund Papers, TG17/3/4.

65 Aitken to Holmes, 12 December 1925, National Gallery Archives, 215.3 Tate Gallery 1923–5.

66 This event was captured by Sir John Lavery in two paintings now at Tate: *King George V, accompanied by Queen Mary, at the Opening of the Modern Foreign and Sargent Galleries at the Tate Gallery, 26 June 1926*; T*he Opening of the Modern Foreign and Sargent Galleries at the Tate Gallery, 26 June 1926*, Tate Gallery. The latter shows Duveen standing at the extreme left of the picture, while Courtauld sits to the right, his back towards us.

67 Stephenson 1994, p. 39.

68 'My "Don Quixote", which is nearly the same size [...] is more interesting, although probably more sketchy'. Courtauld to Aitken, 25 October 1923, Tate Archives, Courtauld Fund Papers, TG17/3/4.

69 Seurat, *Models (Poseuses)*, 1886–8, Philadelphia, The Barnes Foundation. The painting was exhibited in Paris at Galerie Barbazanges, 30 June–10 July 1926.

70 Courtauld to Manson, 5 May 1926, Tate Archives, 806.1.217.

71 Seurat, *Horses in the Water,* 1883–4, purchased by Courtauld in June 1925.

72 Degas, *Miss La La at the Cirque Fernando*, 1879, The National Gallery.

73 Degas, *Miss La La at the Cirque Fernando*, 1879, Tate; bought by Courtauld for himself in 1926, and presented by him to the Tate Gallery in 1933. The pastel has remained part of the Tate collection, whereas the Degas painting of the same subject was transferred to the National Gallery in 1961.

74 The Courtauld Fund Deed of Trust contained a clause written in that sense. See also the letter Courtauld first wrote to Holmes to propose his scheme: Courtauld to Holmes, 25 June 1923, Tate Archives, Courtauld Fund Papers, TG17/3/4.

75 National Gallery Archives, Board Minutes, vol. XI, 11 October 1932.

76 Courtauld to Clark, 19 February 1934, National Gallery Archives, NG26/20/1 Courtauld Fund: Correspondence.

77 National Gallery Archives, Board Minutes vol. XI, 24 October 1933 (for the loan of Manet's *Bar*) and 13 February 1934 (for the loan of Cézanne's *Montagne Sainte-Victoire with Large Pine*, c.1887, Courtauld Gallery).

78 From 1926 to 1961, when transferred to Trafalgar Square.

79 'Cézannah!', *The Times*, 14 March 1934, National Gallery Archives, NG24/1934/4, Press Cuttings.

80 Courtauld to Clark, 15 February 1934, National Gallery Archives, NG26/20/1 Courtauld Fund: Correspondence.

81 Clark to Courtauld, 19 February 1934, National Gallery Archives, NG26/20/1 Courtauld Fund: Correspondence.

82 Courtauld to Clark, 19 February 1934, National Gallery Archives, NG26/20/1 Courtauld Fund: Correspondence.

83 Ibid.

84 Clark to Courtauld's secretary, 6 April 1937, National Gallery Archives, NG26/20/1 Courtauld Fund: Correspondence.

85 Courtauld was elected in January 1931, chairman in 1936–7; re-elected 1939, chairman in 1940–2. He remained a trustee of the National Gallery until a few months before his death. In November 1935 Courtauld was elected as the trustee representing the National Gallery on the Tate Gallery Board (re-elected in this role in 1945).

86 See in the National Gallery Archives, *Memorandum from the Chairman: Distribution of Pictures between National and Tate Galleries*, written by Samuel Courtauld, 30 March 1936: 'Visitors to the N.G. should see something of the branches springing from the Old Masters towards the future: visitors to the Tate should see the roots leading from the past into contemporary growth.'

87 Oliver 2004, p. 18.

88 Titian, *The Vendramin Family*, about 1540–5, and English or French (?), *The Wilton Diptych*, about 1395–9, both The National Gallery. See Courtauld to Daniel, 22 November 1928, National Gallery Archives, NG26/20/1 Courtauld Fund: Correspondence.

89 'May I say again that I am very grateful to you for suggesting visiting the depots as it will be a great relief to me to have your opinion on them.' Clark to Courtauld, 26 June 1940, National Gallery Archives, NG26/20/1 Courtauld Fund: Correspondence.

90 Lists dated 12 January and 12 May 1943, 'New arrivals to Manod', National Gallery Archives, NGA 35/1/3 Wartime storage: non-National Gallery pictures.

91 National Gallery Board Minutes, vol. XIV. The transfer was decided in the wake of the The National Gallery and Tate Gallery Act, in 1954, defining the remits of these institutions' roles and collections, and establishing the Tate Gallery as legally separated from the National Gallery.

92 Monet, *The Gare St-Lazare*, 1877, The National Gallery, bought 1982. Renoir's *The Skiff* (p. 113) was also acquired by the Gallery in 1982, and Seurat's *The Channel of Gravelines, Grand Fort-Philippe* (p. 129) in 1995.

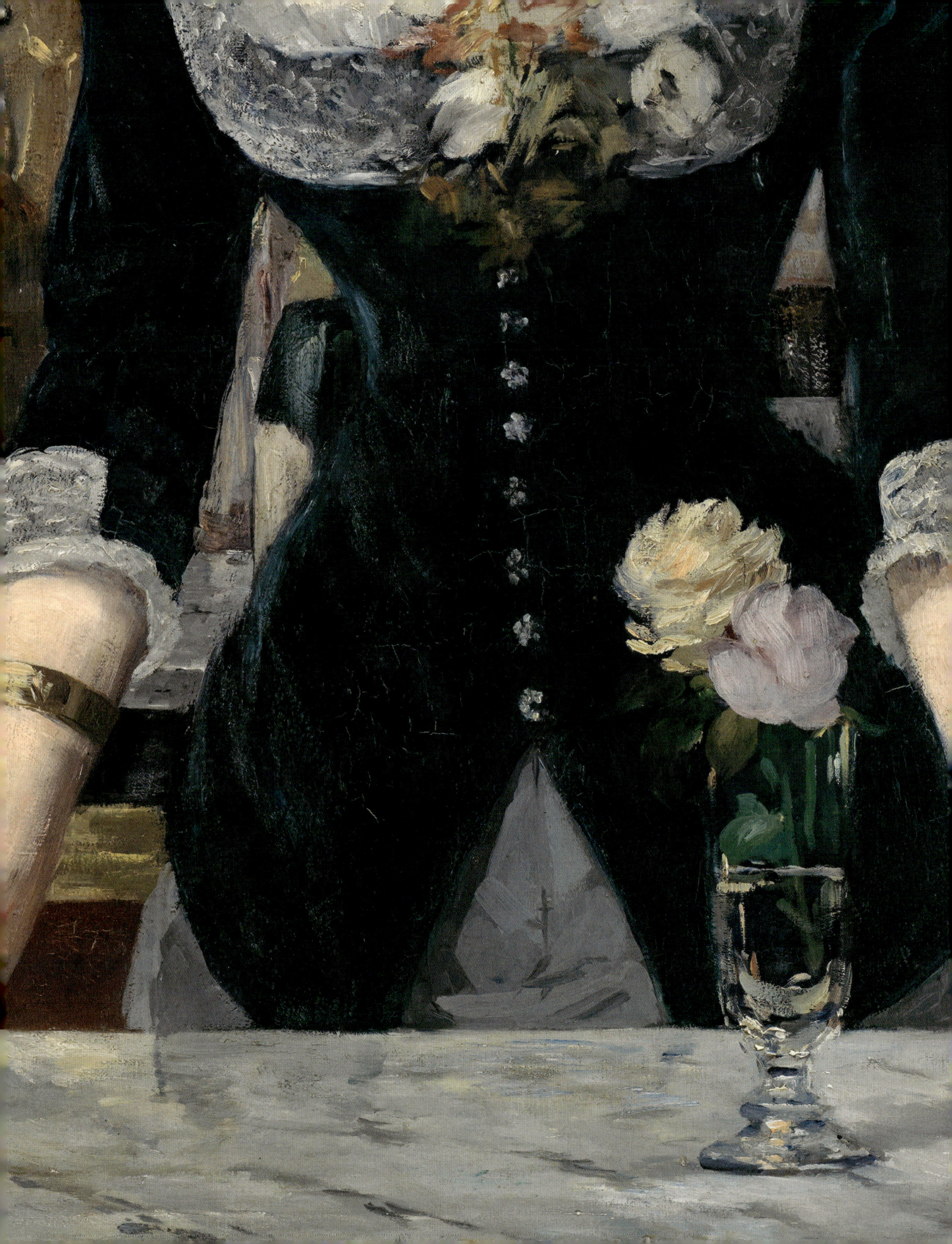

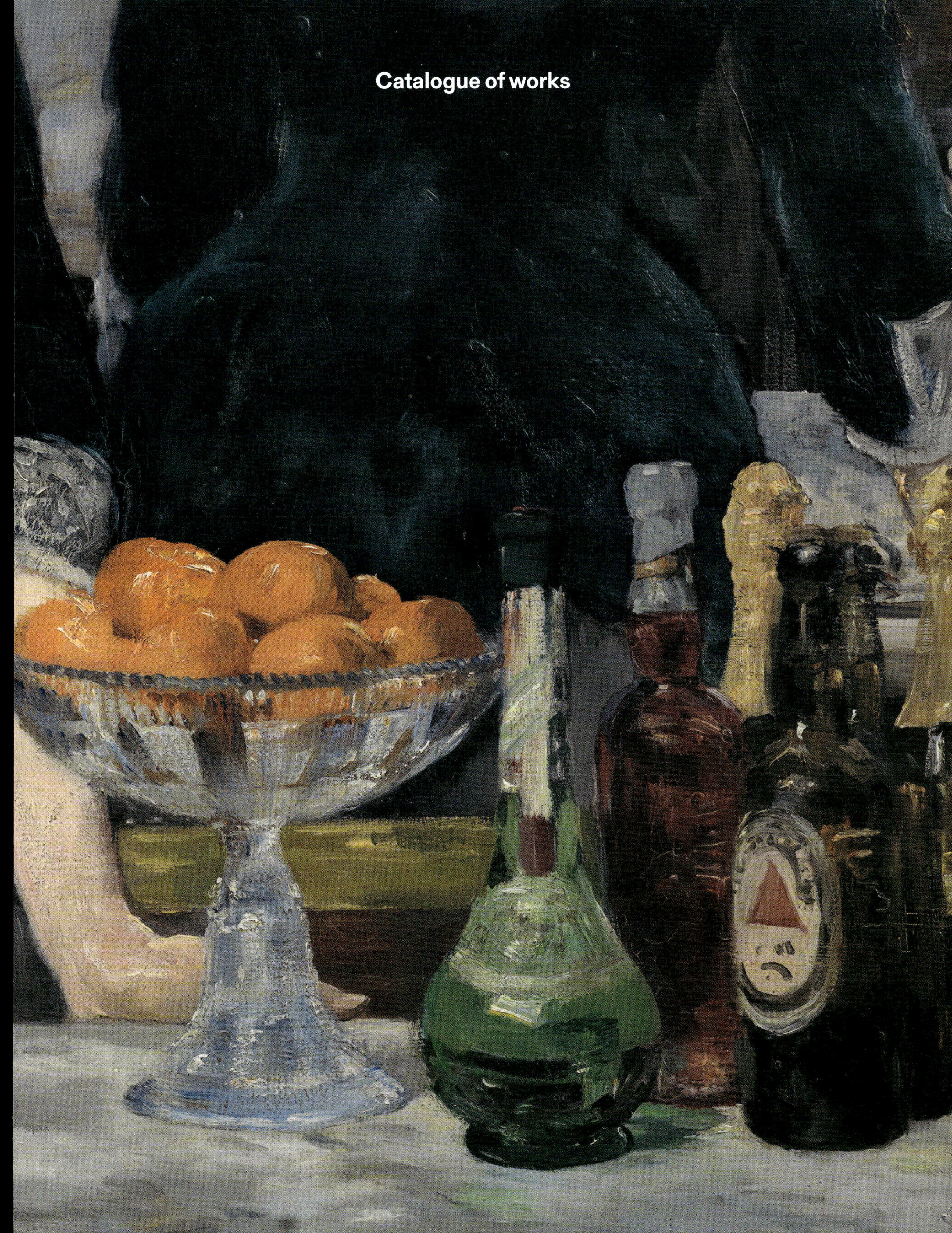
Catalogue of works

Pierre Bonnard (1867–1947)
Blue Balcony, 1910

Oil on canvas, 52.5 × 76 cm
The Samuel Courtauld Trust, The Courtauld Gallery, London
P.1932.SC.33

In the 1900s Bonnard spent less time in Paris to paint in the countryside, working each spring in the valley of the river Seine. In 1910 he rented a house in Vernonnet, a neighbourhood of Vernon situated across the river. He subsequently bought it in 1912. Standing on the Route des Andelys, it was just 3 kilometres from Giverny, enabling Bonnard to exchange frequent visits with Monet. Christened 'Ma Roulotte' or 'my gipsy caravan', it was a modest house of around 1895, set on a hill among trees. Bonnard's friend Thadée Natanson described how 'the upper floor of the "Roulotte", with a wooden balcony, was on the same level as the road, and the small garden fell away steeply to the riverbank where a boat was moored.'

This is one of Bonnard's earliest paintings of the house, whose exterior, particularly the terrace on the first floor, became a recurring theme in his work. Exactly the same corner of the house is depicted in *Sunlight at Vernon* (1920, National Museum Wales, Cardiff), the woodwork painted not in blue, but in pinks and lilacs. Here the pale turquoise of the balcony is echoed in the garden table and chairs just glimpsed at the bottom of the path; a figure on the former (perhaps Bonnard's companion and future wife Marthe) leans forward in an enigmatic gesture. On the left a large white and red striped tablecloth hangs out to dry, the same tablecloth as on the table in *The Terrace* (1918, The Phillips Collection, Washington). The brushwork throughout is free and broad, the trees and grass handled in an array of different greens. The river is conveyed with thick pale paint added between the dark tree trunks. The brickwork on the left is rendered in wide strokes of a pink-orange over a deeper red, and the wall above a yellow over a pinkish red, testament to Bonnard's lifelong obsession with layering glowing colour. Yet overall the tonality is subdued. Under an overcast grey sky the wild and uncultivated garden is painted with muted greens. Even the whites of the blossom and linen drying are tempered with blue-grey. The brightest accents are provided by the red flowers in the right foreground.   SH

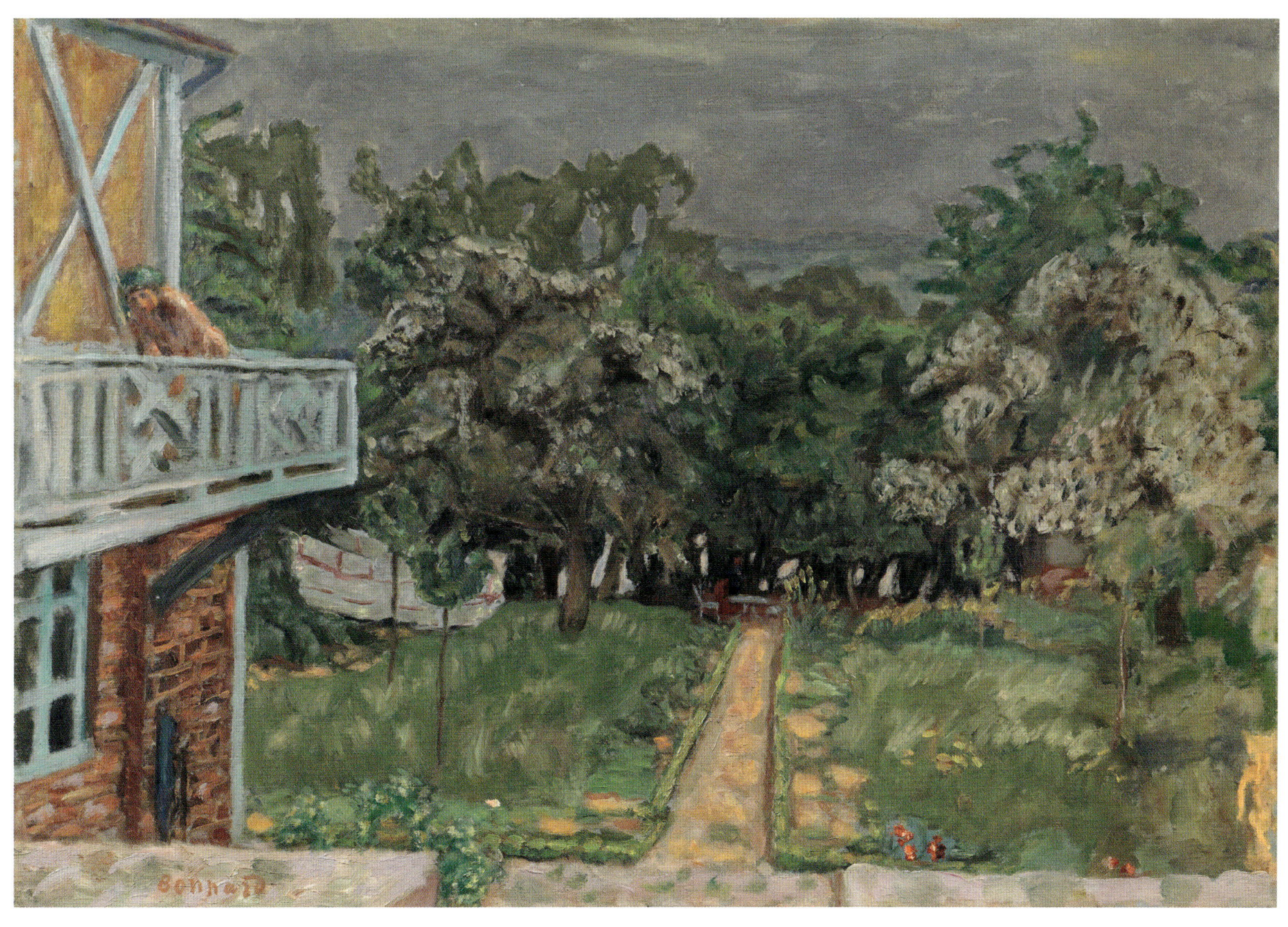

Pierre Bonnard
The Table, 1925

Oil on canvas, 102.9 × 74.3 cm
Tate: Presented by the Courtauld Fund Trustees, 1926
NO4134

From the early 1920s Bonnard spent an increasing amount of time at Le Cannet, a residential suburb of Cannes overlooking the Mediterranean. Here, inside his villa, he observes his immediate surroundings: a comfortable, light-filled dining room dominated by a table laden with baskets and plates of fresh fruit. The artist's wife, Marthe, sits opposite us. Elusive, almost blending into the room and its furniture, she turns her barely visible face to look down at a small dog standing at her feet, its head raised, patiently expecting the food being prepared by its mistress.

The painting's innovative treatment of space derives from Bonnard's early experiments with the Nabis, or prophets, in the 1890s. This group of young avant-garde painters – of which he was a founding member – favoured flat coloured areas and radically cropped compositions, inspired by Japanese woodcuts. Here, the table with the remnants of a meal occupies two-thirds of the picture, its mural, block-like presence harking back to the Nabi aesthetic. It is also reminiscent of Cézanne's still lifes, not least his *Still Life with Plaster Cupid* (acquired by Samuel Courtauld in 1923; see p. 57). Here, as in the Cézanne painting, each object seems to have been observed from a different angle: the fruit dish at the far end is depicted from its side, whereas the basket in the foreground is viewed from above.

The intense, iridescent Mediterranean light casts dramatic shadows around the dishes, baskets and crockery, creating abrupt contrasts of light and dark areas, transforming the table into a pool of radiant whiteness. Bonnard was fascinated by the colour white, the secret of which he said he struggled to understand. His luminous, high-pitched tones applied in small, free touches – owing much to the Impressionists' technique – transcend the ordinary objects while reinforcing the atmosphere of relaxed intimacy.

The second painting by a living artist to have been bought from the Courtauld Fund (in December 1925), and also by far the most contemporary, *The Table* holds a very special place in the history of Courtauld's purchases. Works by Bonnard had been sought by the Fund trustees since the major 1924 Bonnard retrospective at Galerie Druet in Paris. In 1928, Courtauld acquired another picture by Bonnard, *Blue Balcony* (p. 39), this time for himself. Courtauld favoured an 'Impressionist' example of Bonnard's work to fit in his grand interior at Home House, and a more recent, daring painting to hang on the walls of the newly built Duveen Galleries at Millbank.   AR

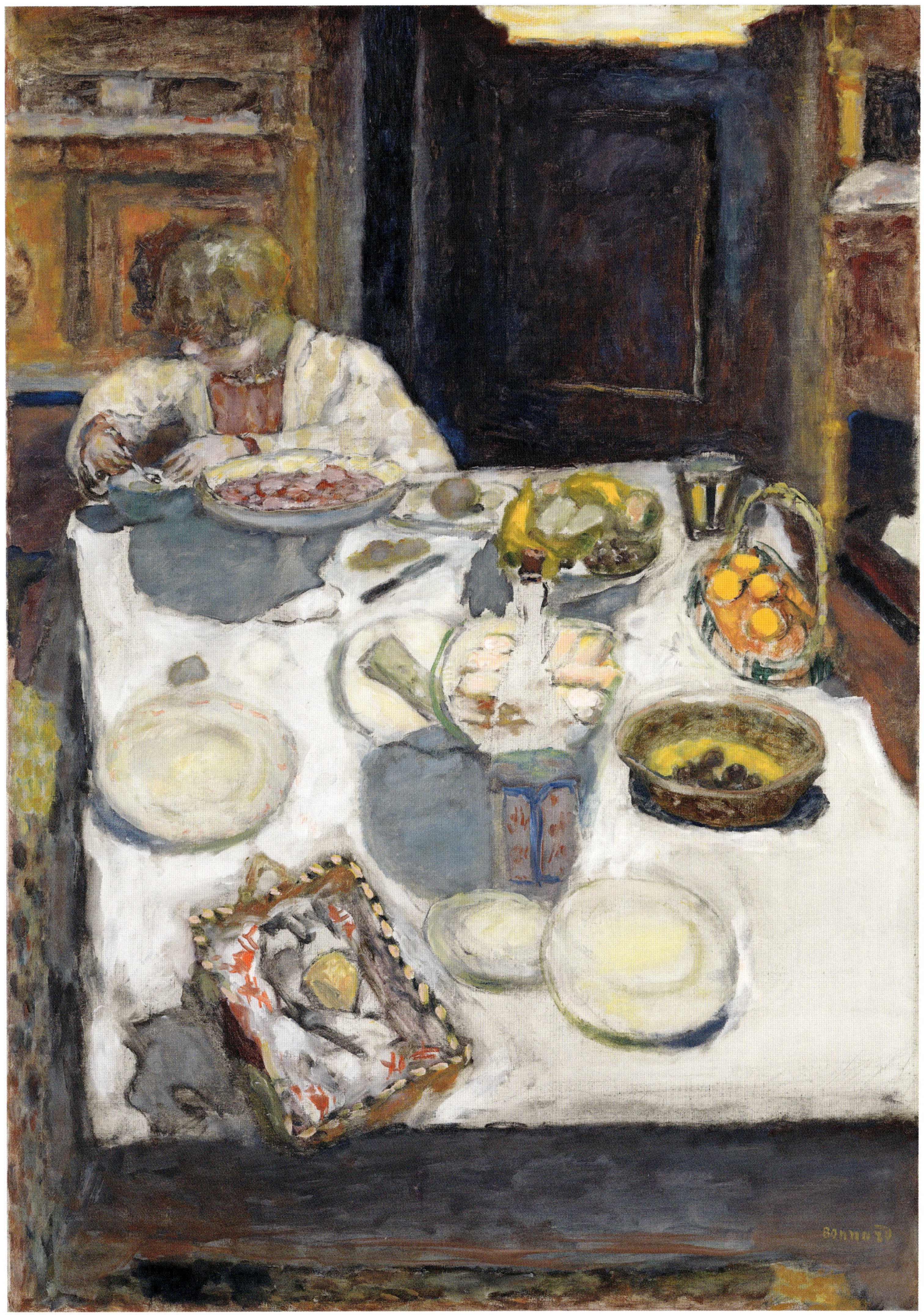

Paul Cézanne (1839–1906)
Self Portrait, about 1880–1

Oil on canvas, 34.7 × 27 cm
The National Gallery, London. Bought, Courtauld Fund, 1925
NG4135

Despite its modest size, this self portrait exudes authority and poise. The artist looks straight at the viewer, his gaze direct and impenetrable. He appears austere and remote. Warm sunlight pouring in from the window on the left illuminates half of his head, while the other recedes into the shadows. A bright ray of light catches the iris of his right eye. Cézanne's balding head suggests he must have been aged about 40 when he painted this portrait in Paris, around three years after largely leaving the capital to lead a hermit-like existence in Provence, no longer being able to bear the vicious critical onslaught on the works he exhibited at the first Impressionist exhibitions.

The artist's domed cranium basking in sunlight dominates the picture plane. The large expanse of his bulbous skull prompted artist and critic Roger Fry to remark that Cézanne 'poses to himself as he wished his sitters to pose, "as an apple", and he looks at his own head with precisely the same regard that he turned on an apple on the kitchen table.' Cézanne constructs the still life of his skull out of a multitude of short parallel strokes of paint: whites, yellows, reds, oranges, but also blues and greens, sometimes mixed straight onto the brush. This dense texture of brushstrokes of colour lends his skull a heavy, earthly presence, in striking contrast with the more thinly and loosely painted dull olive wallpaper of the background.

The bold wallpaper framing Cézanne's head appears in several other paintings from the same period, both portraits and still lifes. In this picture, he observes himself without any emotion, directing his attention to the geometry of forms: the way the diamond pattern of the wallpaper contrasts with the strong organic curves of his domed skull. The diagonal lines on the wall are interrupted before they intersect the head, allowing it to stand out even more clearly against the dark background. The wallpaper's lozenge-shaped motif, however, reappears in Cézanne's ear and eye, lending the picture an audacious formal quality.   JD

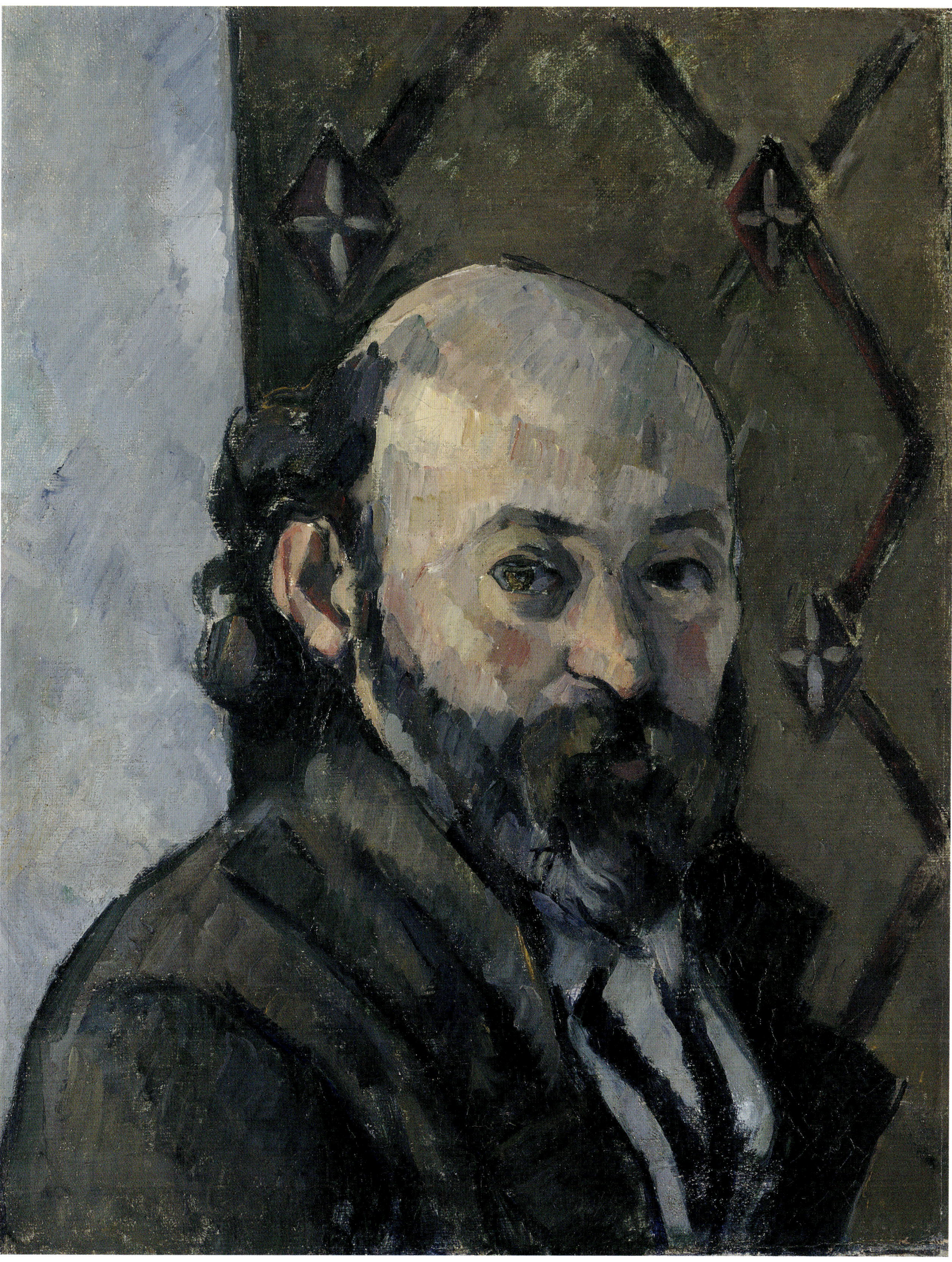

Paul Cézanne
Farm in Normandy, Summer (Hattenville), about 1882

Oil on canvas, 49.5 × 65.7 cm
On long-term loan to The Courtauld Gallery from a private collection
LP.1997.XX.13

This is one of four paintings known to have been executed by Cézanne during a visit to his friend Victor Chocquet in the village of Hattenville, Normandy, in 1882. A Paris-based customs official, Chocquet had met Cézanne a few years earlier – introduced by their common friend Renoir – and bought his first work by the Provençal artist in 1875. In March 1882 Chocquet's wife had inherited several properties in Hattenville, including a farmhouse; Cézanne stayed there the following summer, along with his wife and 10-year-old son, painting the farm grounds.

Typically Cézanne excluded his friends and relatives from these landscapes, as well as the farm itself, to focus on the cool, shaded area of the garden. The artist set up his easel in the orchard, choosing a viewpoint close to the ground, allowing the apple trees to align in a diagonal leading to the centre of the composition. The eye is drawn towards a patch of wall illuminated by golden sunlight, framed by the line of the tree trunks and topped by their gracefully curving branches. These carry a heavy canopy of foliage, filtering soft sunlight through its dense, dark mass of leaves, and casting pale areas on the grass. Unlike his Impressionist friends, Cézanne did not care to depict the celebrated sky of Normandy, yet the painting demonstrates his full assimilation of the Impressionist technique in its rendition of the subtle effects of light. He alternates between thin, parallel touches and more saturated strokes, visible in the area near the trees, where the paint is thicker. He introduces variety in the shape and direction of the brushwork, at times square and assured, mosaic-like, or smooth and almost fused.

Chocquet was the first owner of all four views of the Hattenville orchard and was among the most assiduous collectors of Cézanne's work, acquiring no fewer than 35 paintings and sitting for him on several occasions. It is not known whether Chocquet actually commissioned Cézanne to produce the Hattenville pictures; he is likely to have worked spontaneously, before presenting his host with the paintings. Unlike the other Cézanne paintings in the Chocquet collection, the artist left these unsigned, possibly planning to rework them on a later occasion. This may account for less resolved passages in this work, such as the truncated saplings to the right. It is not impossible, however, that Cézanne might have intended his experimental technique to show through. They do, in any event, give a fascinating insight into Cézanne's deeply personal and innovative working process.   AR

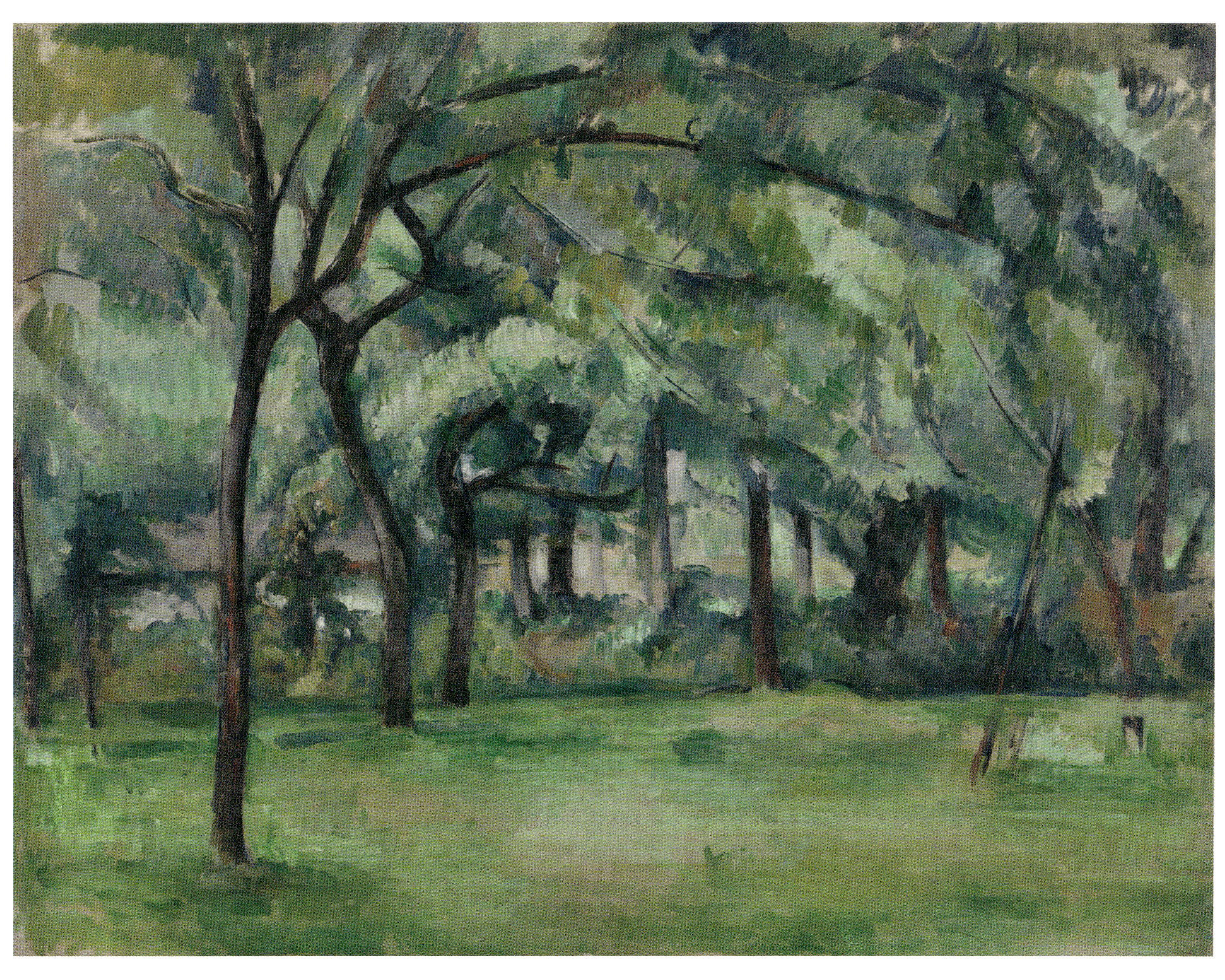

Paul Cézanne
Tall Trees at the Jas de Bouffan, about 1883

Oil on canvas, 65 × 81 cm
The Samuel Courtauld Trust, The Courtauld Gallery, London
P.1948.SC.54

This is one of the first two landscapes by Cézanne acquired by Samuel Courtauld for his private collection. It was through seeing a landscape by Cézanne at an exhibition in 1922 that Courtauld experienced a revelation regarding his art: 'at that moment I felt the magic', he said, and was forever converted.

This painting shows a site that was particularly familiar to Cézanne: the garden of the Jas de Bouffan, the country estate acquired by his father in 1859. Located just outside of Aix-en-Provence, it comprised a mid-eighteenth-century *bastide* (or manor house) set in vast grounds, which included a farmhouse and vineyards. Cézanne constantly returned there to find the peace and solitude he relished. Never tiring of the variety of motifs it offered, he sketched and painted its garden pool and statues, and its different species of trees that changed with the seasons; he also enjoyed the open views of the surrounding countryside.

Located by the west wall of the estate's grounds, the group of trees seen here appear in several of Cézanne's paintings. He was no doubt drawn to their near symmetrical arrangement, their elegant silhouettes and graceful grouping in two clusters of three. Their trunks are gathered at the base before widening in their upper branches, which carry a splendid summer leafage. Surrounding a central, lozenge-shaped patch of sky, they deploy themselves on both sides of this focal point, their leaves seemingly flickering in the warm sunlight. The foliage looks ruffled under a soft summer breeze, an effect achieved thanks to Cézanne's dazzling technique. Small, parallel strokes across the surface animate the picture with a remarkable dynamism, evoking the vibration of wind, or light, in the gently rustling foliage. Although varying in direction, these brushstrokes give the picture its unified texture and remarkable overall coherence.

Rendered in vertical brushstrokes, the luminous grass in the foreground and the farm buildings provide a solid, stable base to these trunks. Cézanne's motif, its subtle range of modulated greens and warm browns, is offset by the golden tones of the cottages and straw-coloured fields against the summer sky. The painting conveys Cézanne's sense of wonder in front of a familiar scene, captured on a magnificent day. It also demonstrates the astonishing surety of hand of an artist who, even in the 1920s when Courtauld acquired this painting, was still criticised for his alleged technical shortcomings, and would continue to polarise opinions in Britain for decades.   AR

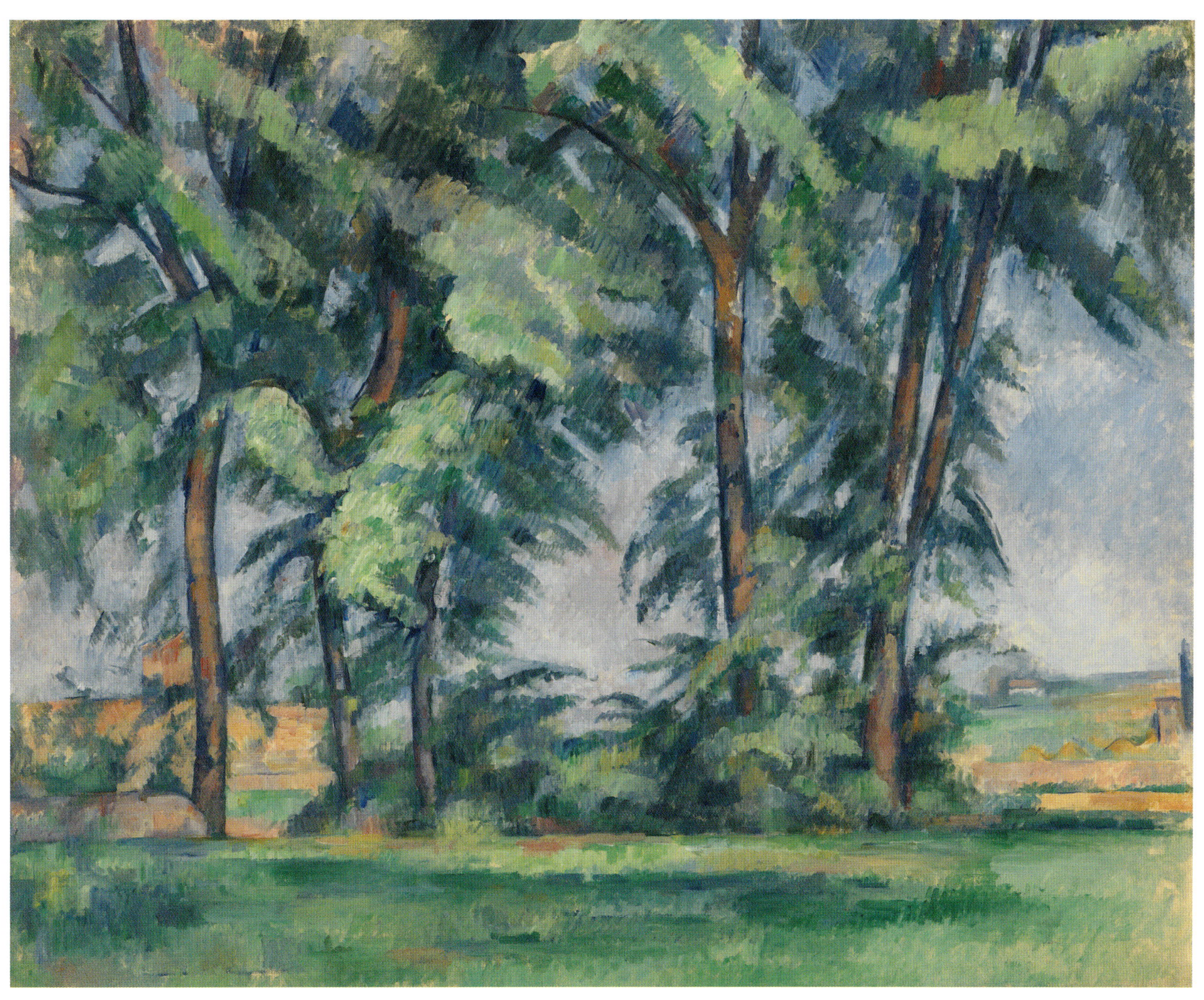

Paul Cézanne
Pot of Primroses and Fruit, about 1888–90

Oil on canvas, 46 × 56.3 cm
The Samuel Courtauld Trust, The Courtauld Gallery, London
P.1948.SC.56

Cézanne started painting flowers in the 1870s. Fascinated by their natural grace and the infinite variety of their shapes and colours, he was also frustrated by their ephemeral quality. For an artist who needed to analyse his subjects for protracted periods of time, flowers wilted too fast. Potted plants such as the one featured here must have suited him better. Conveniently, they grew in the greenhouse at the Jas de Bouffan; the artist drew and painted them *in situ* or incorporated them into his still lifes in his converted studio on the second floor of the manor house, where this picture is likely to have been executed.

The Chinese primrose depicted here takes centre stage, dominating the composition. Observing the plant from a slightly elevated position, Cézanne emphasises its solidity, to the detriment of its prettiness: only one flower looks in bloom, the stems appear rather thick and its leaves stiff, delineated by dark contours that accentuate their rigidity. It is flanked by a plate with two pears, one seen from its base, inscribed in a perfect circle; a third fruit lies in front of the pot, having possibly rolled from the plate to fall on its side. The soft curves of the pears and the plate's festooned edges echo the scalloped contours of the plant's indented leaves; all contrast with the severe, semi-abstract network of lines animating the wall. Cézanne may have learnt this formal trick from his friend Pissarro, who would often enliven the background of his still lifes with the straight lines of wallpaper, or with pictures hanging on the wall, using their vertical and horizontal edges as a strict structure contrasting with the bends and gentle ovals of leaves and petals.

In Cézanne's still lifes, however, these background lines serve a further purpose. Whether ornamental moulding, painted decorative lines or studio props, they are not immediately legible. They distort the picture plane and throw the composition out of balance. Here, behind the plant, a stretcher seems to have been propped up in the space between the wall and the table, the top edge of which drops abruptly to the right. The stretcher appears to be resting on the table's edge, pushing the composition towards the viewer, as if plant and fruit, thrown out of balance, may fall off the table. Yet this tension and slight sense of insecurity are admirably counterbalanced by Cézanne's harmonious brushwork and delicate palette: soft colouring and luminous tones, enlivened with warm accents, are distributed throughout the picture.   AR

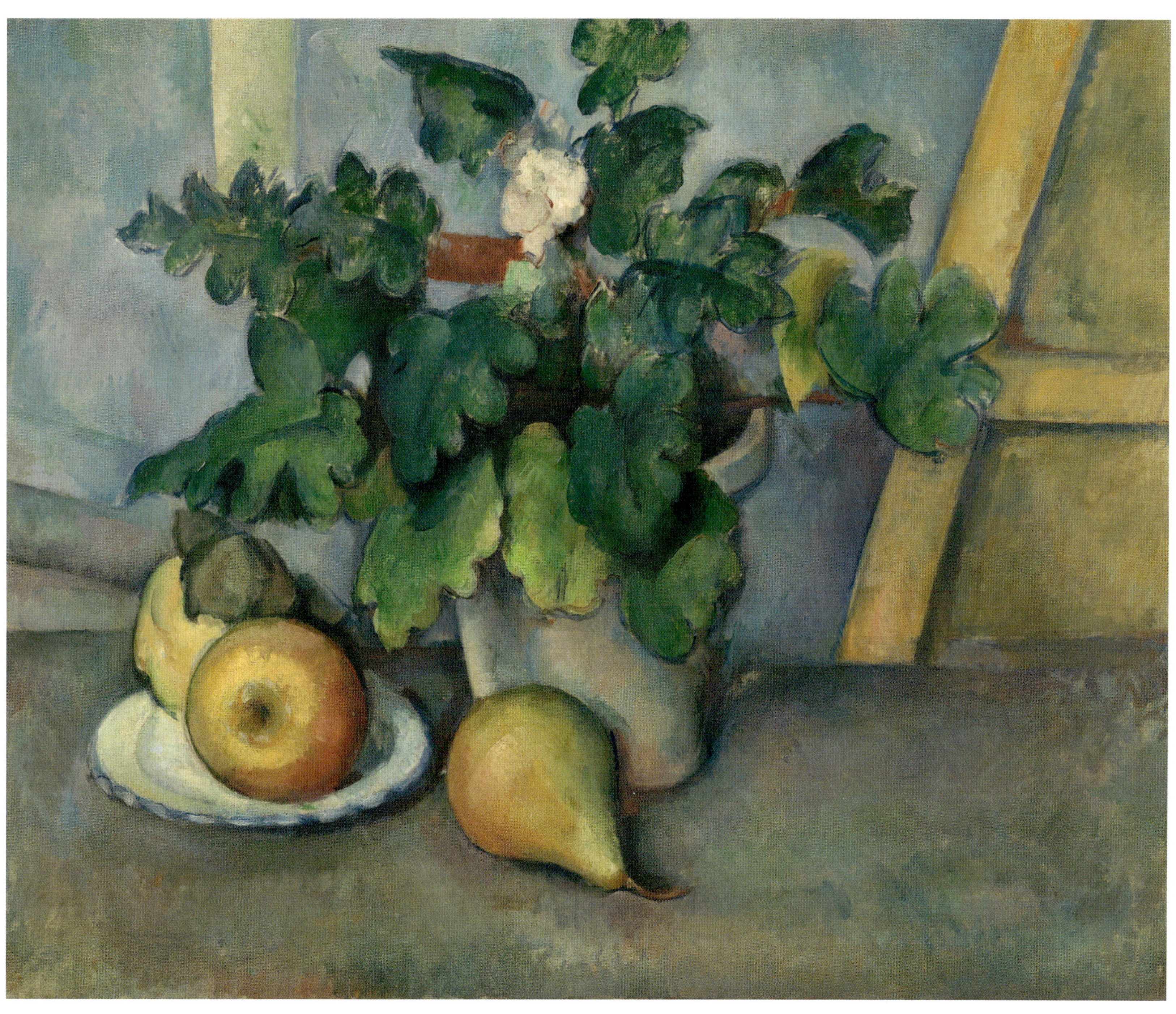

Paul Cézanne
Hillside in Provence, about 1890–2

Oil on canvas, 63.5 × 79.4 cm
The National Gallery, London. Bought, Courtauld Fund, 1926
NG4136

This painting is imbued with a profound sense of place: the area around Aix-en-Provence, which Cézanne knew intimately by wandering its dusty paths throughout his career. Cézanne captures the characteristic landscape, the effects of the southern light, but he also titillates the viewer's senses, evoking the smell of pine trees in the scorching heat of the sun, or the repetitive background sound of crickets. While it has the appearance of a painting executed quickly in the open air, its simple composition belies the care with which each element was placed in order to attain a solid and harmonious whole.

The wall of angular, protruding rocks is the main subject of the picture, set off between the smooth dusty road of the foreground and the fuzzy foliage of the pines above. The pays d'Aix has its own distinctive geology and topography, and Cézanne seems to have had a particular interest in understanding the geological specificities of the region, reportedly saying: 'In order to paint a landscape well, I first need to discover its geological structure…I need to know some geology… since such things move me, benefit me.' Cézanne took great care in carving the spectacular ragged rock formation out of a bold interplay of light and dark, using short parallel strokes of complementary colours to create dramatic contrasts: the orange-red rocks drenched in sunlight become violet-blue in the cool shadows.

Above the rocks and the trees, a discreet farmhouse in the middle distance serves as the only indication that the land is inhabited, its geometric shapes almost invisible amid the squares of the fields gently sloping behind it. While the mountains are less remarkable than the rocks in the foreground, the brownish red and the complementary greens of the fields give a tonal vibration, animating the landscape with a sense of shimmering atmosphere. Cézanne painted much of the colour in thin, diluted washes of oil paint, giving the picture an effect akin to watercolour. The primed pale blond canvas is visible throughout the composition, which is suffused with the warm glow of a southern landscape drenched in sunlight.   JD

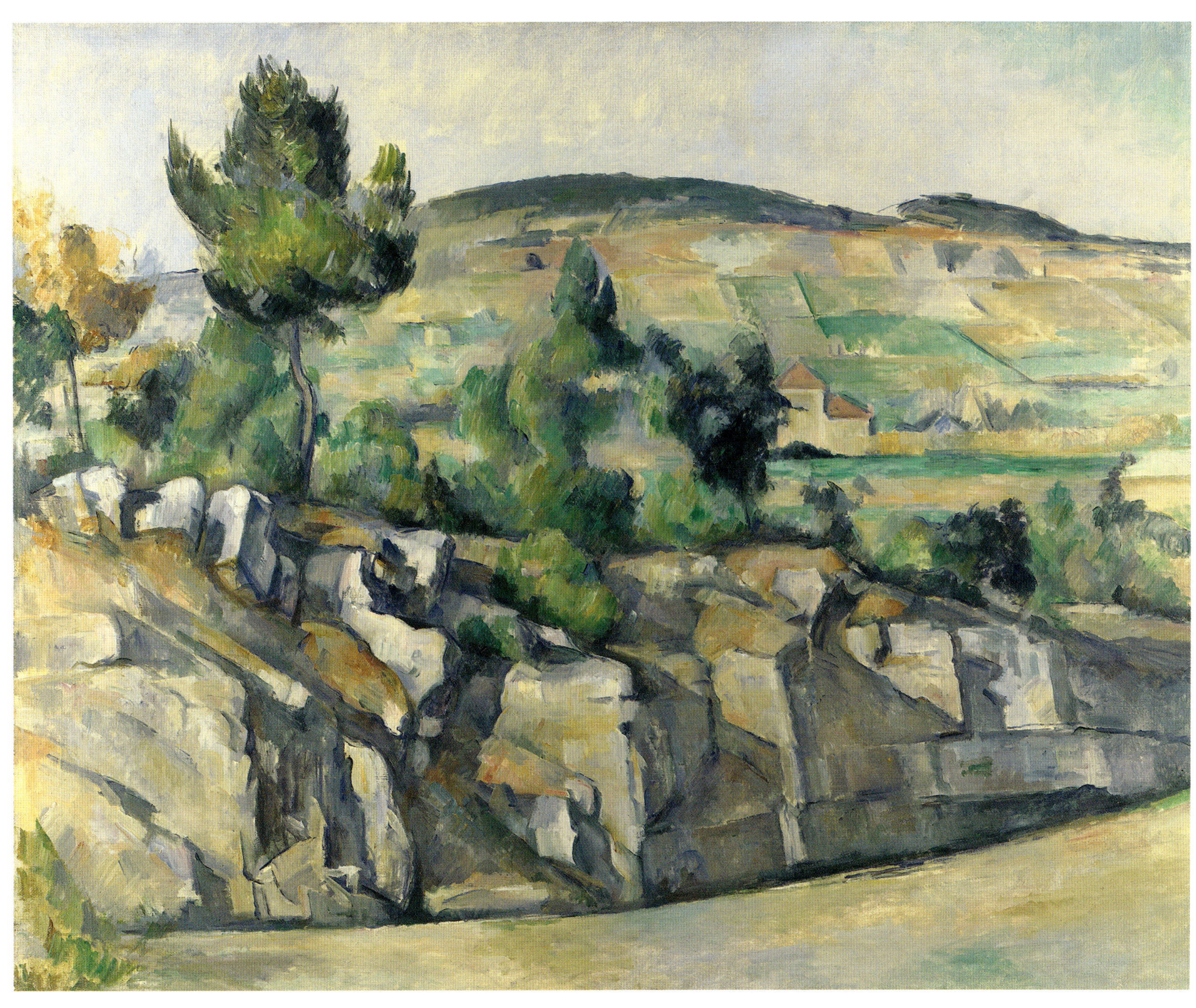

Paul Cézanne
The Card Players, about 1892–6

Oil on canvas, 60 × 73 cm
The Samuel Courtauld Trust, The Courtauld Gallery, London
P.1932.SC.57

This is one of five pictures showing men playing cards that Cézanne painted in the 1890s. They differ in size, setting and in the number of figures they depict: from five to just two protagonists. The three canvases with two players facing each other – such as this one – form a coherent group, showing the same dark interior and compact arrangement of figures. With brown wainscoting or wood panelling, and what could be the blurred surface of a mirror, the room has sometimes been identified as a café, yet is more likely to depict the farmhouse of the Jas de Bouffan, the country estate that had belonged to Cézanne's father, and where the artist painted regularly. His sitters are peasants and servants who lived and worked on the farm. After a day labouring in the fields, they relaxed by playing cards, a pastime then popular in Provence.

The atmosphere is one of quiet concentration as the players focus on their game. While evoking seventeenth-century Dutch or French genre scenes in its configuration and setting, the picture exudes a sense of peace and silence at odds with these Old Master paintings of gamblers in rowdy taverns. It is devoid of moralising undertones and free from any narrative or anecdote. With no hint of camaraderie between them, the figures, along with the table, chairs and bottle, are like elements of a tautly structured still life. This sense of disconnection between the players may be explained by Cézanne's working methods and his staging of the scene. He posed his models separately, making drawings and studies of each individual figure and using them as visual aids, before combining them on the canvas.

This may account for the perspectival distortions of the composition, where the table leans dangerously to the left while the head of the man to this side looks more remote than his body. Like his sitters, Cézanne's brushstrokes are disjointed, loosely applied then filled in with vibrant touches, in subdued tones.

In 1919 Cézanne's early biographer, Gustave Coquiot, hailed his paintings of card players as 'equal to the most beautiful works of art in the world'. Ten years later Samuel Courtauld paid £12,500 for this painting, his second most expensive Cézanne; he even considered exchanging his *Lac d'Annecy* landscape (see p. 58) – itself a masterpiece – for this work, which shows how eagerly he coveted it. Courtauld ended up spending more money on works by Cézanne than by any other artist.   AR

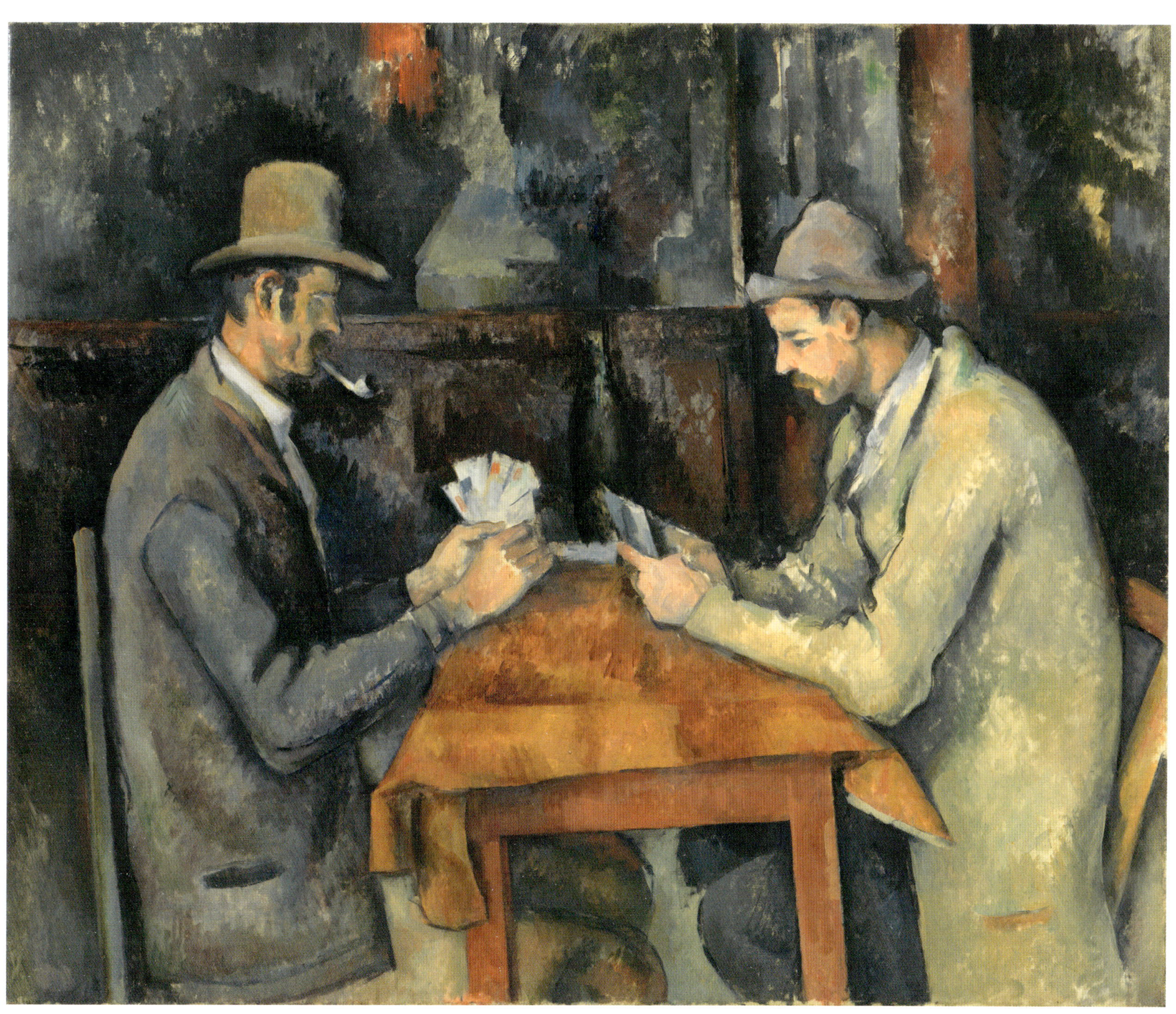

Paul Cézanne
Man with a Pipe, about 1892–6

Oil on canvas, 73 × 60 cm
The Samuel Courtauld Trust, The Courtauld Gallery, London
P.1932.SC.58

Cézanne painted a number of pictures showing individual peasants and farmworkers: some of them as single-figure oil studies for his group paintings; others as independent works, such as this one. This picture of a smoker is related to Cézanne's paintings of card players: its sitter appears as the man to the left of the three two-figure compositions (this would not have escaped Samuel Courtauld's attention as he sought to acquire *The Card Players* (p. 53); he enjoyed these connections between artworks within his collection). Whereas most of Cézanne's card players sit in profile, here the smoker faces us, on a neutral background animated by only two horizontal lines.

Wearing a rough coat and smoking a clay pipe, his hair and moustache unkempt, the man depicted here was employed on the Jas de Bouffan estate, which Cézanne's father had acquired in 1859. By the early 1890s Cézanne had known some of its employees for three decades and would have felt comfortable asking them to sit for him, whereas he was notoriously uneasy using professional models. Here the smoker's near absence of facial expression belies the alleged familiarity between sitter and artist. His calm, stolid features barely betray his lassitude after the labours of the day; instead his hunched posture conveys his exhaustion. His wide frame, slightly tilted towards us, structures the composition, his broad shoulders pointing downwards as if dragged by tired, heavy arms. The bell-shaped, rounded contour of his back echoes the curve of his hat, while its narrow, turned-up brim chimes with the clearly defined outline of his ears.

The room is bathed in dimmed natural light, possibly filtered by a window facing the sitter. This produces specks on his face, clothing and on the background wall, creating a sense of volume and bringing him to life. Cézanne's palette is restricted to warm browns, dirty ochres, olive-greens, earth colours and greys, with delicately distributed blue and pink highlights. He applied pigment in light, loose diagonal strokes, allowing the primed pale canvas to show through in places, to achieve an effect of texture and depth. Dark lines, sometimes tentative – for instance on the edge of the smoker's waistcoat – reinforce the sense of volume: the irregular contours add vibrancy. Cézanne's idiosyncratic approach to finish and drawing was still derided in Britain in the 1920s, despite Roger Fry's energetic praise of his unique abilities as a draughtsman. Courtauld was not dctcrrcd, acquiring *Man with a Pipe* in October 1927.   AR

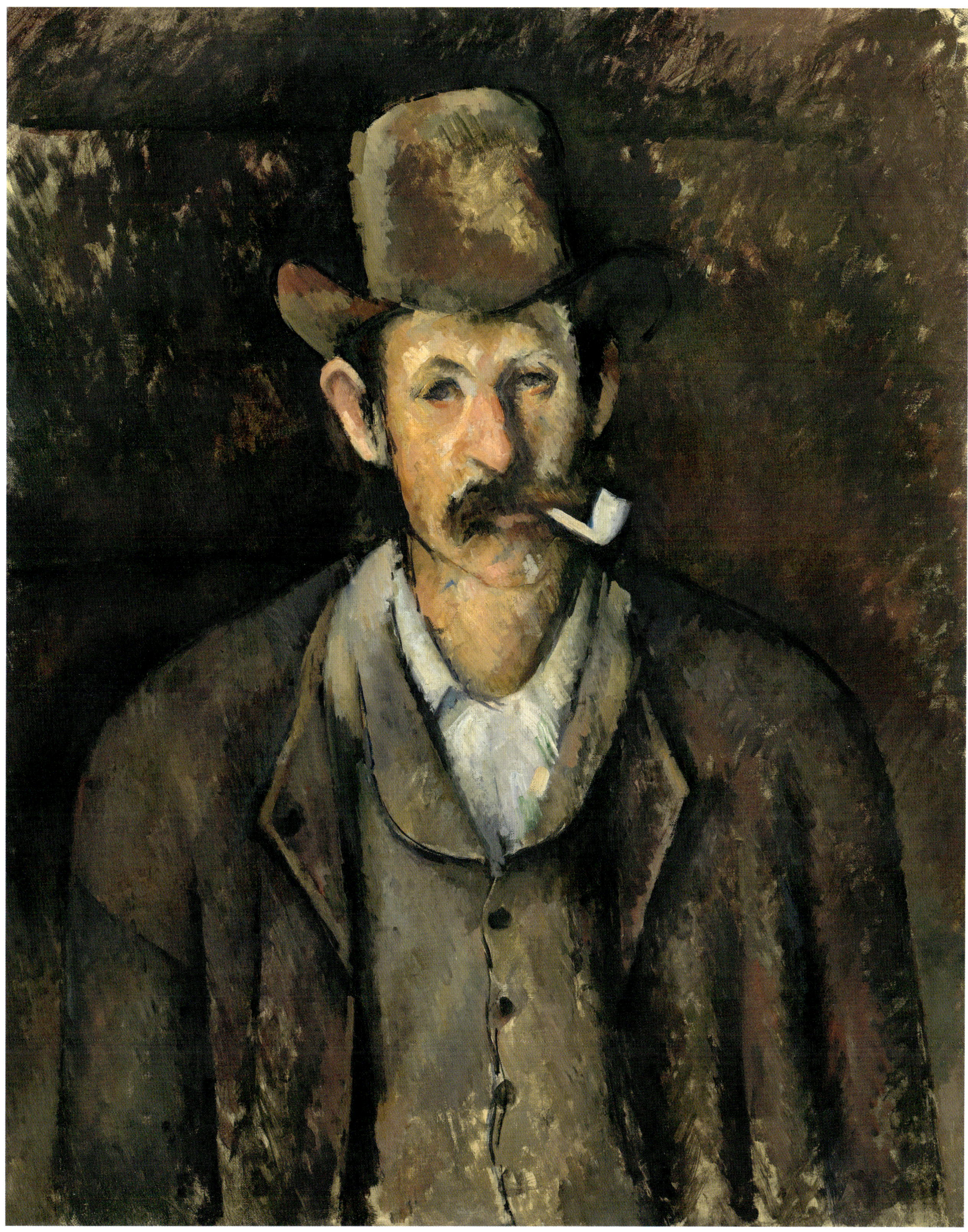

Paul Cézanne
Still Life with Plaster Cupid, about 1894

Oil on paper on board, 70.6 × 57.3 cm
The Samuel Courtauld Trust, The Courtauld Gallery, London
P.1948.SC.59

With its complex composition and multilayered meaning, this painting remains one of Cézanne's greatest works, as well as among the most puzzling. On a portrait-oriented canvas, unusual for still lifes, foodstuff and studio props are arranged around the plaster cast of a cupid. Cézanne particularly treasured this statuette, then attributed to the seventeenth-century sculptor Pierre Puget – a fellow Provençal artist he much admired – taking it with him from one studio to another and sketching it in a number of drawings.

Viewed from above, the putto spirals upwards, towering over a range of objects. Apples and onions lie on a table against which canvases are propped up; a large painted still life of fruit nestling in blue drapery is wedged between the table and the wall to the left; and a small canvas of an *écorché* after Michelangelo hangs, or sits, at the top.

By showing objects both real and painted with no clear limits between them, thus playing games with the idea of representation, Cézanne departs radically from the traditional depiction of a still life. In the ambiguous studio space, the busy foreground contrasts sharply with the empty, flat, trapezoidal area to the right, which is hardest to decipher. Is the floor tilting towards us, and if

so why is the most distant fruit not rolling down its slope? The cupid's torso leans back, his belly projecting forward; however the lower part of his body is differently oriented. His elongated, muscular legs, emphasised by a dynamic line, look disconnected from his plump upper body, as if belonging to another sculpture altogether. The thigh and calf stretched forward, foot gracefully tilted, are reminiscent of Puget's *Milo of Croton* (1671–82, Musée du Louvre, Paris), the large, dramatic sculpted group that Cézanne studied in a dozen drawings. It is not impossible to think that Cézanne – who found in still life an ideal ground for experimentation – may have given his dimpled putto the legs of this sixth-century BC Greek wrestler, fusing his memories of Puget's masterwork with this small, directly observed studio plaster.

This is the first work by Cézanne to have entered Samuel Courtauld's private collection, which was to include no fewer than 11 paintings by the artist. A critic visiting Courtauld's home in 1928 described Cézanne as 'the hero of this collection'. Within it, this work held exactly that place: Courtauld kept it close at hand and heart until his death in 1947.   AR

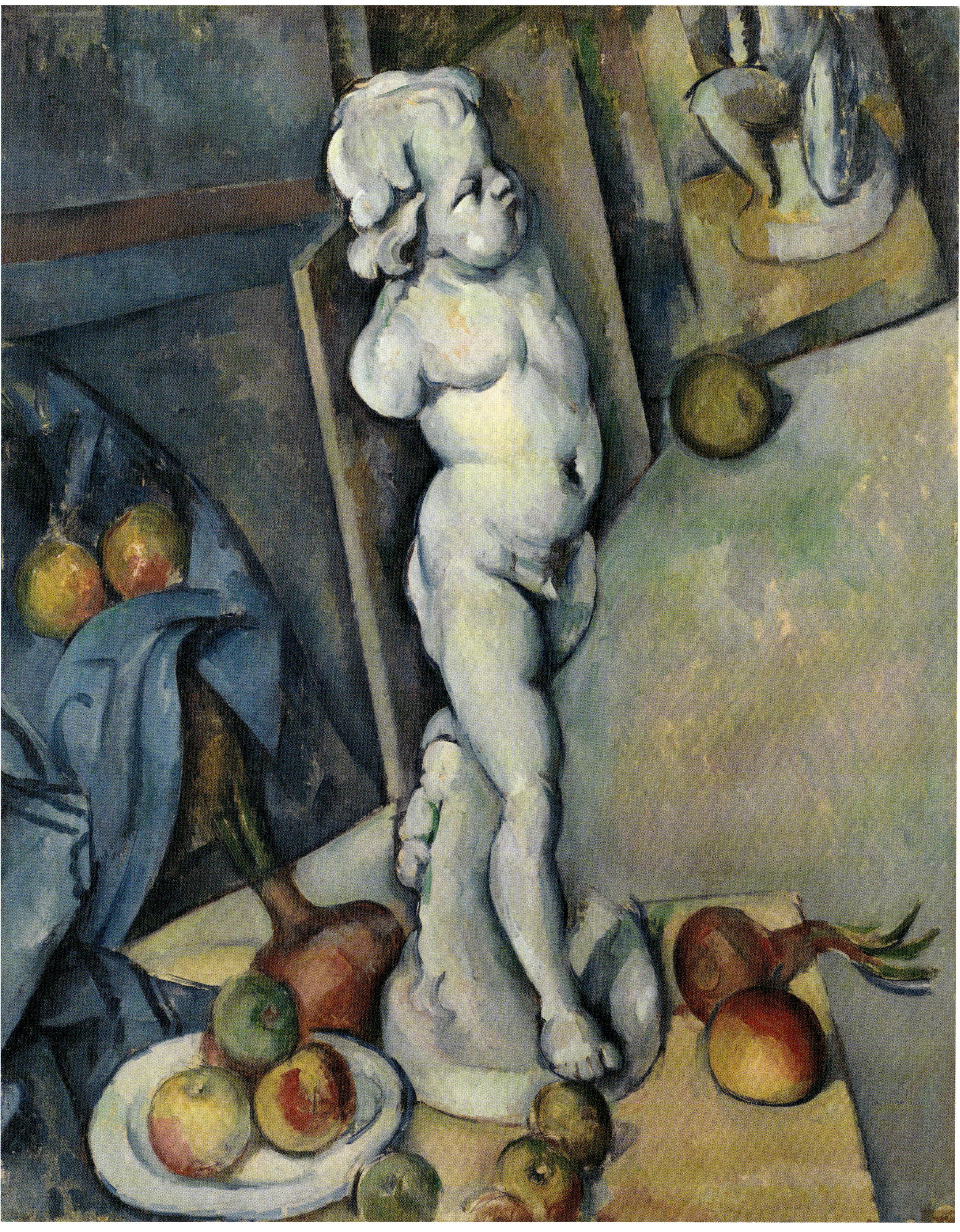

Paul Cézanne
Lac d'Annecy, 1896

Oil on canvas, 65 × 81 cm
The Samuel Courtauld Trust, The Courtauld Gallery, London
P.1932.SC.60

Alongside his depictions of Montagne Sainte-Victoire, this glorious landscape is one of Cézanne's best known and most accomplished; unlike his images of the Provençal mountain, which he depicted ceaselessly, the artist seems to have painted this view only once. The picture was executed in July 1896, when Cézanne, persuaded by his wife, was taking a holiday in the Haute-Savoie region of France, staying by the scenic lac d'Annecy. The abbaye de Talloires where the couple stayed – a medieval abbey recently converted into a hotel – offered spectacular views of the distant shore and alpine panorama.

Cézanne hardly ever travelled – he left France only once, for a trip to Switzerland in 1890 – and was easy prey to ennui on such holidays. Writing to a friend, he begrudgingly acknowledged the evident beauty of the view: 'To relieve my boredom I'm doing some painting; it's not much fun, but the lake is very fine with big hills around…It's not as good as our country.' The site was no doubt dismissed by Cézanne as looking too much like a postcard. 'The Lake…seems to lend itself to the linear drawing exercises of young ladies', he reported. 'It is still nature, of course, but a little bit as we have learned to see it in the sketchbooks of young lady travellers'. Yet the crystalline water, with a castle jutting out on the lake, and the majestic backdrop of mountains inspired him to paint this masterful work.

Not entirely avoiding pictorial conventions, Cézanne made the castle the focal point, framed by a large tree to the left, which creates a sense of depth. Its branches shelter the lake's surface, while their descending diagonals contrast with the ascending lines of the hillside contours, hit by the warm, golden-pink rays of the morning sun. The landscape is glowing in this radiant light, which illuminates the massive trunk, the castle's pale blond stone and the mountain pastures. Cézanne's palette of dark blue-greens, soft pinks and gold-yellows evokes the fresh mountain air and pure lake water. These rich colours are subtly adjusted in a complex pattern of distinct brushstrokes. Fluid and diluted in the foreground when describing the water – cut through by long reflections on the lake's mirror-like surface – they become denser and more heavily worked in the distance, on the hillside slopes, where they shimmer like the facets of a precious stone. The English writer and critic Roger Fry, who saw this painting in Paris before Samuel Courtauld acquired it, thought it, rightly, 'unsurpassed'.   AR

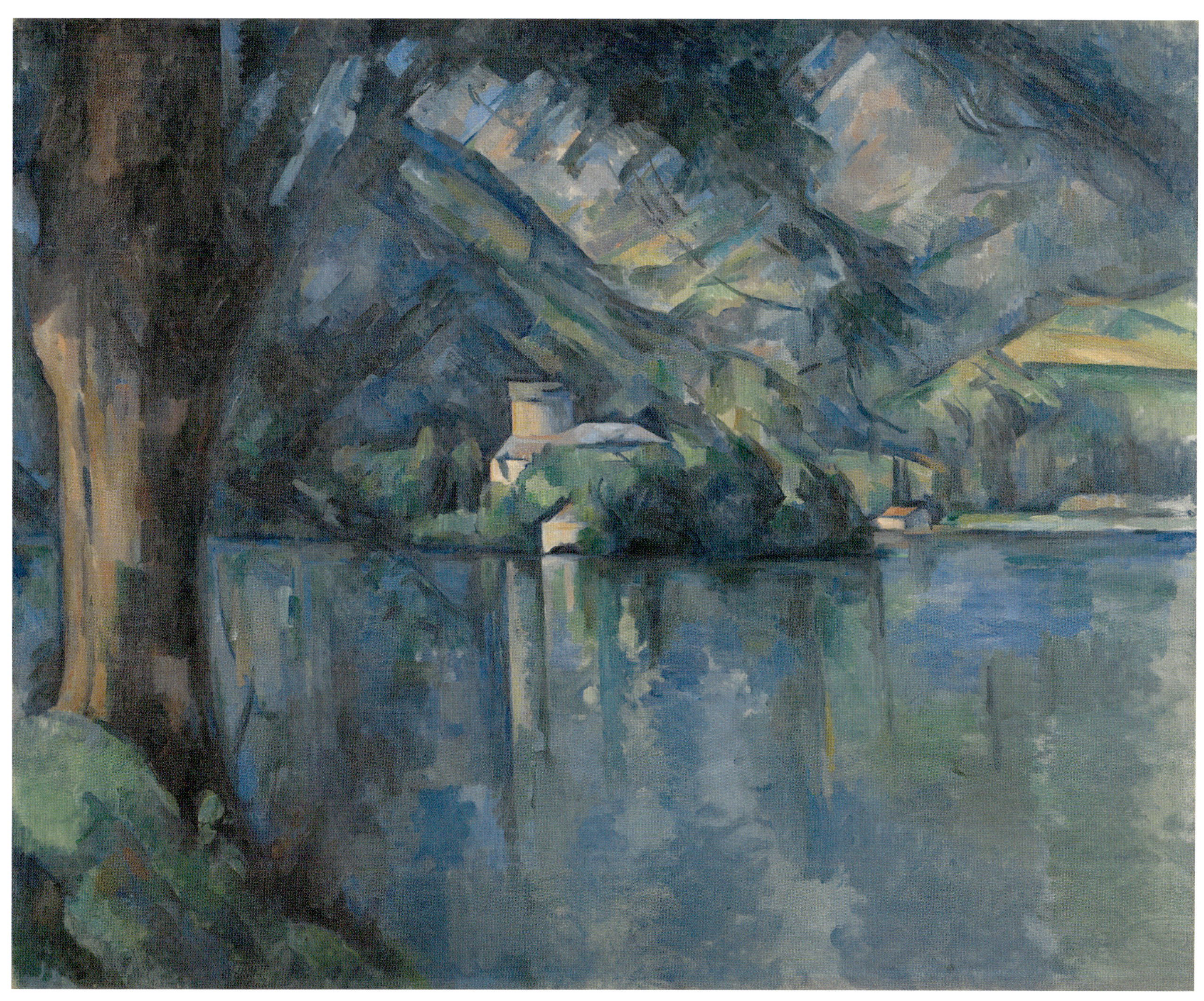

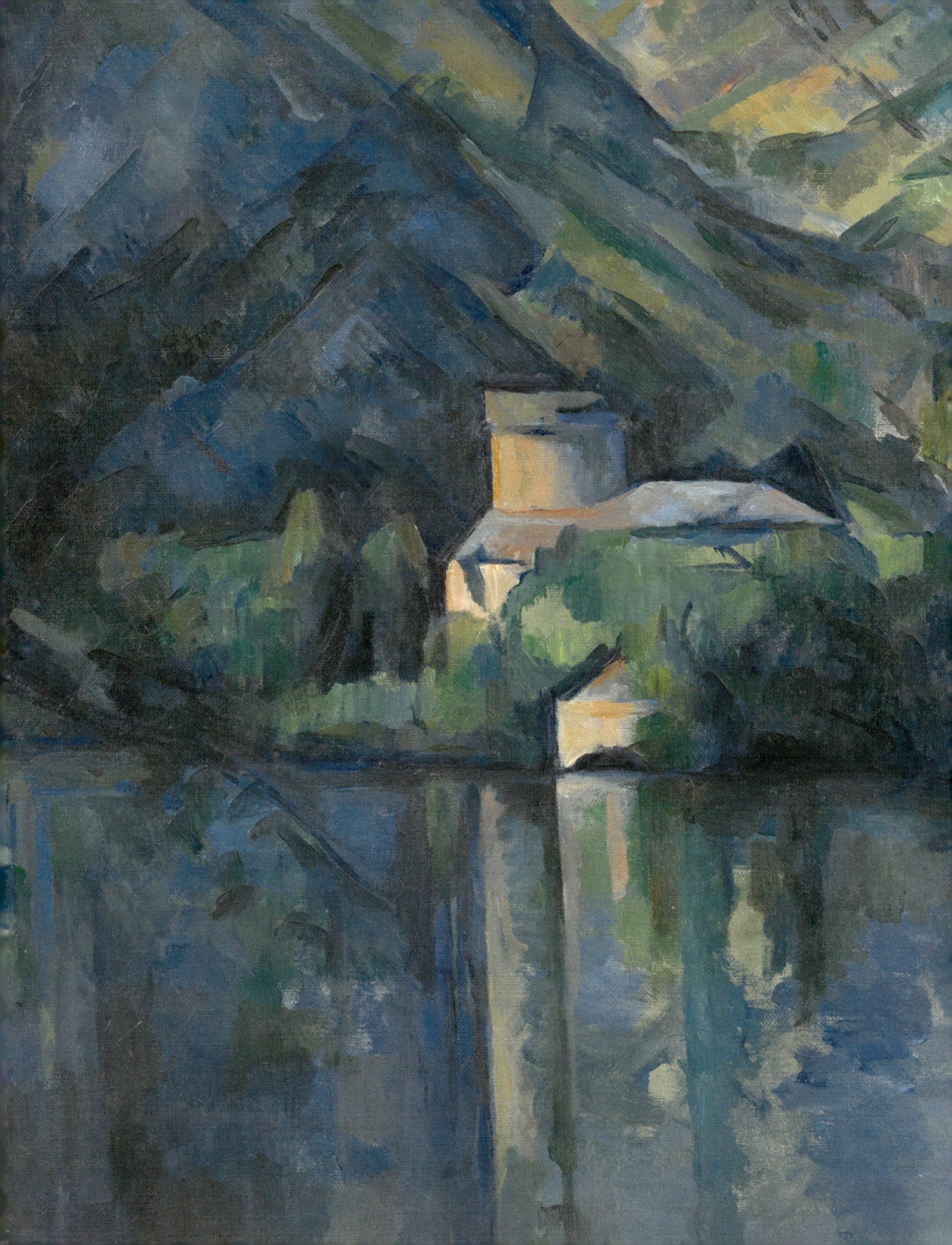

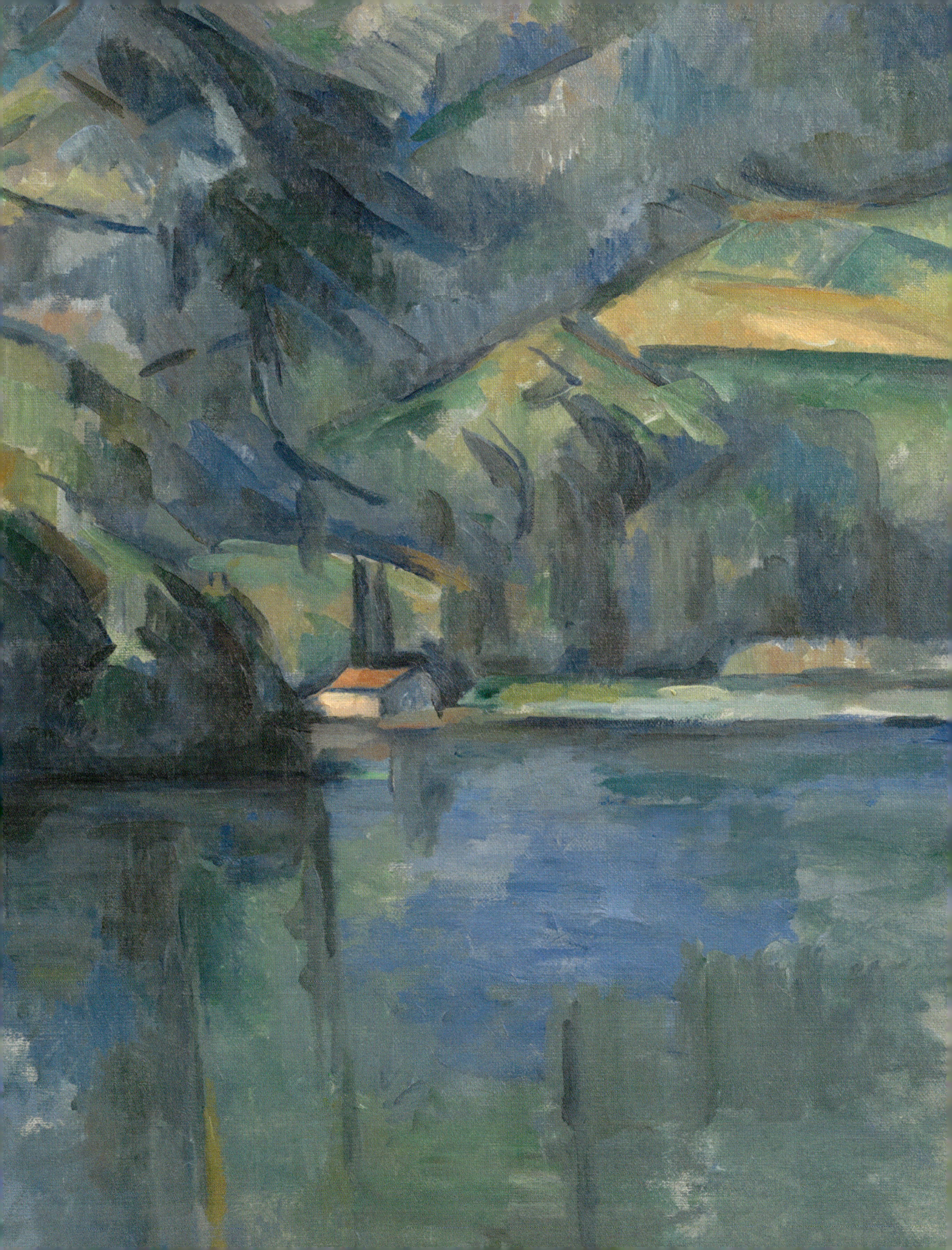

Honoré-Victorin Daumier (1808–1879)
Don Quixote and Sancho Panza, about 1855

Oil on oak, 40.3 × 64.1 cm
The National Gallery, London. Sir Hugh Lane Bequest, 1917
NG3244

This oil sketch shows the two protagonists of *Don Quixote*, Miguel de Cervantes's seventeenth-century satirical tale of knights and chivalry. From 1850 onwards, Daumier made numerous drawings and paintings of these characters, not always from specific episodes in the novel. This work is a preparatory study for a larger work depicting an episode from part 1, chapter 18, in which the idealistic Don Quixote heroically charges at two advancing armies in the distance, only to discover that the dust clouds are caused not by soldiers but herds of sheep.

While the dust clouds and sheep themselves cannot be seen in this study, Daumier – a caricaturist of great repute – clearly renders the differing personalities of the two men. To the left, the elderly noble Don Quixote on his equally elderly horse Rocinante charges into the middle distance, lance at the ready. His trusty squire, Sancho Panza, unable to restrain his master, remains static on his mule, which looks on impassively at Don Quixote. Sancho Panza's hands appear raised towards his face; here he may seem to be taking a swig from his drinking bottle, but in the final picture his hands are clasped together, perhaps imploring Don Quixote not to charge.

The strong psychological contrast between the figures is matched by extreme lighting effects within the picture. The dramatic shadow in the foreground, and the clearly delineated forms of the men and their mounts, are typical of Daumier, who was better known as a printmaker. Yet the artist chose to make only drawings and paintings of this subject, asserting his status as a fine artist. His hand is very evident in this loosely painted work, in which the underdrawing is visible and an earlier sketch of the pair can be seen in the sky. Daumier seems to have used the end of his brush to outline the figure of Sancho Panza.

Daumier would have been familiar with the many illustrated editions of *Don Quixote* in French translation. By the mid-nineteenth century, a craze for the novel, referred to as 'Don Quixotisme', was rife among Romantic authors and artists. Daumier, like some of his contemporaries, associated his own creative personality with the inseparable and complementary pairing of the roguish Don Quixote and the more philosophical Sancho Panza.

Courtauld admired the work in Hugh Lane's collection and in 1923 acquired his own version. RMcK

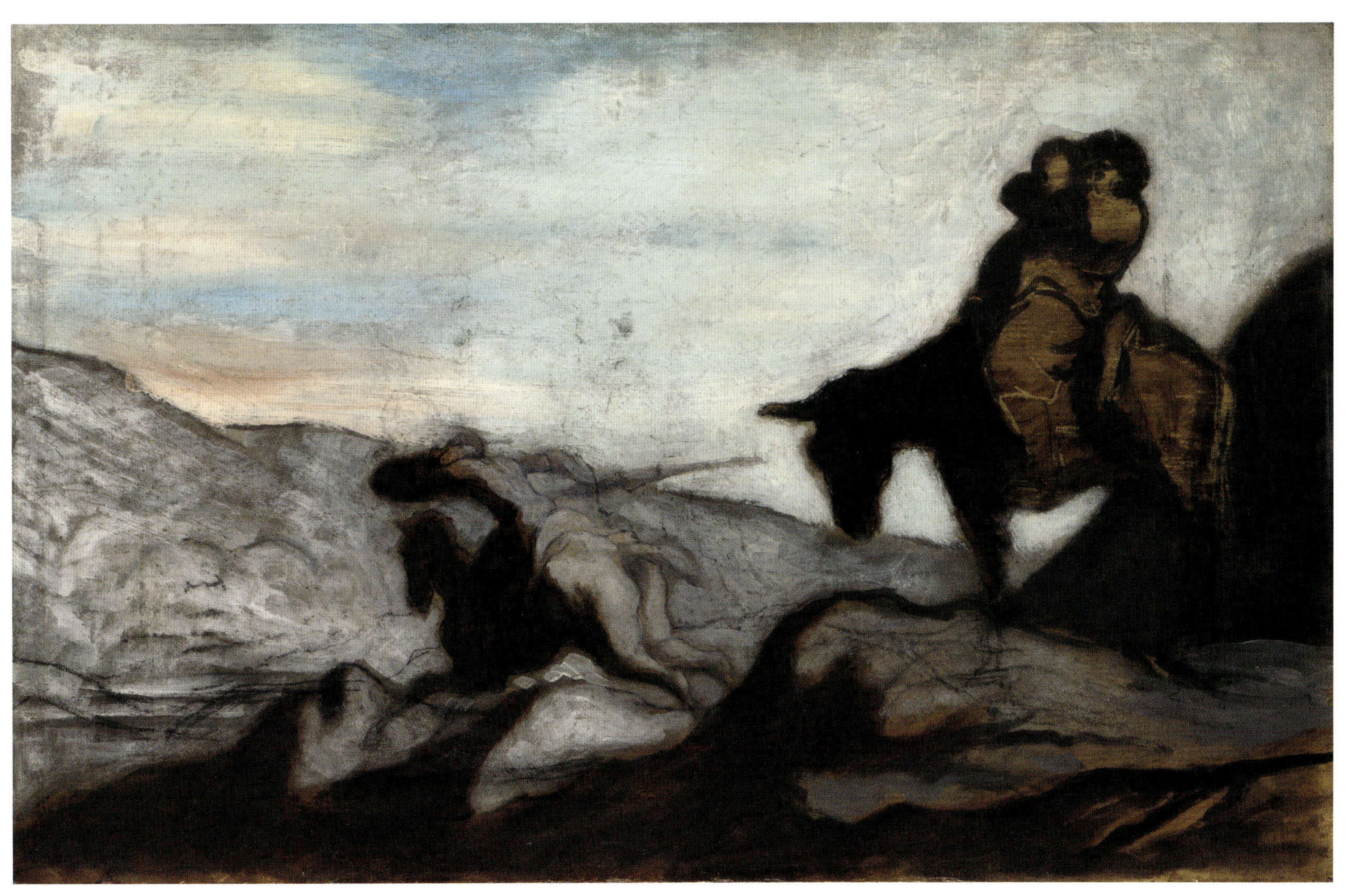

Honoré-Victorin Daumier
Don Quixote and Sancho Panza, about 1868–72

Oil on canvas, 100 × 81 cm
The Samuel Courtauld Trust, The Courtauld Gallery, London
P.1932.SC.86

Daumier was always attracted to the characters of Don Quixote and Sancho Panza. Miguel de Cervantes's hero, Don Quixote, featured in his first submission to the Paris Salon in 1851, and Daumier seems to have delighted in returning to the subject of this deluded, paranoid, idealistic knight and his improbable earthbound companion throughout his career. Daumier would have sympathised with Sancho Panza's earthly realism and found in the ambitious knight's disillusions a poignant reminder of his own thwarted aspirations.

This is one of Daumier's last paintings of the subject. A dark and mysterious picture, it depicts Don Quixote accompanied by his faithful long-suffering servant Sancho Panza riding across an oppressive mountainous gorge, only a sliver of sky appearing at the top right. Two faceless beings, they are an inseparable yet odd pair: the skeletal elongated silhouette of Don Quixote and his horse Rocinante is in stark contrast to the rotund, short shape of Sancho Panza riding his mule. One is tall, dignified and alert, the other squat, prostrate and exhausted; the knight's head held high, the servant's meekly pointed towards the earth, like his mule. They are ridiculous in their disparity and yet offer a moving reflection on the complexities of human relationships.

The deep spirituality of the work is reinforced by Daumier's daringly emotive application of paint. The armature-like form of the figures progressively appears out of a whirlwind of strokes of fluid brown paint, identified as either burnt umber or burnt sienna. The paint seems muddled and drips over the white ground of the canvas at the bottom of the picture, reinforcing the pathetic raggedness of the figures. Further modelling is achieved through the use of transparent white and grey brushstrokes, particularly to define Rocinante's proud head and Don Quixote's pointed shoulders, raised like the bones of a skeleton. At first glance restrained and sparse, the picture unfolds as an illustration of a creative performance, every step, layer and mark of its intricate production left visible.   JD

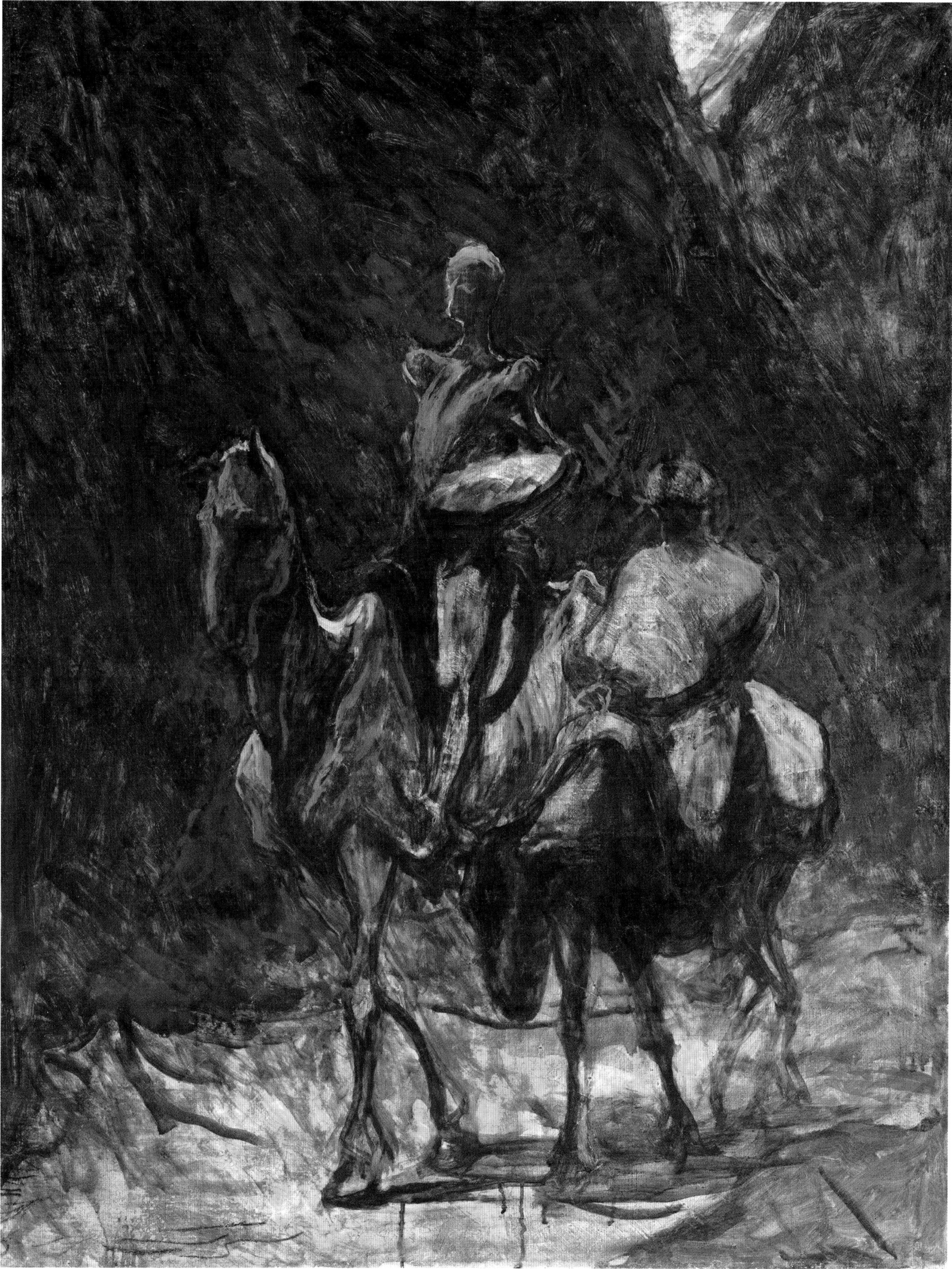

Hilaire-Germain-Edgar Degas (1834–1917)
Young Spartans Exercising, about 1860

Oil on canvas, 109.5 × 155 cm
The National Gallery, London. Bought, Courtauld Fund, 1924
NG3860

Early in his career Degas aspired to emulate the Old Masters, imagining he would follow the respectable path of history painting: large, learned compositions filled with figures of the ancient or medieval past. This picture is one of Degas's few history paintings ever to have made it beyond a myriad of preparatory drawings and oil sketches. Its subject matter was unconventional: Degas chose to depict a rather obscure passage from the work of the Greek philosopher Plutarch, detailing the manly upbringing of Spartan girls, who were encouraged to join boys in wrestling contests. While it was begun around 1860, Degas kept on reworking it through the 1870s, the 1880s and maybe even the 1890s, when he is thought to have repainted the background in broad strokes of pinks and greens, emulating the appearance of pastel. It is both an early and a late work, encapsulating the whole of the artist's career.

Degas felt a particular affection towards this picture, which held pride of place in his studio well into the twentieth century. Despite its many reworkings, it still bears witness to the characteristic way in which Degas varied the level of finish of different parts of his compositions. While the figures' features are carefully defined – the boys offering a variety of reactions to the girls' taunting and the faces of the central two girls exquisitely overlapping – their limbs have a sketch-like quality; the group of girls appears to hover above a cloud of legs. Degas's earlier sketches for the work contained more Hellenistic elements, such as a Greek temple in the background, but he progressively removed them as he developed his increasingly spare composition, imbuing the scene with a timelessness.

This work does more to bring in the contemporary world than first meets the eye. Aside from its classical subject matter, *Young Spartans* also evokes nascent adolescent sexuality and the meeting of the sexes on an equal footing. Degas's Spartan youths are not idealised classical bodies inspired by the antique sculptures he knew so well; they are contemporary Parisian types transposed into a scene from ancient Greece. One can recognise the svelte bodies of his future dancers in the Spartan girls, while his boys appear to be modelled on youths from Montmartre, where he lived. Under the respectable veneer of the classical, we can decipher that a keen interest in the modern world that surrounded him was present from the very outset of Degas's career.   JD

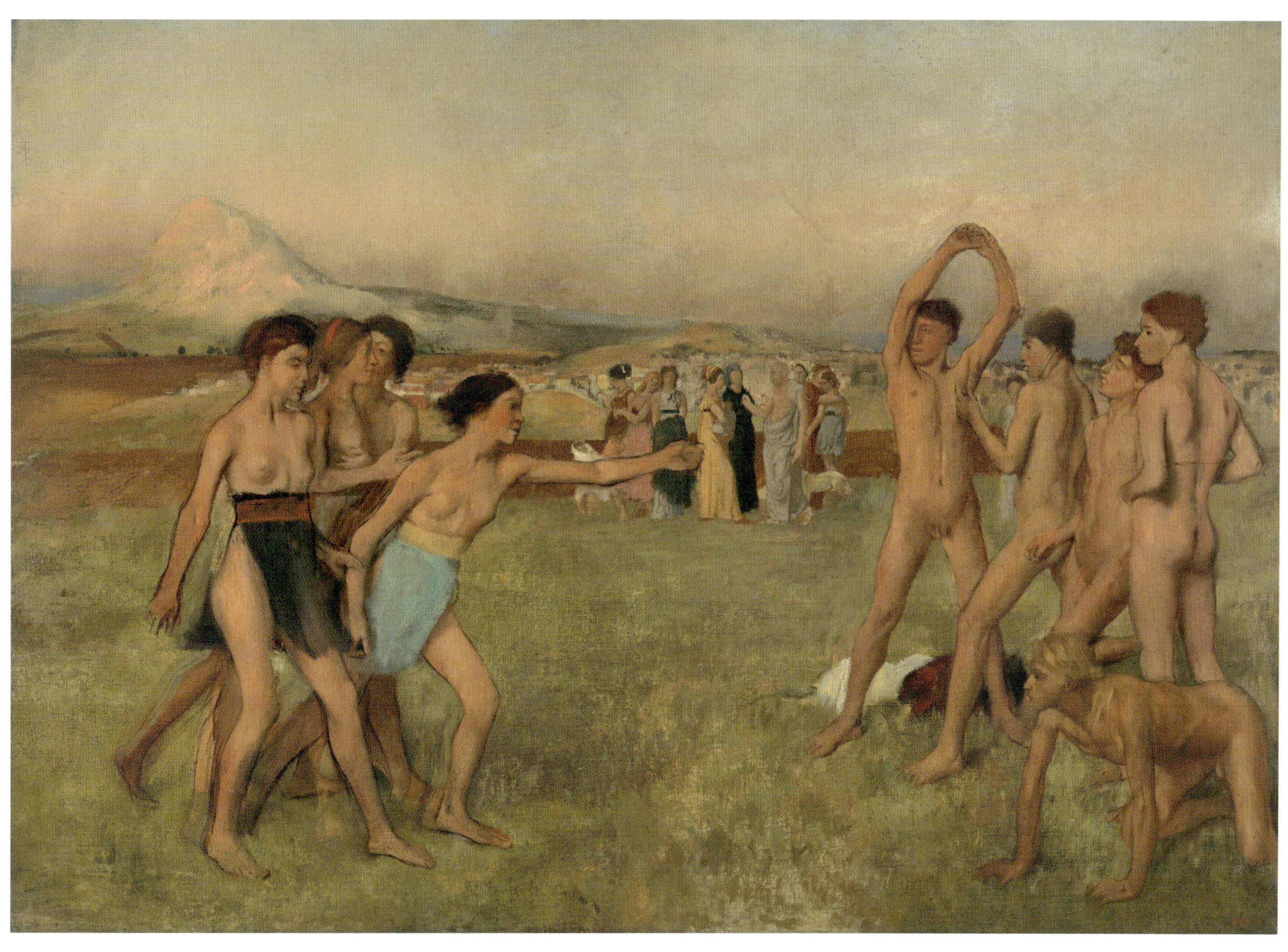

Hilaire-Germain-Edgar Degas
Woman at a Window, 1871–2

Oil on paper, 61.3 × 45.9 cm
The Samuel Courtauld Trust, The Courtauld Gallery, London
P.1932.SC.88

It was in the late 1850s that Degas began to use essence, paint drained of oil and thinned with turpentine, which produced a result very like watercolour, relatively transparent, and often matt. In the 1860s and 1870s he painted a small number of pictures purely in essence, of which this is one. It is worked using an extreme economy of colour; the dark paper support that stands in for areas of shadow is overlaid almost solely with black and different shades of white and cream. The woman's figure is outlined with rapid fluid brush drawing and then blocked in with thin washes of black essence. In the window, the absolute focus of light in the picture, a mass of thick white strokes is applied at random, overlapping the buildings and defining the sitter's profile. A brilliant shaft of light on the window frame overlies her black sleeve. Typically, Degas has reworked the outlines, particularly her back, and the white that contours her shoulder and right arm redefines its outline. With her face in shadow, the woman's two most striking features are her hands, with the finely observed play of light on their delicately curled fingers.

This painting was bought by the artist Walter Sickert in around 1901–2 for his former wife. A friend of Degas, whom he first met in 1883,

Sickert recorded the artist's reminiscences concerning the picture: that the sitter was a *cocotte*, that he painted it 'during or soon after' the siege of Paris during the Franco-Prussian war, when food was extremely scarce, and how he presented her with a piece of meat 'which she fell upon, so hungry was she, & devoured it raw.'

Her half-starved state is not evident in this serene and composed image of a woman seated calmly by a window, her face subtly turned towards the light. Degas had a particular interest in *contre-jour* lighting and had already explored the subject in a sketch of around 1860 of a figure silhouetted against a window. In such works as *A Woman Ironing* (1873, Metropolitan Museum of Art, New York), a dramatic dark form is outlined against the whites of the wall, the ironing and the diffuse light of a curtained window. It was this contrast of dark and light that fascinated Degas in so many of his portrayals of working women, whether actively labouring or, as here, posing for the artist.   SH

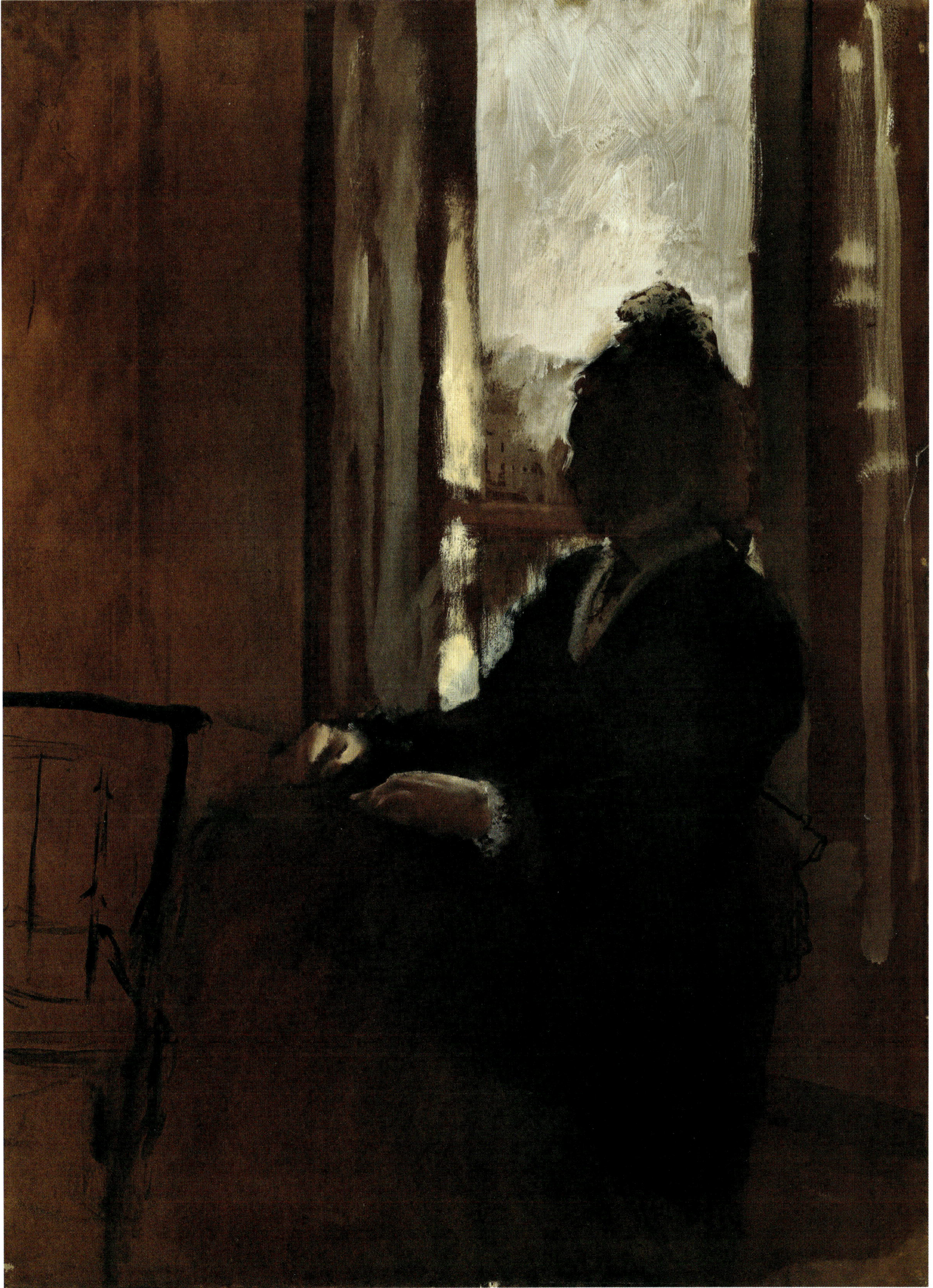

Hilaire-Germain-Edgar Degas
Two Dancers on a Stage, 1874

Oil on canvas, 61.5 × 46 cm
The Samuel Courtauld Trust, The Courtauld Gallery, London
P.1932.SC.89

Degas had a lifelong love of the ballet, portraying actual performances, classes and rehearsals, as well as making countless studies of individual dancers. Here two dancers perform on a largely empty stage in front of scenery painted to evoke exuberant foliage. The principal dancer, *sur pointes*, is set just to the right of centre; her supporting dancer is in fourth position, with her arms in *demi-seconde*. A third figure is just glimpsed on the far left. The first has a pink bodice, deep cerise roses in her skirt and a headdress of pink flowers. The second is in yellow, with additional green sepals over her skirt. Both wear black velvet ribbons around their necks. They have been identified as dancers in the *Ballet des Roses*, a love story between flowers and butterflies that was performed as part of Mozart's opera *Don Giovanni* at the theatre of the Paris Opéra in the rue Le Peletier. The same pair of dancers appears on the right of *The Ballet Rehearsal on Stage*, which exists in three versions: a grisaille of 1874 in the Musée d'Orsay, Paris, and two versions of around 1874 in the Metropolitan Museum of Art, New York. The two figures replicate those in the Orsay picture, although set further apart, so that more of the secondary dancer is visible. It was entirely characteristic of Degas to reinvent figures in this way, using drawings and studies (of which

a number exist of both dancers, presumably made before October 1873 when the theatre burned down) as reference points, even making tracings to facilitate placing them in reverse.

The paint surface is fairly highly worked, with, typically for Degas, final layers of paint incompletely covering the underpaint. The dancer's face has a top layer of thick white paint over her cheek and chin. The tulle skirts are also painted in white paint of varying thickness, so that in places their legs show through.

This picture was exhibited by the Parisian dealer Paul Durand-Ruel at the Ninth Exhibition of the Society of French Artists in London in November 1874. It was the first painting by Degas bought by the notable collector Captain Henry Hill, who later also purchased one of the related paintings now in the Metropolitan Museum of Art. The latter was acquired at Hill's estate sale in 1889 by the British artist Walter Sickert, a former owner of *Woman at a Window* (see p. 69).   SH

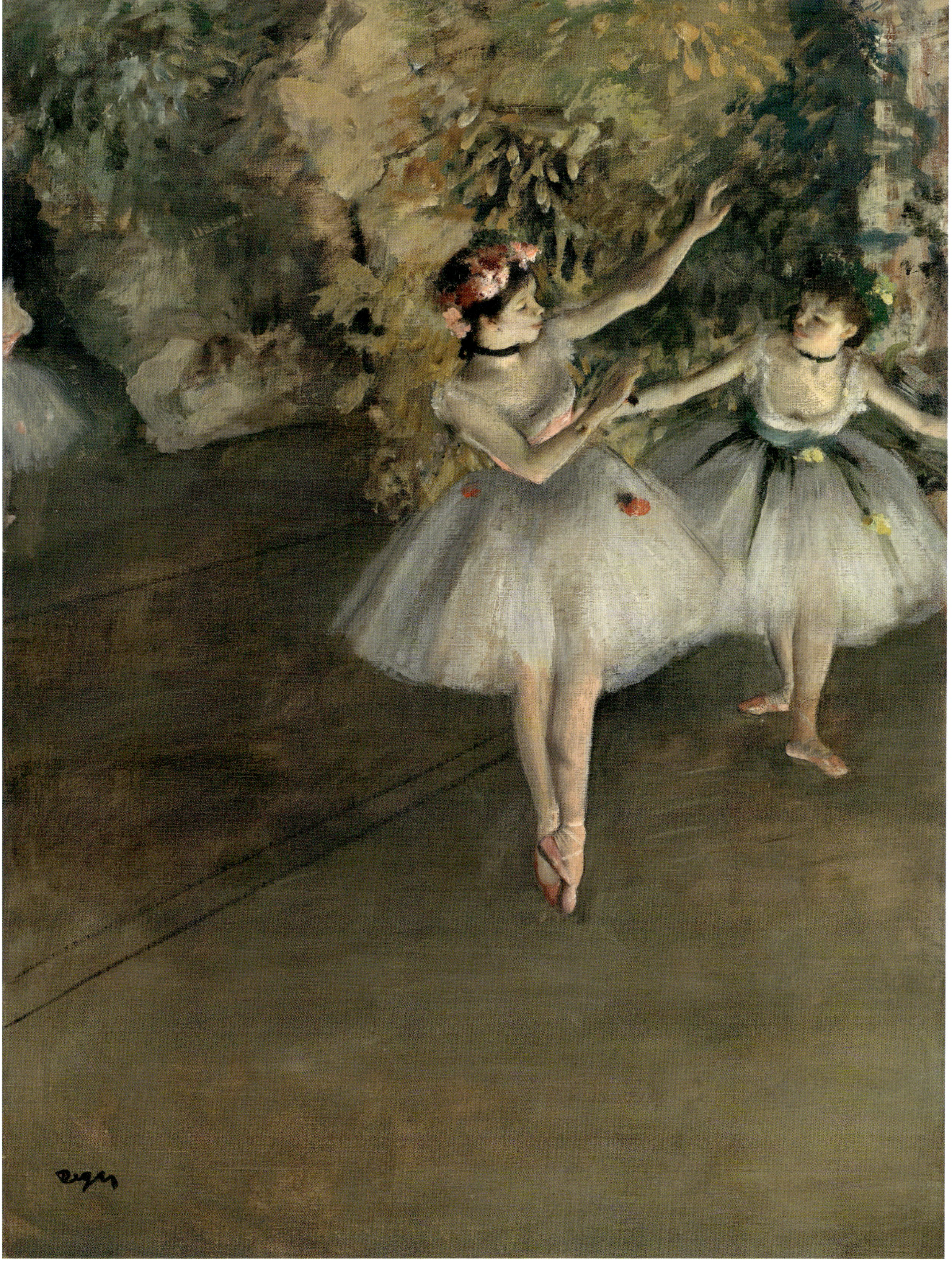

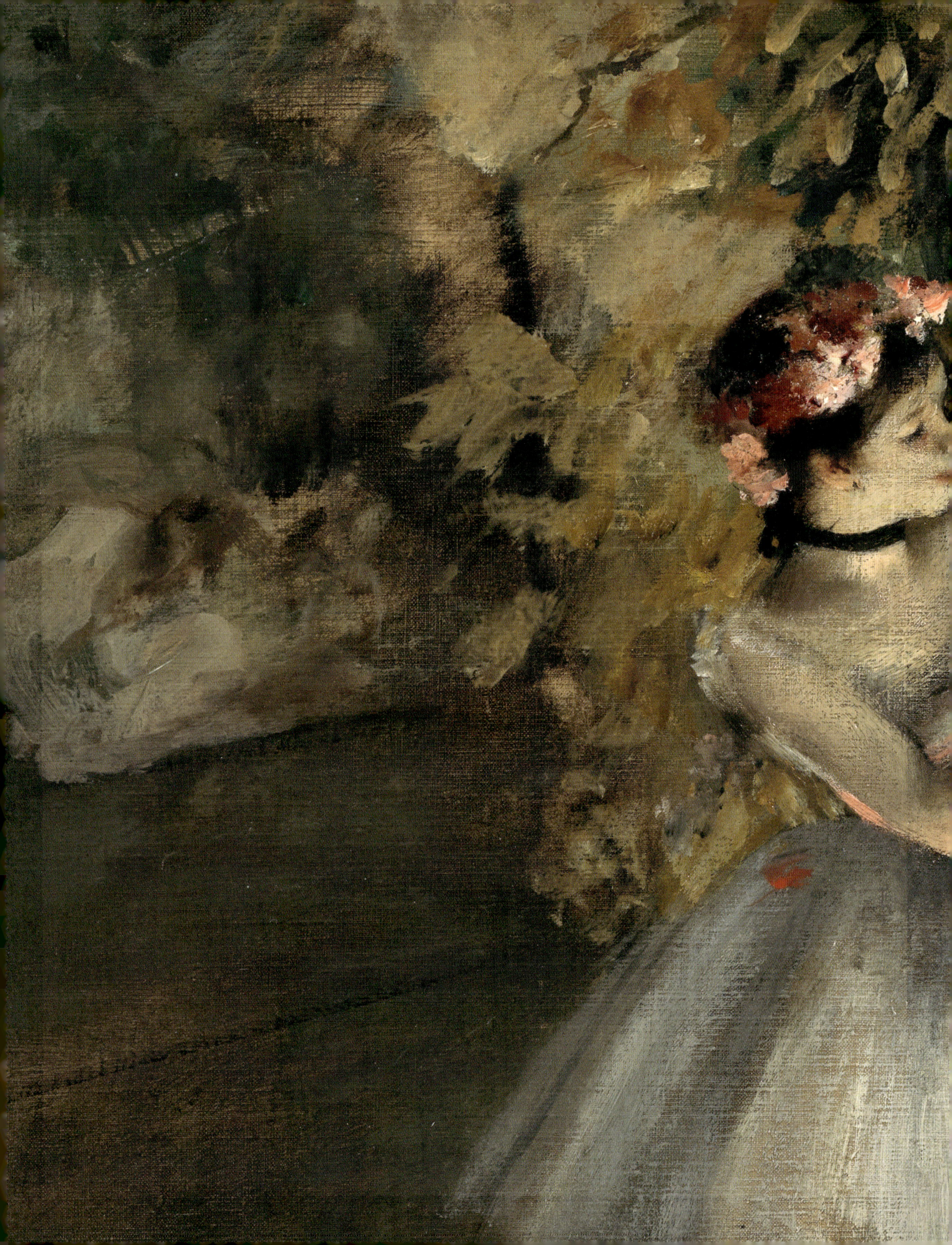

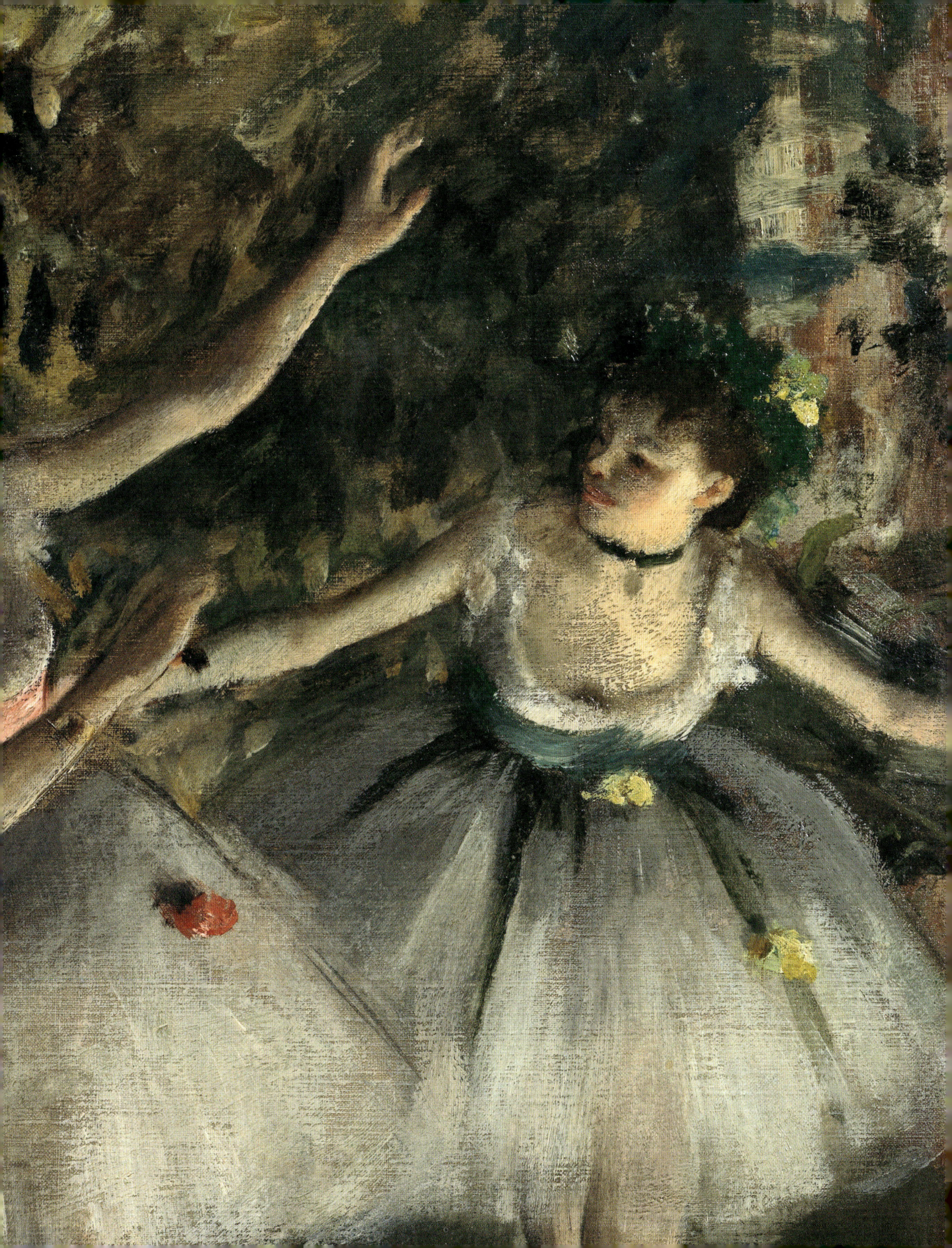

Hilaire-Germain-Edgar Degas
Portrait of Elena Carafa, about 1875

Oil on canvas, 70.1 × 55 cm
The National Gallery, London. Bought, Courtauld Fund, 1926
NG4167

This portrait is of Degas's first cousin, Elena, aged about 18. Her mother, Stéphanie, Marquesa di Cicerale and Duchessa di Montejasi, was the youngest sister of Degas's father and like most of Degas's extended family they lived in Naples. Degas's paternal grandfather had made a fortune establishing himself as a banker in the city, after allegedly narrowly escaping the guillotine during the French Revolution. Degas often travelled to Naples in his early career, and this portrait could have been painted when he returned with his dying father in the winter of 1873–4, or when he was again in the city for the funeral of his uncle, Achille, in 1875.

Degas did not produce portraits on commission, preferring to depict his circle of friends and family, imbuing the rare instances with a unique sense of intimacy and immediacy. This work is no exception. Elena slouches somewhat awkwardly in a flower-patterned armchair, her fingers nervously fiddling with the pages of a book. Her gaze is aimed straight at the viewer: it is that of a self-assured young woman combined with hints of the playfulness of childhood from which she has just emerged. Technical examination, however, has revealed a startling change of pose: Degas originally painted Elena lost in her thoughts, looking away with a downcast and unfocused gaze. He made this fundamental alteration with relatively little overpainting, by simply extending the left side of Elena's face, and amending the direction of her eyes. It is as if Degas may have reacted to a spontaneous movement during the sitting, his young cousin engaging more directly with him after an initial period of shyness.

As is customary in his oeuvre, Degas used varying degrees of finish in order to focus and guide the viewer's eye. Elena's face is clearly defined, as are her hands, emerging from a whirlwind of black brushstrokes evoking her lace sleeves. Her shawl is made of a series of short strokes of blue-green paint rapidly applied over part of the chair, which in turn is built up of equally quick zig-zagging brushwork of white paint, overlapped with dabs of red, pink and green to suggest its patterned fabric. One of the painting's most striking features is the red flower in Elena's hair, appearing out of a few dazzling brushstrokes of vermilion, which also find their way onto the curtain to the left.   JD

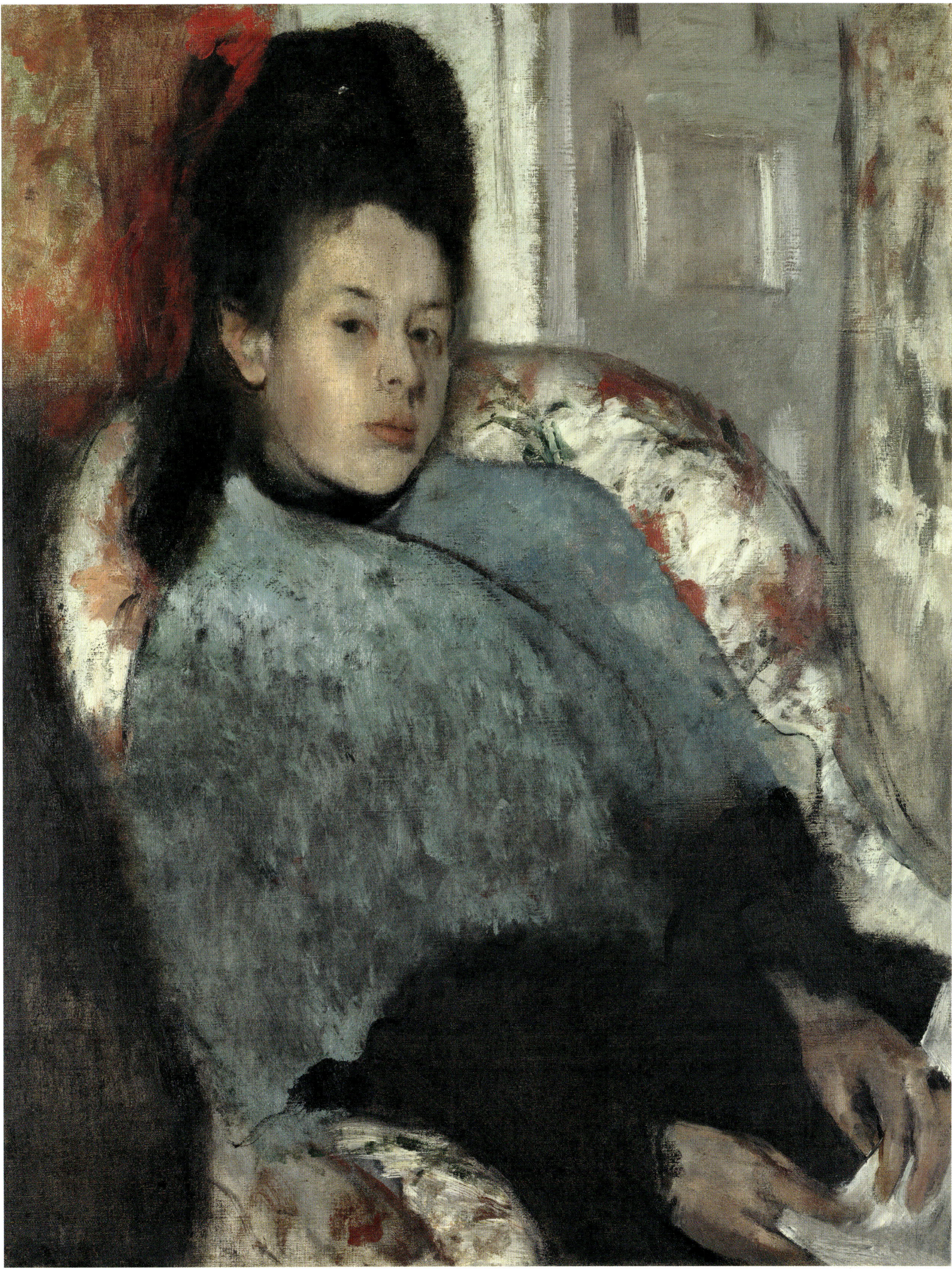

Hilaire-Germain-Edgar Degas
Carlo Pellegrini, about 1876–7

Oil on laid paper, strip-lined, 62.6 × 34.2 cm
Tate: Presented by the Art Fund, 1916
NO3157

Painted in rapid fluid brushstrokes of paint, this portrait is of Carlo Pellegrini, a well-known caricaturist based in London where he regularly contributed to *Vanity Fair* under the pseudonym 'Ape'. Degas may have been introduced to him by either of their mutual artist friends, Whistler or Tissot, on a visit to London in the 1870s. In about 1876–7, Pellegrini produced a half-length portrait caricature of Degas, with the artist's forehead enlarged and his eyebrows turned into long drooping diagonals, giving him a pained and somewhat quizzical expression. Pellegrini inscribed his work 'à vous/Pellegrini' and presented it to Degas. The present portrait, inscribed 'à lui/Degas', is thought to constitute Degas's return present, which Pellegrini kept until the end of his life.

Degas seems to have had Pellegrini's *Vanity Fair* caricatures in mind when he produced this portrait: not only is this work closer to caricature than any other he produced, but it also emulates the narrow upright format, exaggerated proportions and amusing distinctive attitudes that Pellegrini employed. On the other hand, Degas's portrait is executed in his characteristic idiosyncratic experimental technique. Most of the picture is painted in essence, a medium often used by Degas, which he made by draining paint of its oil before diluting it with turpentine. This allowed him to paint in fluid brushstrokes, flowing and blending like watercolour, staining the surface of the paper and drying quickly to a matt finish. Pellegrini's head, however, is painted in a few thick brushstrokes of traditional oil paint, giving the caricaturist's head a comical, lumpy texture.

Sir Joseph Duveen surely inspired Courtauld. He gave *Pellegrini* to the nation in 1916 and financed the galleries for modern foreign paintings at Tate where Courtauld Fund works would first be shown.   JD

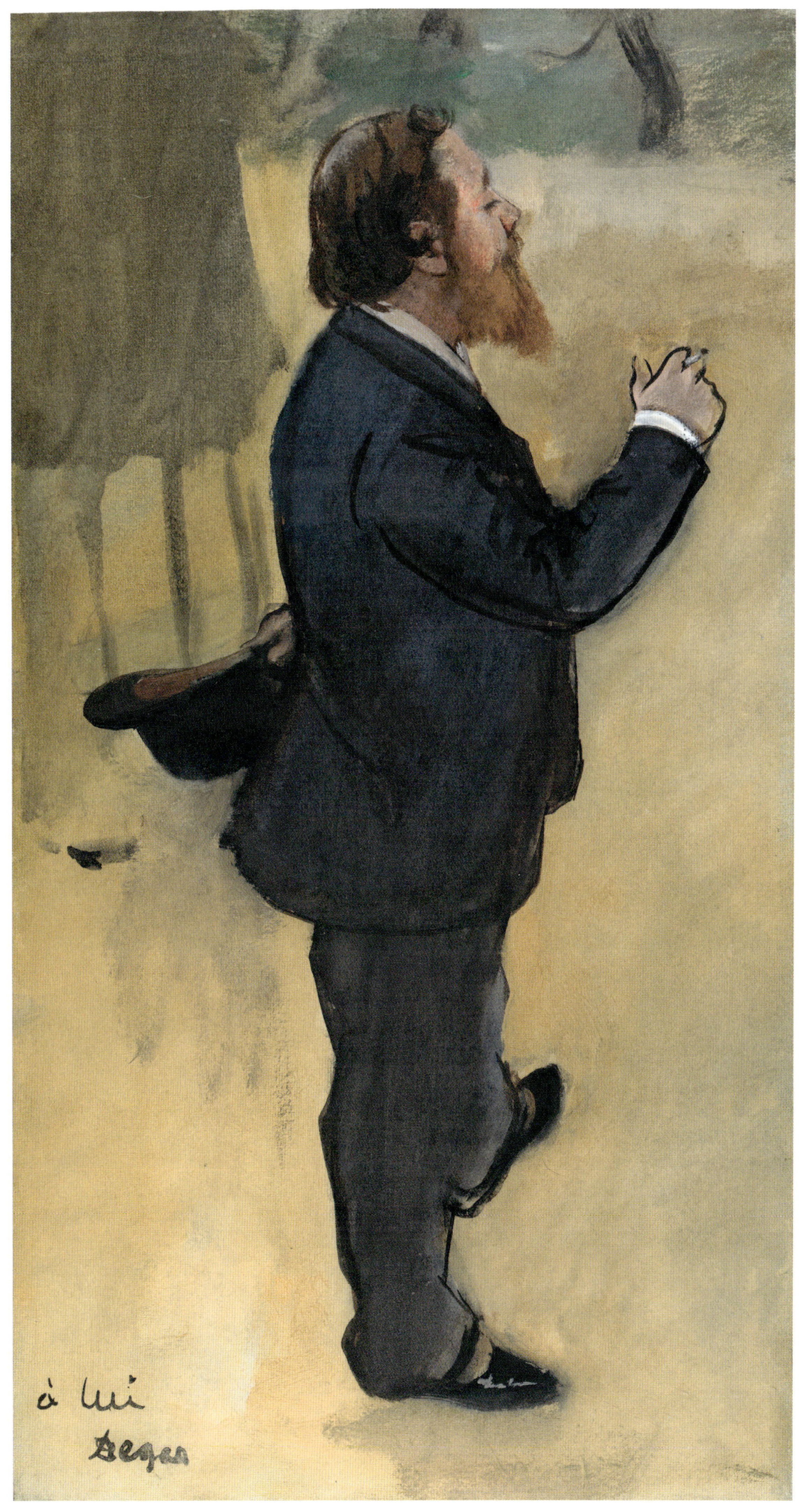

à lui
Degas

Paul Gauguin (1848–1903)
The Haystacks, 1889

Oil on canvas, 92 × 73.3 cm
The Samuel Courtauld Trust, The Courtauld Gallery, London
P.1932.SC.162

This harvest scene in Brittany dates from the early autumn of 1889, some nine months after Gauguin's sojourn in Provence the previous year, when he had painted and lived in the same house together with Van Gogh. That *mésalliance* ended in aesthetic differences between the two strong-willed artists, which escalated to recriminations, violence, madness and Van Gogh's commitment to a sanatorium. Gauguin fled. It was also irrefutably a moment of intense creative advancement for the two men as, rubbing against one another, they both perceived the mature direction their art henceforth would take.

Early in 1889 Gauguin returned to Brittany where he had worked on and off since 1886, establishing himself this time at the small and isolated town of Le Pouldu. There, he observed the 'timeless' way of life, peasant customs, super-stitions and the 'harsh' Breton language. He had long sought an escape from Paris's sophistication and while he complained of Le Pouldu that 'every-thing is…very closed-in (forever, it seems)', it suited his nostalgia for what he supposed to be the 'primitive' and allowed him to press forward with some of the aesthetic intuitions that had come to him in Provence.

A new colouristic clarity and simplification of form emerged in the landscapes Gauguin created there in 1889–90. Here, seven peasant women harvest and stack hay. Their forms are rounded, generalised, like the haystacks themselves. In the foreground a young man leads yoked oxen past the workers. The artist's viewpoint is eccentric, as if he were floating in the air and looking down on the oxen; they become a flattened, angular pattern at the bottom of the canvas. Conversely, the horizon line is daringly high up, determined by the piled haystacks, with only a few trees and rooftops visible, and little sky. Individual details are suppressed in favour of bold patterning in large areas of pure, largely unmodulated colour. Those colours are jewel-like and strongly contrasting. Many brushstrokes resemble Cézanne's parallel hatchings, independent of the forms they depict. The image derives not so much from natural observation as from observation filtered through an intense will to stylisation and simplification of form. In that, it harks back to Gauguin's aesthetic arguments with Van Gogh, who remained dedi-cated to direct observation of nature, Gauguin insisting instead that the modern artist must synthesise, stylise and abstract the motif as he transposes it to canvas, moving towards decoration.   CR

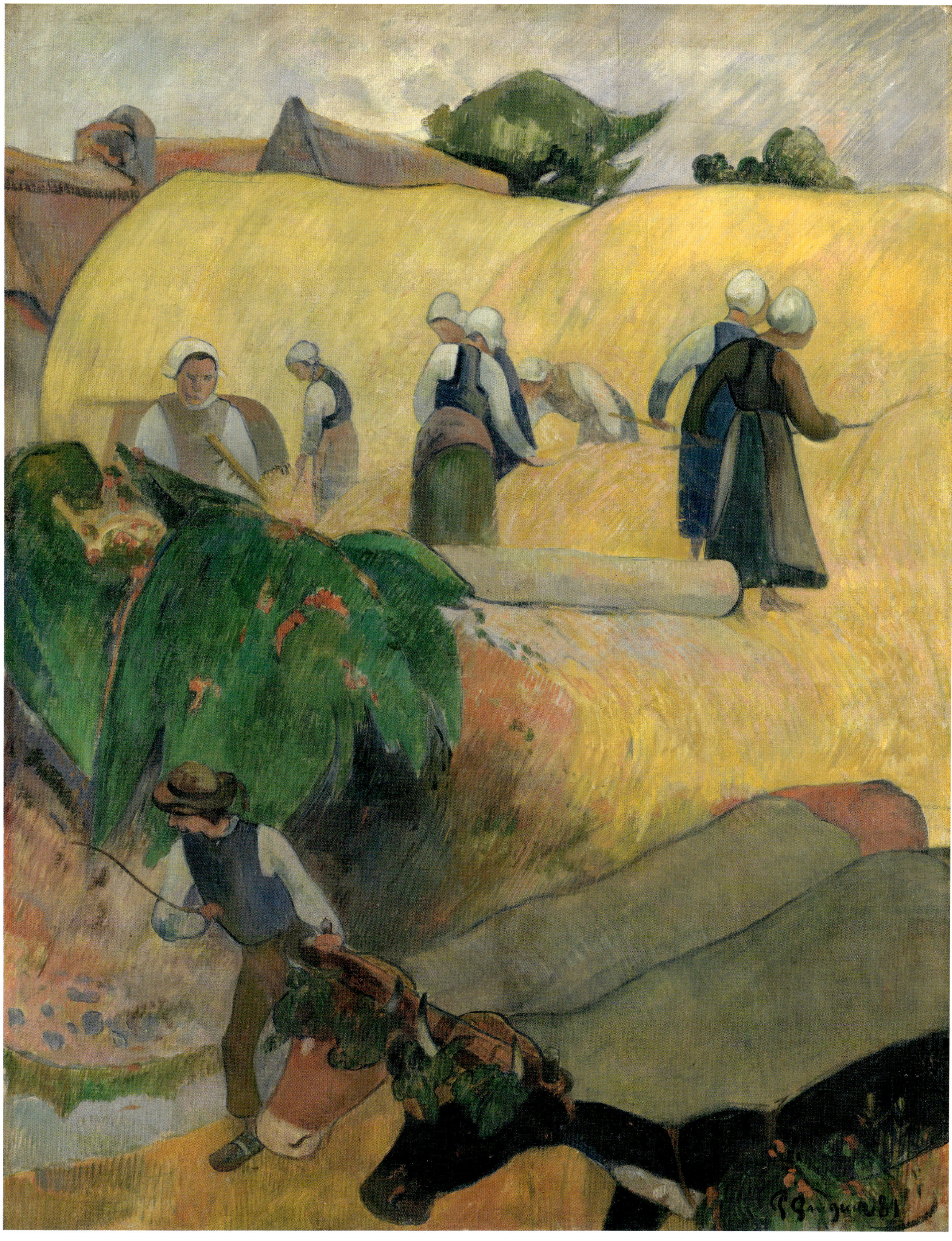

Paul Gauguin
A Vase of Flowers, 1896

Oil on canvas, 64 × 74 cm
The National Gallery, London. Bought, 1918
NG3289

Unequivocally disillusioned with Paris, the art world and Western civilisation, Gauguin set off for a second time to Tahiti in 1895, never to return. There, in a Polynesian Eden that was mainly the product of his delirious imagination and sexual fantasies, he produced some of the most important and vibrant works of his career. Still lifes are rare in Gauguin's oeuvre, his paintings usually featuring figures and landscapes, often in combination. If flowers are ever present, they assume a decorative, graphic quality, adorning the head of his lascivious vahines (Tahitian women). When his dealer Ambroise Vollard asked him to send more flower paintings a few years later, he replied coarsely: 'I am not a painter who works from nature – these days even less than before. Everything with me takes place in my wild imagination. And when I am tired to make figures (my predilection) I start a still life which I finish without a model.'

In Tahiti, perhaps more than anywhere else, Gauguin was not interested in reality. While this painting most probably began as an observation of real flowers, he could well have left the blooms to wilt in their vase by his easel and completed it from his imagination. Positioned against a dark, golden background, the flowers spring out of a simple clay vase: fiery red bougainvillea and hibiscus, white and yellow speckled frangipani and delicate white tiaré. These strange, exuberant native Polynesian flowers appear as an explosion of colour and undulating shapes. They are arranged to highlight their contrasting colours, forming a relatively symmetrical pattern, with the broad blue leaves framing the white and the red of the flowers. A few petals have fallen onto the dark wooden table, rendered in quick dabs of luminous colour.

Degas purchased this picture from Gauguin's friend George-Daniel de Monfreid in 1898. Four years earlier, when Gauguin returned from his first voyage to Tahiti, Degas had been instrumental in helping him organise his exhibition of Tahitian paintings. While the show was a resounding critical and commercial failure, Degas was one of the first collectors to understand the importance of Gauguin's Polynesian works, and amassed a collection of 11 of his paintings. This still life must have enthralled the ageing Degas: in the last phase of his career, he was influenced by a younger generation of artists spearheaded by Gauguin and Van Gogh who were taking colour and form to a new level of expressivity.

The Courtauld Fund acquired no Gauguins, perhaps because the national collection already contained this canvas, acquired in 1918, and *Faa Iheie* (1898, Tate), presented by Duveen in 1919.   JD

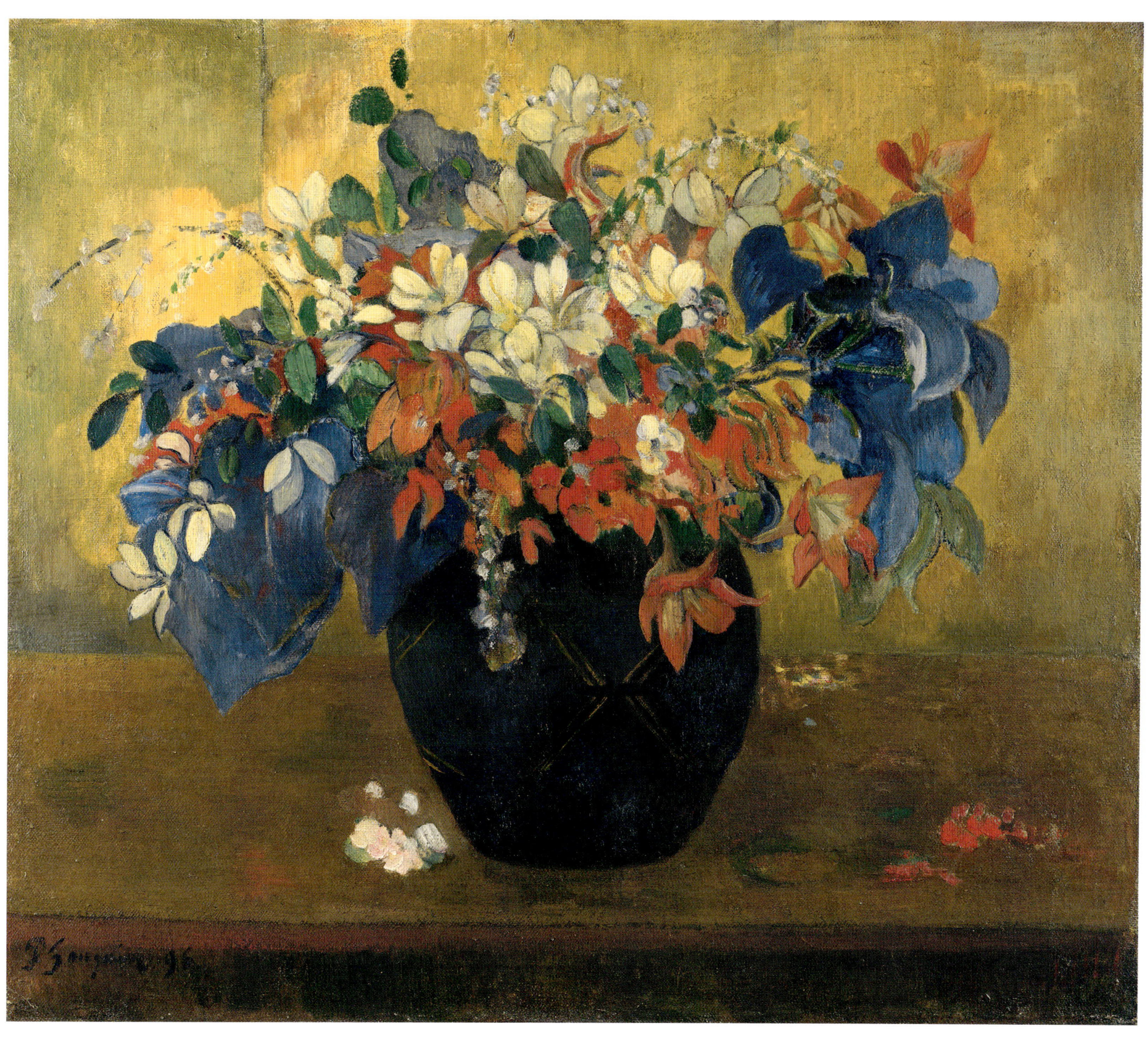

Paul Gauguin
Nevermore, 1897

Oil on canvas, 60.5 × 116 cm
The Samuel Courtauld Trust, The Courtauld Gallery, London
P.1932.SC.163

The young Tahitian woman Pahura entered Gauguin's life early in 1896 on his return to the South Pacific from a sojourn in Paris. At the end of the year she gave birth to his daughter, who died soon after. By February 1897 he was painting this portrait of a pensive and melancholic model, who may well be Pahura, reclining nude on a richly ornamented bed. Her eyes are alive as she glances back warily at a bird that has perched above her. As the painting's ominous title suggests, the unsettling conjunction may have something to do with Edgar Allan Poe's *The Raven*, although the level of Gauguin's engagement with that famous poem of longed-for love is the subject of speculation. Behind the girl, two figures in an adjacent room exchange whispered confidences that are not any clearer. Mystery pervades a canvas that is meant to evoke what the artist called 'a certain long-lost barbaric luxury' compound of sensuality, strange ornamentation, bright colour and dread. It was not unlike the richly ornamental interior of the house Gauguin was then building for himself.

Gauguin called the painting a 'simple nude' and worried that it was not well executed. In fact, it alludes to a long tradition of reclining female nudes in European art from the sump-tuous Venuses of Titian to the odalisques of Ingres ensconced in Oriental opulence, to his friend Manet's frank and provocative Parisian courtesan *Olympia* (1865, Musée d'Orsay, Paris). It is painted on an unusually long horizontal canvas of rough hemp, which has been heavily primed in white – a landscape with a seated figure lies underneath – and then carefully painted wet-on-wet so that subtle colour distinctions are achieved, especially in the flesh tones. The background is divided into rectangles by insistently vertical, richly decorated architectural members that set off the model's undulating body.

The first owner of *Nevermore* was the English composer Frederick Delius, who acquired it in Paris in 1898. Did he intuit something musical in the picture's languorous rhythms?   CR

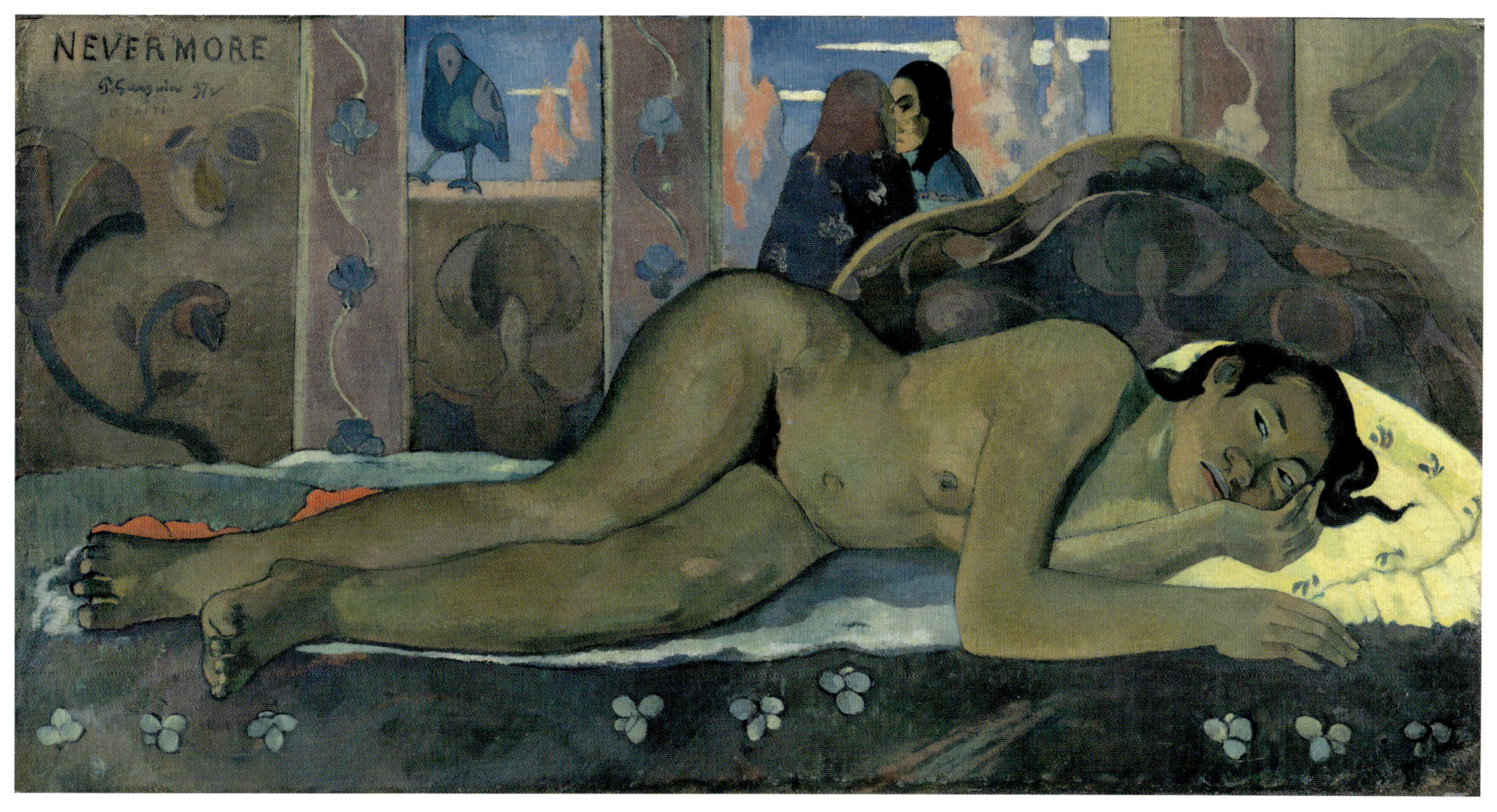

NEVERMORE
P. Gauguin 97
O TAÏTI

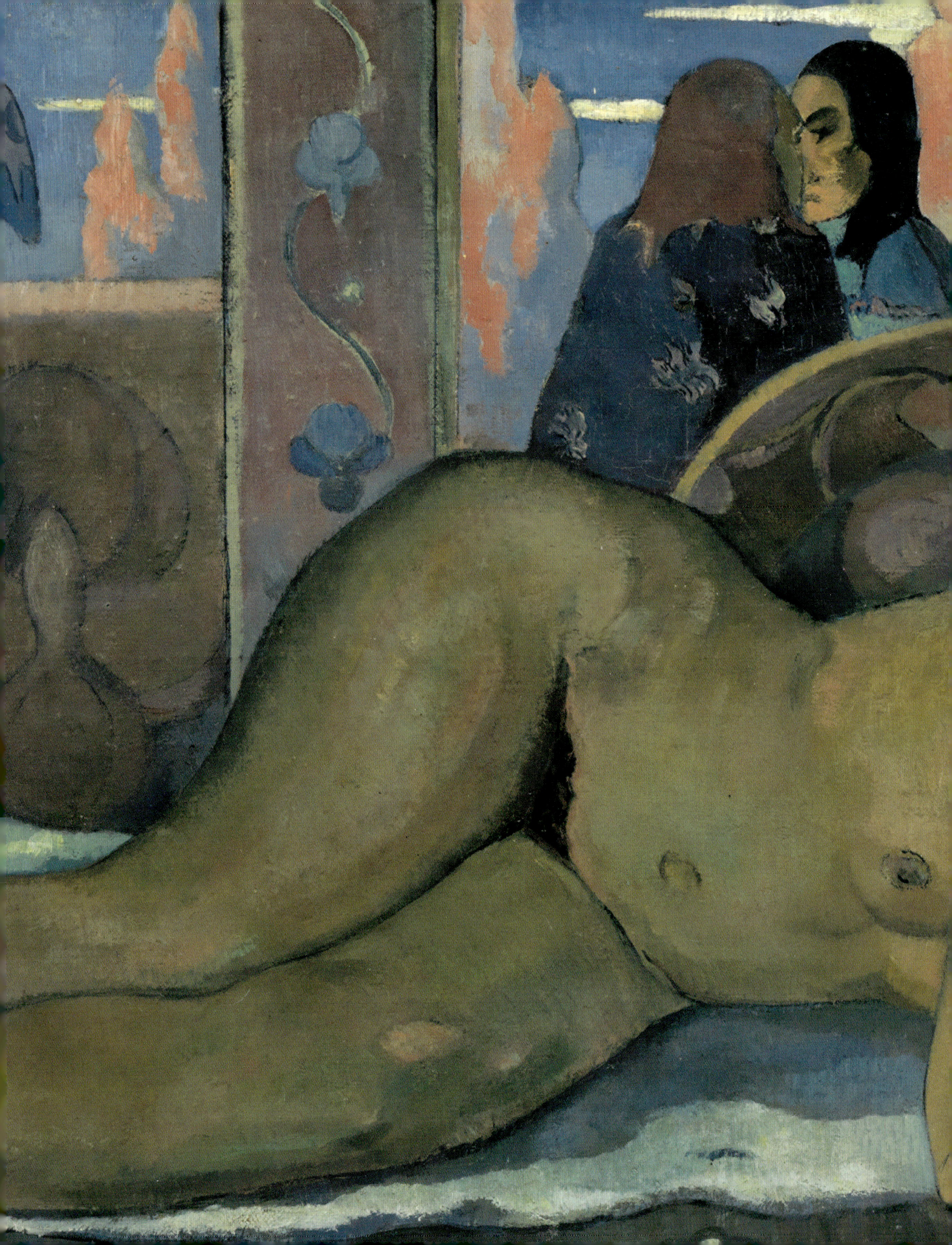

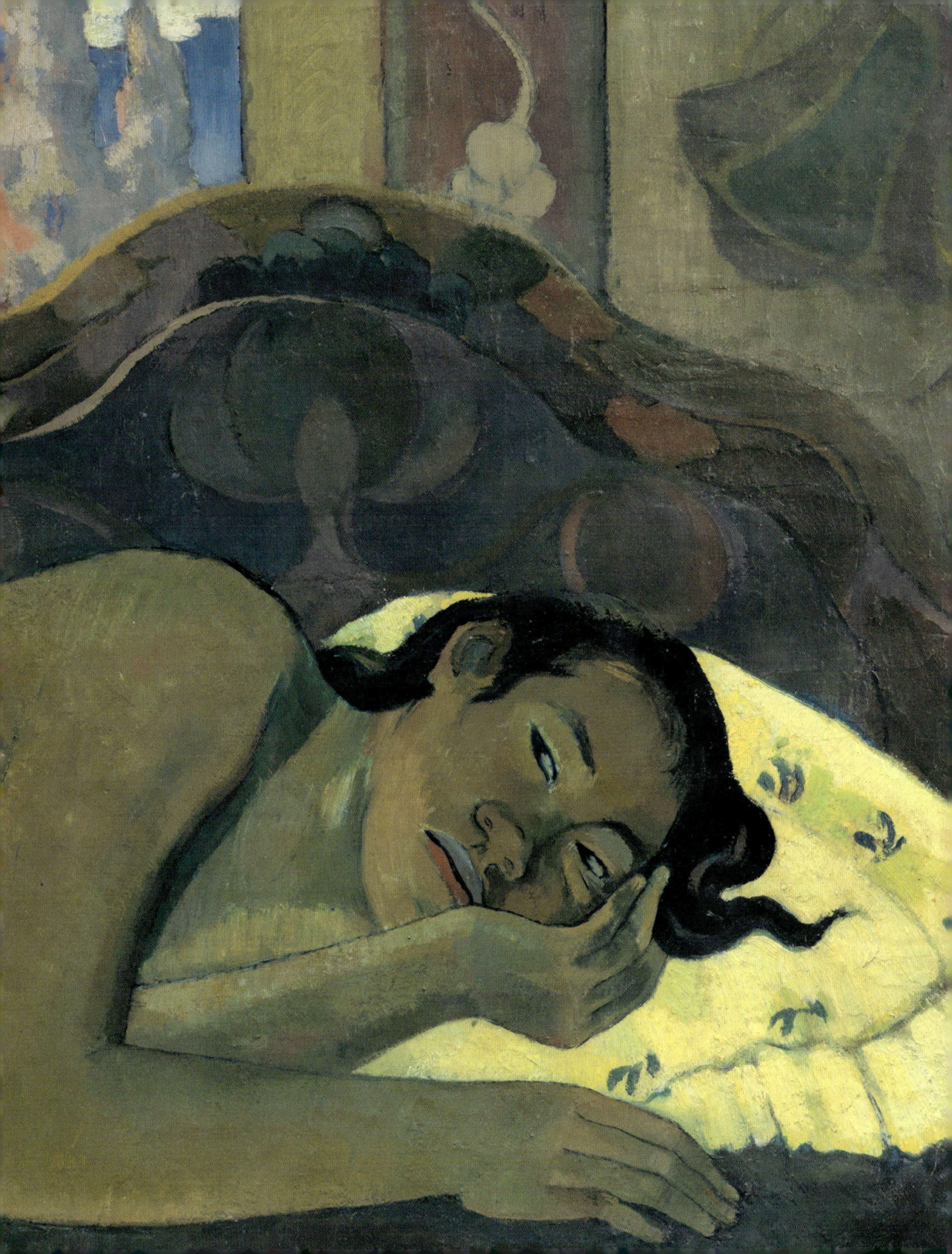

Paul Gauguin
Te Rerioa, 1897

Oil on canvas, 95.1 × 130.2 cm
The Samuel Courtauld Trust, The Courtauld Gallery, London
P.1932.SC.164

In March 1897, about a month after he completed *Nevermore* (p. 83), Gauguin was preparing paintings to be sent back to France by ship. At almost the last moment – the sailing had been delayed – he added this painting to the shipment. It had been executed quickly and thinly in around 10 days, but was, he wrote to his Paris friend Georges-Daniel de Monfreid, 'even better than the rest'. It is a masterpiece of ambiguity. Meant to evoke a dream, it remains intentionally unclear whose dream it is: the sleeping child, the mother lost in thought, the sculpted figures of the opulent wall decoration or the distant horseman. Perhaps, Gauguin hinted, it was 'the dream of the painter' himself. An aura of otherworldly reverie accentuated by fantastical details like the extravagantly carved crib permeates the image.

The work is one of a series of monumental canvases executed during the artist's second Tahitian residence. Many are situated in richly decorated interiors, such as the one Gauguin was preparing at that moment in his own new house. The decorations are a compendium of motifs the artist had picked up on his travels: the crib, for example, is based on a Maori pot noted in Auckland; the local goddess Hina presides on the right, as if copied from a relief carving.

Rather than an ethnographic report on Tahitian ornamental traditions, the interior is a syncretic amalgamation of wide-ranging cultural forms and figures intended to suggest a 'primitive' culture saturated in symbolism and eroticism – note the couple making love on the wall on the left – and presided over by deities whose unending presence must not be ignored. Many of these works also are dominated by large-scale nude or semi-nude Tahitian women such as the mother and her companion here. Their silent watchfulness brings the surrounding forms to hallucinatory life. 'Real' and sculpted humans and animals demand equal visual attention in this dream world.   CR

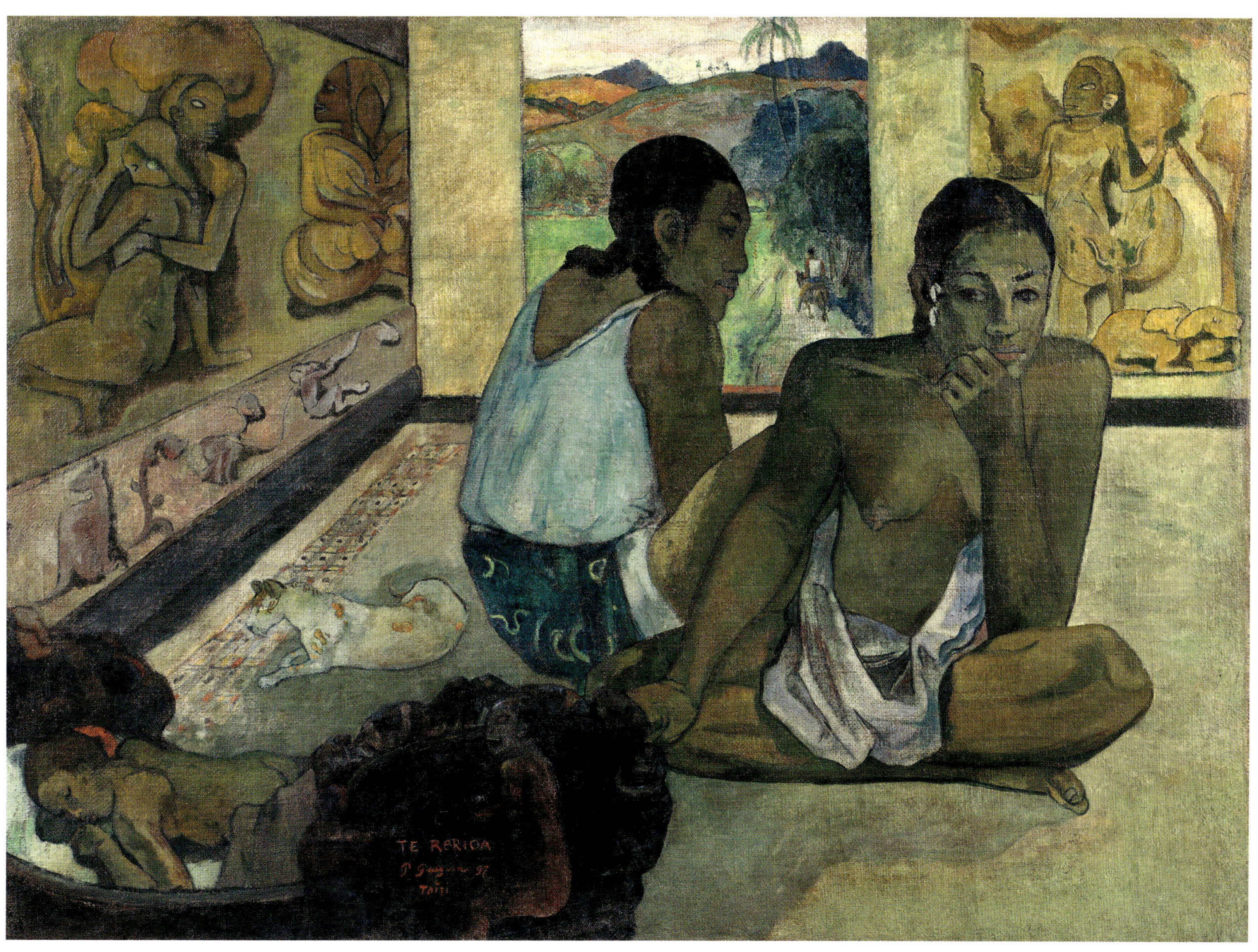

Edouard Manet (1832–1883)
Music in the Tuileries Gardens, 1862

Oil on canvas, 76.2 × 118.1 cm
The National Gallery, London. Sir Hugh Lane Bequest, 1917
NG3260

A fashionable crowd has gathered in the shade of the chestnut trees in the Tuileries Gardens to listen to a military brass band. The musicians are nowhere to be seen; the artist wittily locates the viewer where the orchestra would have been. This picture was Manet's first major work depicting modern Parisian life and predictably attracted much criticism when it was exhibited in 1863: critics saw it as an offence against the rules of high art, both in its loose painting technique and contemporary subject matter.

Manet and his friend, poet and essayist Charles Baudelaire, would often meet at the Tuileries in the afternoons around the time when Manet painted this picture and Baudelaire was writing his seminal *The Painter of Modern Life*, in which he argued that scenes of the contemporary world could be as heroic as academic high art. The two companions were mesmerised by Paris, which before their eyes was transforming into the first modern metropolis, a whirlwind of colour, a city in constant flux changing the very nature of vision itself. Painting, Baudelaire argued, could convey the fleeting essence of modernity better than any other art form. Manet's loose brushstrokes emulate the transitory nature of the city, while carefully observed details, such as dresses of the latest fashion and the wrought-iron chairs that had only just replaced the garden's old wooden seats in the summer of 1862, firmly situate the painting in the present.

This picture was also a highly personal work. The crowd conversing under the canopy of the trees as if in a large fashionable salon is constituted in part by Manet's friends and family: he included himself, gazing straight at the viewer at the left edge of the composition, his brother Eugène, fellow painters Henri Fantin-Latour and Frédéric Bazille, the composer Jacques Offenbach, and poets Théophile Gautier and Baudelaire himself. Manet probably executed the painting in his studio, based on studies he made in the garden, as well as on portrait photographs. Despite each figure appearing, in the words of Emile Zola, as 'a simple, barely delaminated fleck, in which the details become lines and black dots', Manet recorded the defining features of these characters in a few quick masterful strokes of paint, varying the focus and the precision with which he depicted each one. He sought to capture the optical experience of looking at a crowd, when the eye invariably focuses on a few faces, the others remaining a blur outside one's field of vision.

Hugh Lane's bequest was shown at the National Gallery in 1917 where Courtauld singled out *Music* for praise.   JD

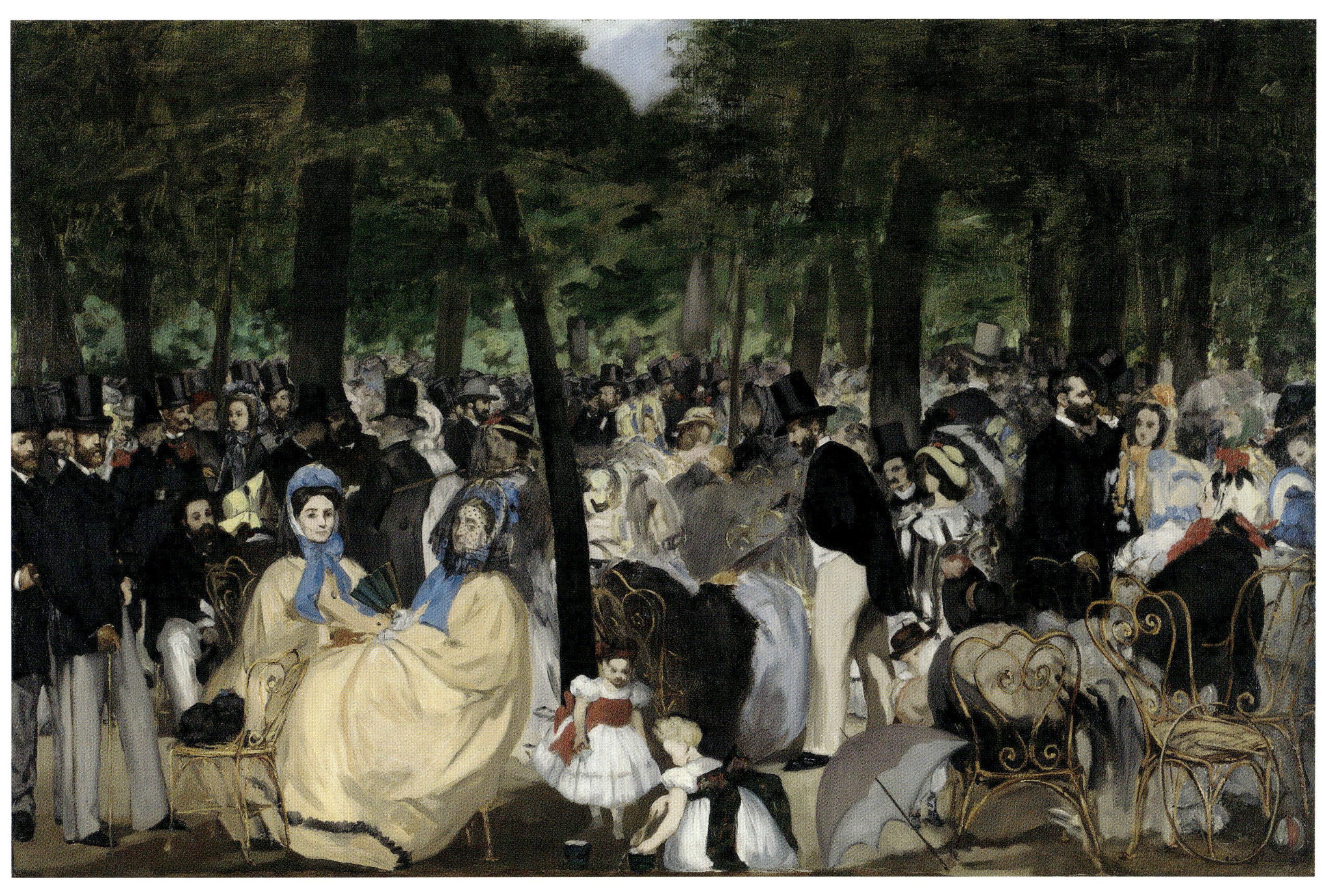

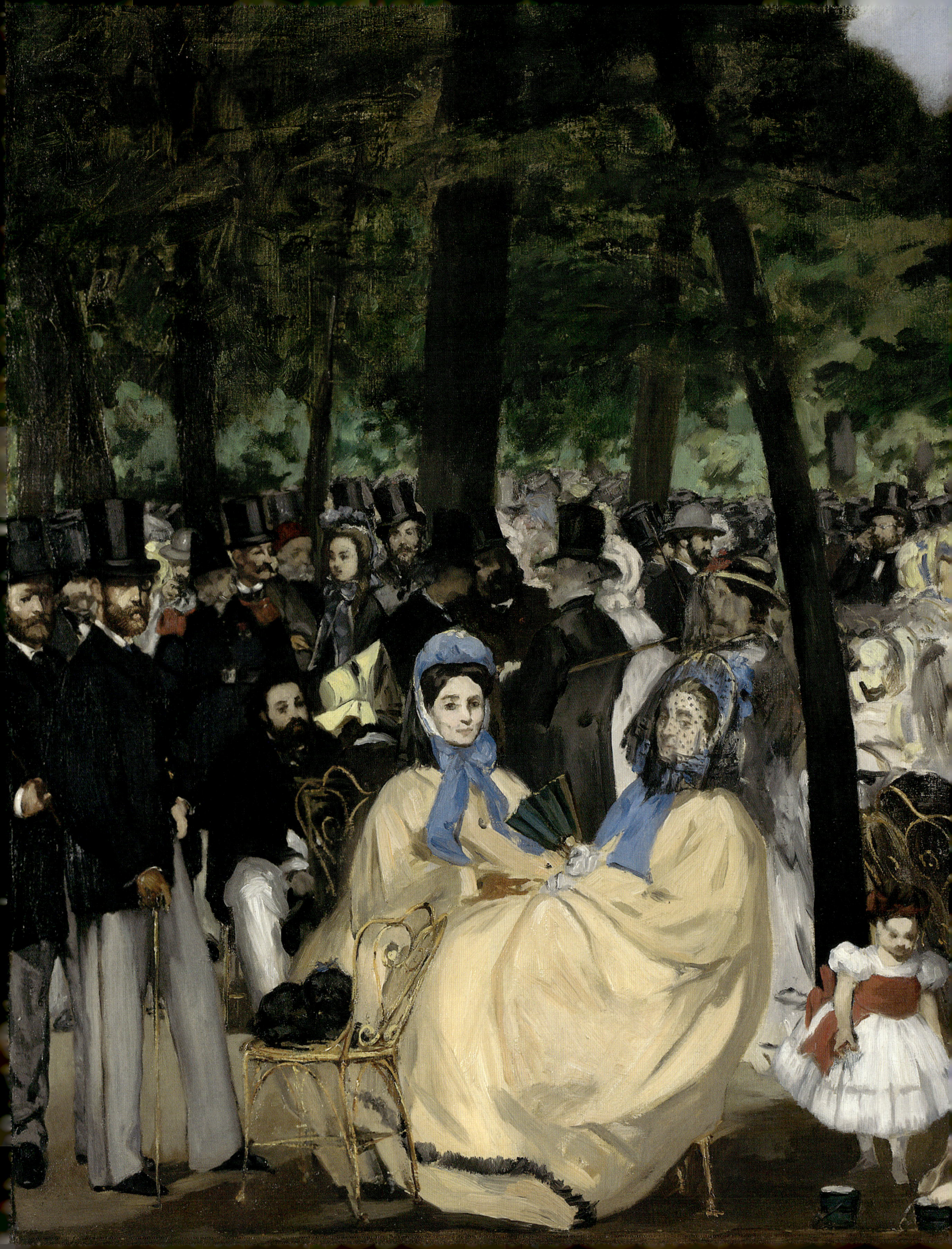

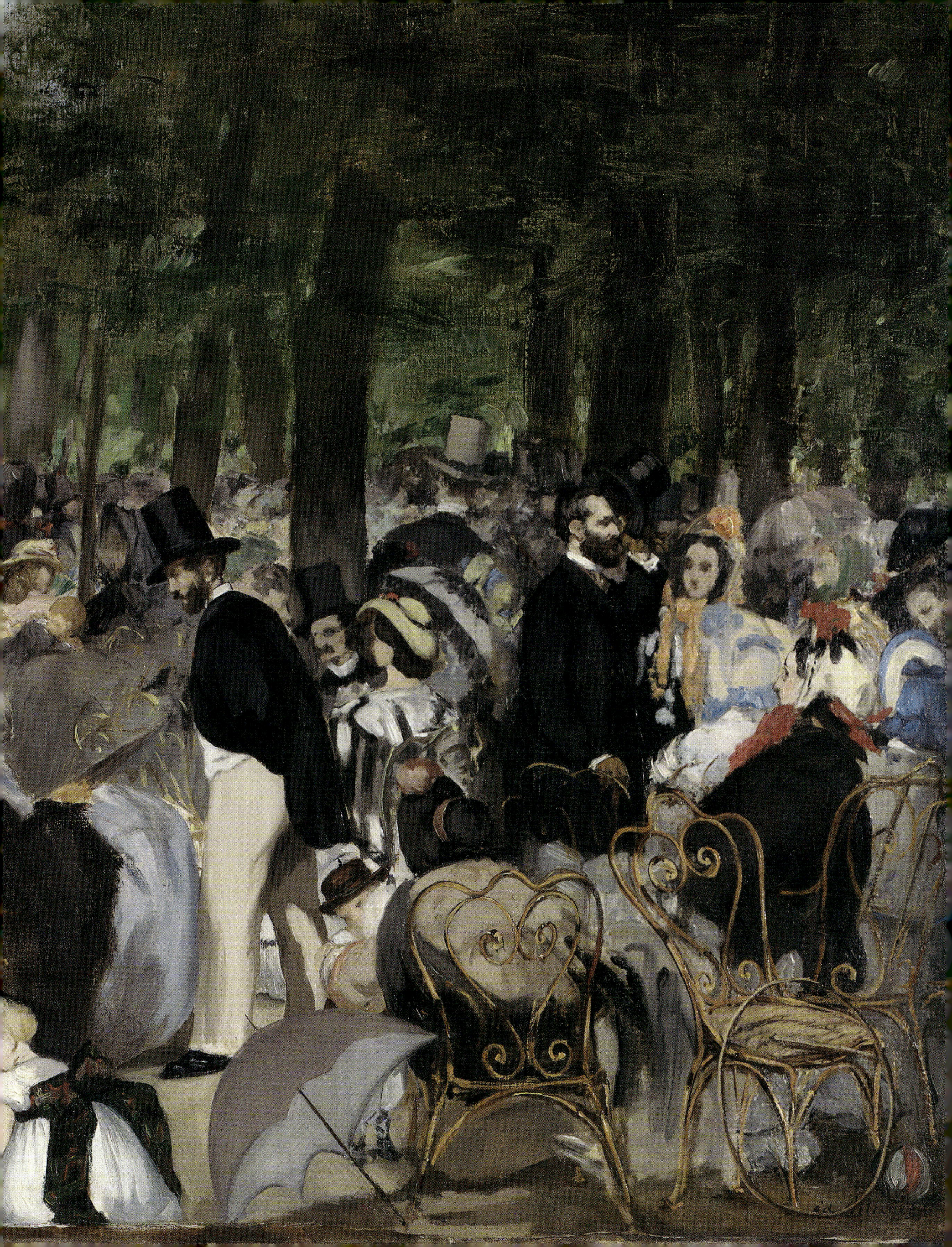

Edouard Manet
Déjeuner sur l'herbe, about 1863–8

Oil on canvas, 89.5 × 116.5 cm
The Samuel Courtauld Trust, The Courtauld Gallery, London
P.1932.SC.232

Technical examination has revealed that this painting is not a preparatory study but a smaller version of Manet's infamous large canvas that was dismissed by the jury of the 1863 Paris Salon and exhibited instead among the rejected works at the Salon des Refusés where it attracted a vitriolic reaction from the critics. Far from hurting Manet's career, the scandalous reception of the work – followed by the even more vociferous outcry surrounding the exhibition of his *Olympia* two years later – firmly established him as modern painting's foremost exponent. While Manet refused to exhibit with them, the Impressionists recognised these two works as milestones in the development of modern art. Cézanne exclaimed: 'It's a new state of painting. Our Renaissance dates from that point.'

The picture constitutes a blend of tradition and modernism. Bathers have been a recurrent subject throughout the history of art and Manet sought direct inspiration from the Old Masters: the motif of a female nude sat among dressed men came from Giorgione's *Pastoral Concert* (about 1509) (now ascribed to Titian), while the poses of the figures echo the configuration of a group of nymphs and river gods in an engraving after Raphael's *Judgment of Paris*. The figures, however, are distinctly modern: Manet portrays his model Victorine Meurent accompanied by his brother-in-law Ferdinand Leenhoff and a second man, a synthesis of Manet's two brothers, Gustave and Eugène. The two men are dressed in the bourgeois/bohemian fashion that was widespread among the Parisian avant-garde, Manet's hybrid brother incongruously wearing an eccentric velvet smoking-cap. The subject of scandal was of course Victorine: her naked, unidealised body catches the light, in stark contrast to the dark attire of her two male companions, and her direct unashamed gaze only adds to the provocation. Her fashionable dress, crumpled into the foreground under a still life of a basket and fruit, accentuates her nudity: she is undressed, naked, as opposed to nude.

The *Déjeuner* was thought indecent and infuriated critics with its suggestive parody of contemporary 'high art', elevating this scene of artistic bohemian life to the heroic scale usually devoted to religious, allegorical or historical painting. While Manet valued provocation, often not devoid of a dose of humour, he also approached this work with ambition. Taking on the Old Masters and adapting their work to the context of modernity, he produced a defining contemporary masterpiece truly of its time.

The attribution is questioned, even if in Courtauld's time one reviewer praised it as superior to the large painting.   JD

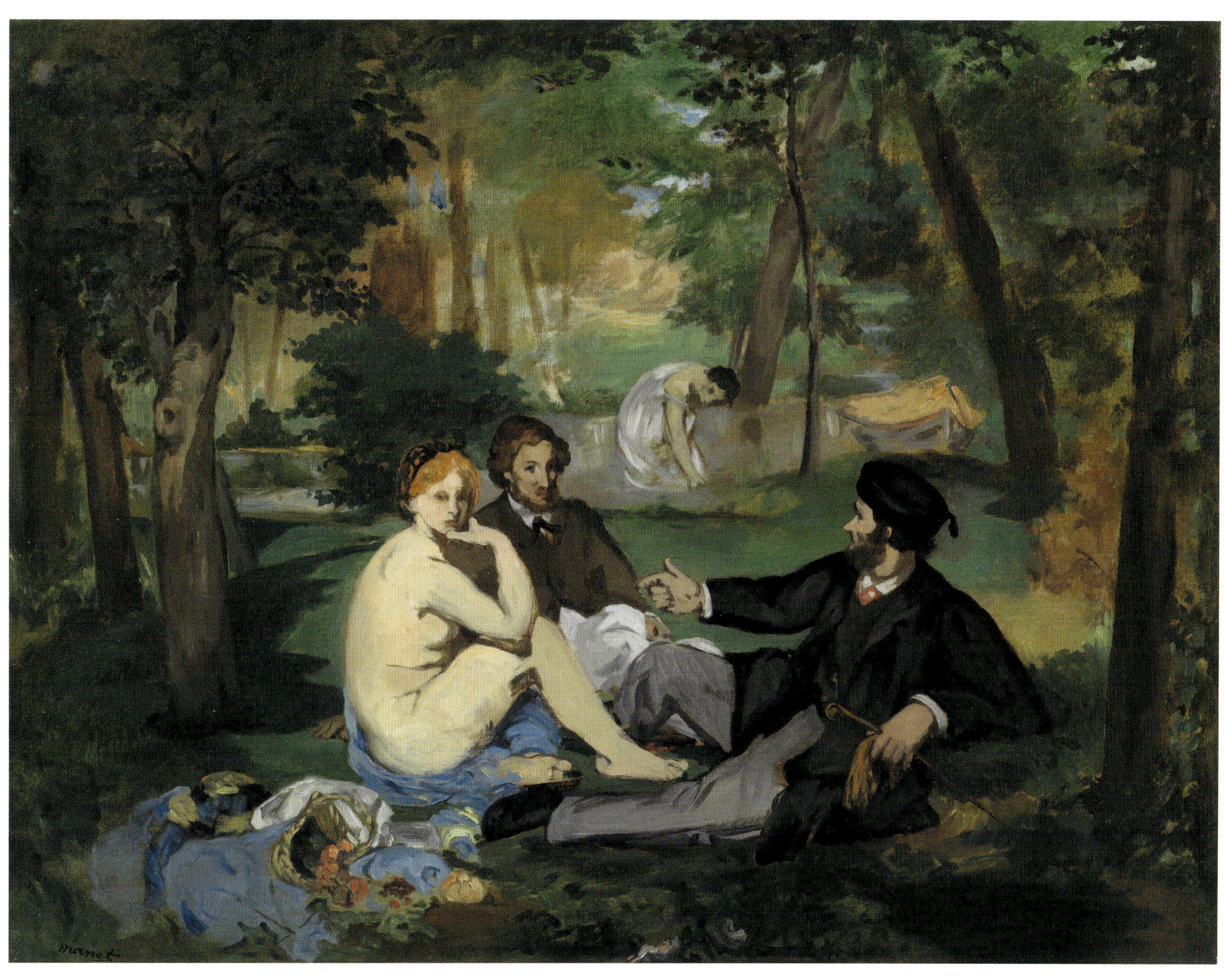

Edouard Manet
Banks of the Seine at Argenteuil, 1874

Oil on canvas, 62.3 × 103 cm
On long-term loan to The Courtauld Gallery from a private collection
LP.1997.XX.14

Manet painted this picture when he visited Monet in Argenteuil in the summer of 1874, a few months after declining to take part in the First Impressionist Exhibition. While he preferred to continue to provocatively show his work at the annual Salon, Manet was close to some of the Impressionist painters, notably Monet, whom he supported financially through difficult times. The two models in this picture were probably Monet's wife Camille and their seven-year-old son Jean, revealing the close personal relationship between the two artists.

This picture marks Manet's most deliberate attempt at Impressionist plein-air painting, and it is thought to have been executed at least partly outdoors. While it shares many characteristics of Impressionist paintings, like broken brushwork and the juxtaposition of vivid colours, Manet made an abundant use of black – a pigment that seldom featured on the Impressionists' palettes – for some of the most important parts of the composition: the hull of the boats and the clearly defined ribbon of Madame Monet's hat. The rest of Camille's figure is painted in a deeply Impressionistic way, her striped dress built up of a quantity of broken brushstrokes conveying the effect of shimmering light fabric: bright white and purple-pink paint in the area hit by a ray of bright sunlight, while the rest of her dress in shadow is constructed from a series of cool greys and blues.

Camille and Jean stand right on the edge of the riverbank, serenely contemplating small elegant sailing boats moored in front of them, the barges on the opposite bank of Gennevilliers drenched in sunlight and in the distance, beyond the high horizon, almost imperceptibly smoking industrial chimneys. Manet conveys the unique sensation of a hot summer day where time appears to stand still, and yet the whole surface of the canvas is animated by a flurry of brushstrokes. The riverbank itself is vividly painted in a wide range of greens, almost as lively as the river beyond. The wavelets on the surface of the water, disturbing the reflection of the boats, are indicated by a series of fluid, zigzagging brushstrokes of blues, intermingled with a variety of whites, which Manet sometimes mixed straight onto the brush.   JD

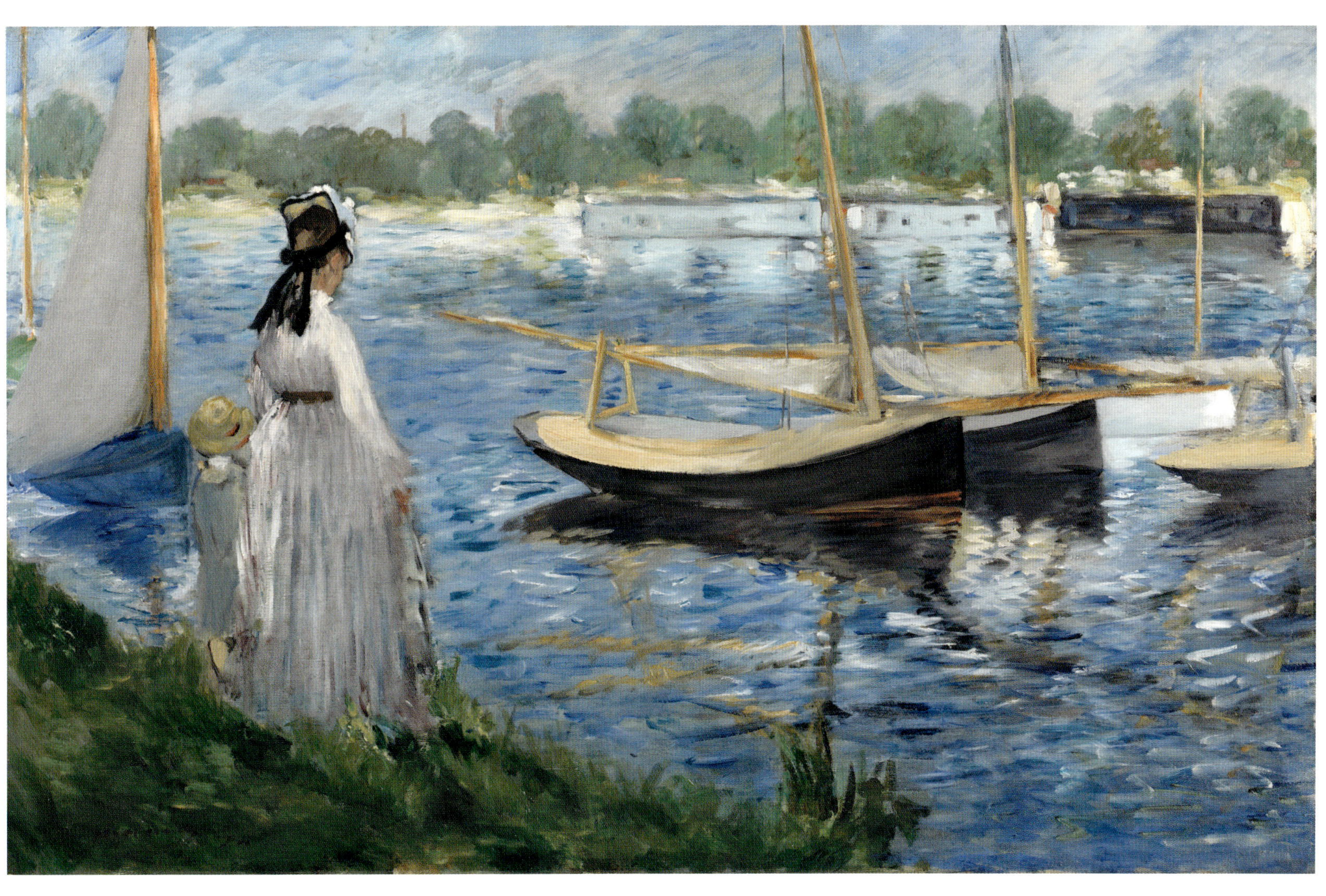

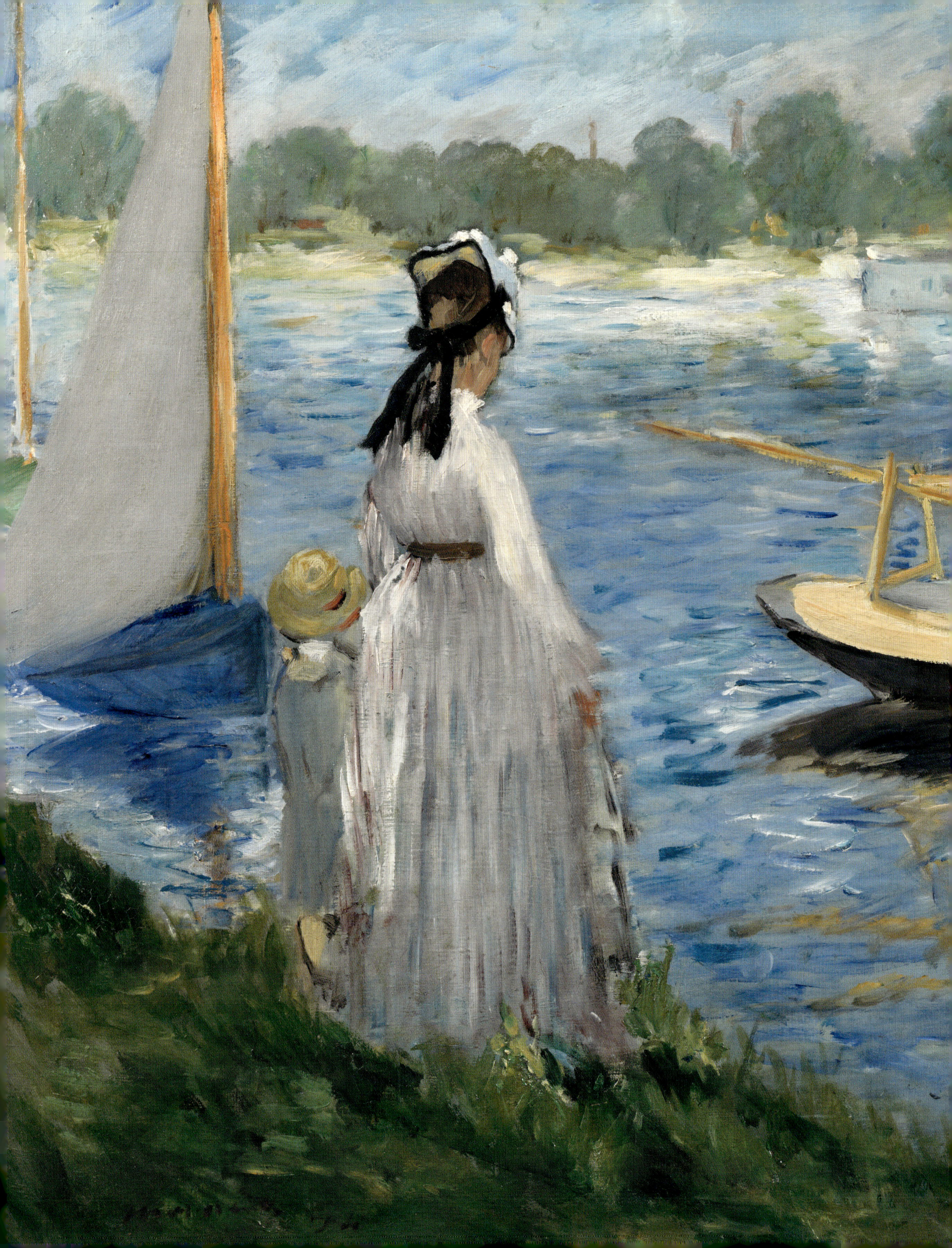

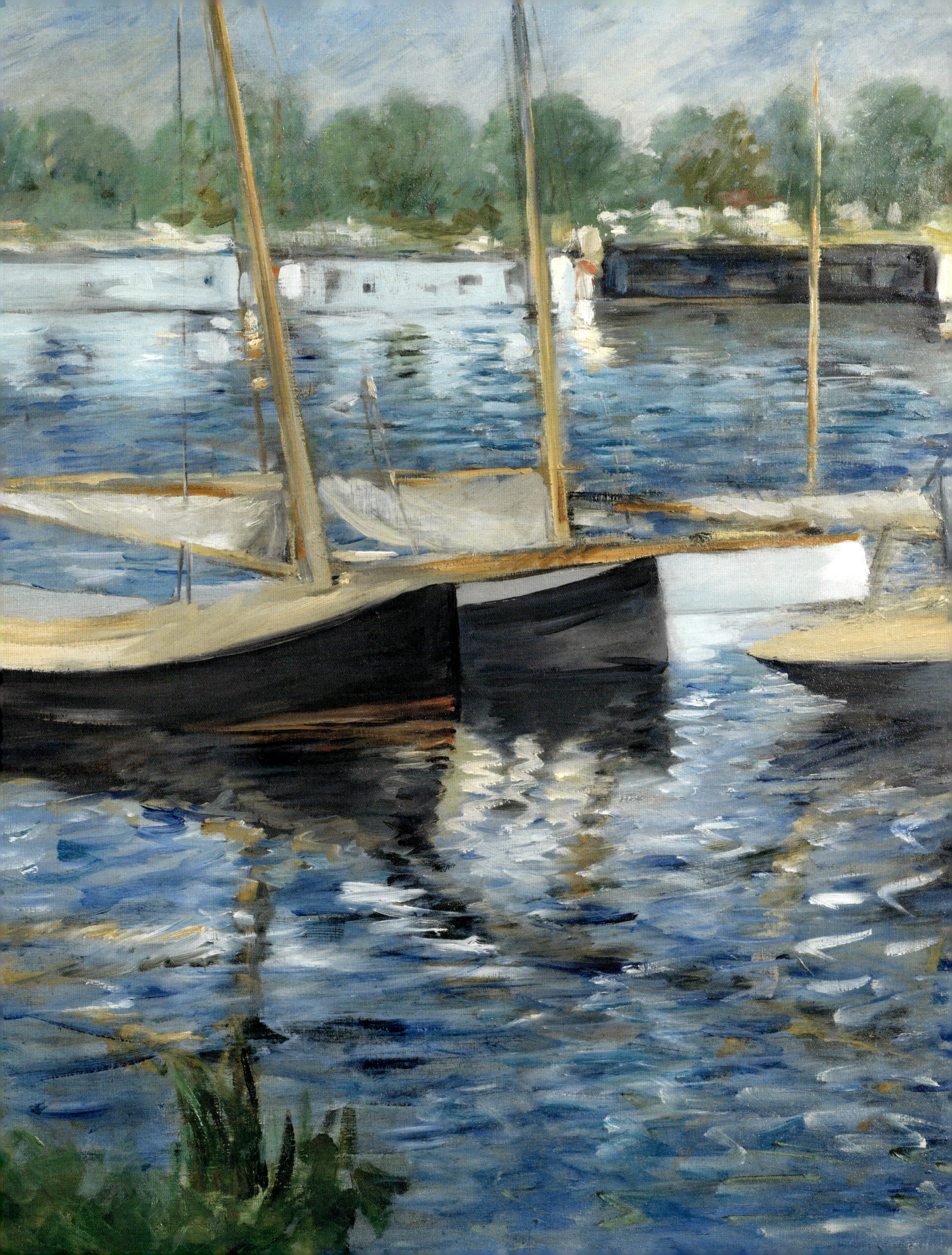

Edouard Manet
A Bar at the Folies-Bergère, 1882

Oil on canvas, 96 × 130 cm
The Samuel Courtauld Trust, The Courtauld Gallery, London
P.1934.SC.234

The scholarly literature on Manet's last completed major painting is immense and contradictory. The problem – on this all agree – is that the picture makes little visual sense. The reflections in the mirror simply do not match what is supposedly being reflected. How can the back of the barmaid we see at the centre of the canvas skew so far to the right? Where does that man come from who seems to stand in the viewer's place directly in front of the girl? Why do the bottles of drink not line up with their mirror images? Recent attempts using computers to whip the picture, and the artist, into logical shape become ever more baroque and convoluted. Manet was not an early master of fractal geometry. As a work of naturalistic observation *A Bar* fails, but as John House has pointed out, nonetheless it remains a penetrating analysis of social, sexual and class relations in the Parisian *demi-monde* of the 1880s, not least for the sense of discomfort and dislocation it occasions. It is about its uncertainties.

Manet made sketches at the popular night spot just below Montmartre and painted at least two preparatory studies for the picture he would submit to the Paris Salon of 1882. They are spatially unambiguous. The model, named Suzon, an actual barmaid from the Folies-Bergère, came to the artist's studio to pose amid bottles and glasses. He worked and reworked the final canvas, however; X-rays reveal various stages of manipulation of figures, objects and reflections as he intentionally moved from naturalism to something stranger. The picture remained in his studio at his death, was sold at his posthumous auction, and passed through the hands of discriminating collectors attuned to Manet's rich ambiguities until acquired by Samuel Courtauld in 1926. Perhaps because the National Gallery already owned major, large-scale works by Manet, or perhaps because it was just so odd, *A Bar* went to his private collection rather than the nation.

We leave the last word to one of the most penetrating recent puzzlers over Manet's elusive art, the sociologist Pierre Bourdieu: 'We go on as though Manet had painted this picture in order to provide scholars with a problem to solve, whereas in fact he could not have cared less: he did not create a problem but a work.'   CR

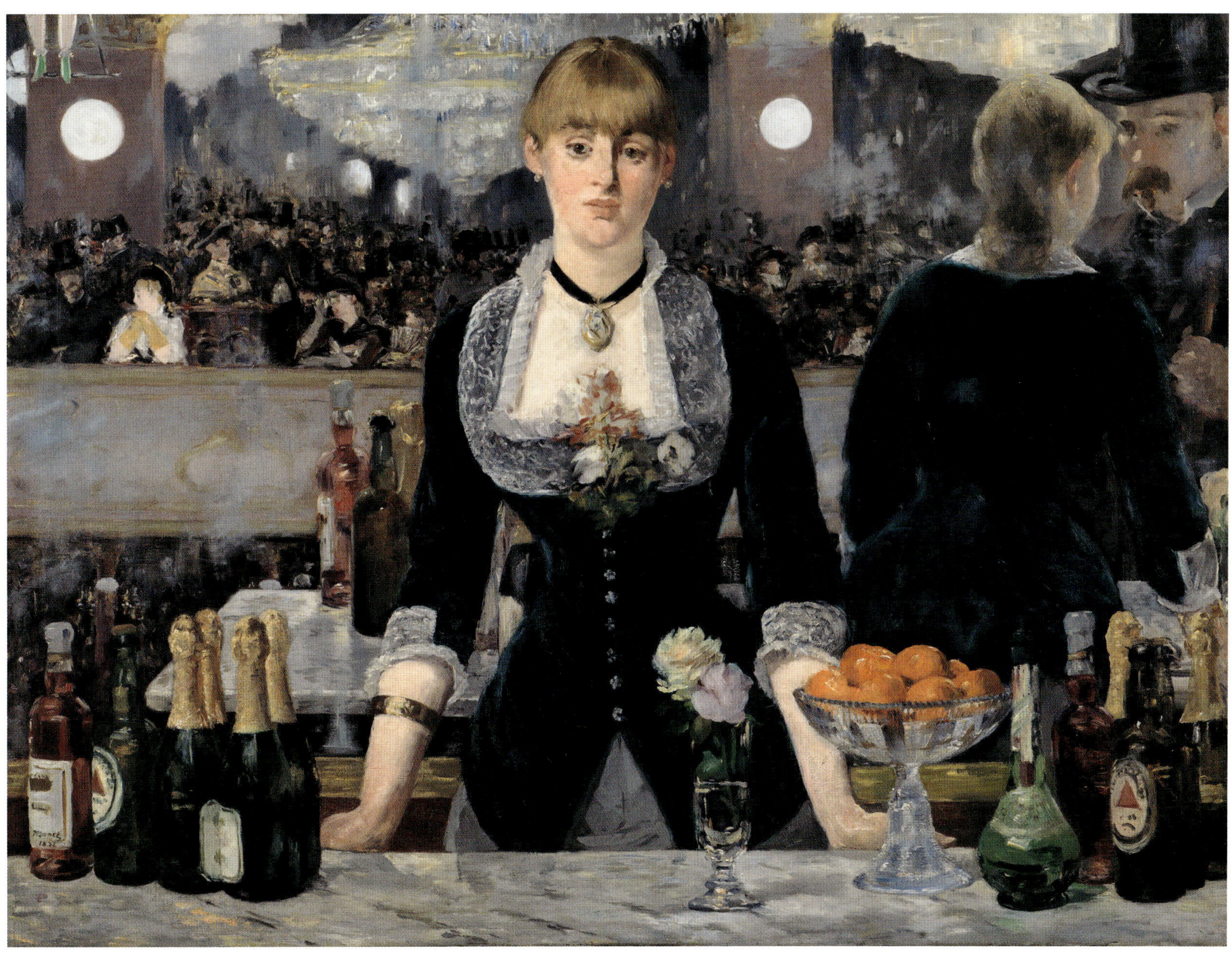

Claude Monet (1840–1926)
Autumn Effect at Argenteuil, 1873

Oil on canvas, 55 × 74.5 cm
The Samuel Courtauld Trust, The Courtauld Gallery, London
P.1932.SC.274

Between 1871 and 1878 Monet lived in Argenteuil, a small town north-west of Paris along the river Seine, with a growing population thanks to commuter railway links and local industry. This expansion is evoked by buildings at the centre of this composition, especially the conspicuous factory chimney. Yet Monet's vision of Argenteuil is still dominated by the natural environment. The buildings appear in the same blues and whites as the sky and river and the leaves turning from summer green to autumn gold are redoubled by the reflection in the water.

The golden hues of the leaves – painted in oranges, yellows and pinks – produce a bold contrast with the blue of the sky and the water. This is most apparent in the foreground, where touches of blue are interlaced with the warm tones of the reflected foliage, the complementary oranges and blues adding to the overall luminosity. The short horizontal brushstrokes, known as *taches* (spots), which so effectively convey the effect of light reflected off water, had been developed by Monet with his friend Renoir at the end of the previous decade. Larger in the foreground than the distance, these horizontal strokes give a sense of recession into space. In the sky, Monet loosely renders the scattered clouds with more freely improvised strokes.

Throughout his long career Monet tried to capture in paint the visual effect of specific conditions of light and weather, referring to this as the *effet*, a word used in the French title of this painting. He worked outdoors, witnessing first-hand the play of autumn sunshine on the water and the rich tones of the autumnal trees. Despite its apparent instantaneity and freshness, it seems that Monet reworked this canvas. Uncharacteristically, he scraped away paint, probably with the handle of his brush, presumably to prevent the surface from looking overly worked. This is most evident in the right-hand tree.

The composition is far from improvised. Against the established norms of landscape painting, Monet bisects the canvas with the horizon, and emphasises this horizontal with the thick blue line of the river's main channel, which visually links the two banks of trees. The balanced structure invites the viewer to contemplate, rather than enter, the scene.   RMcK

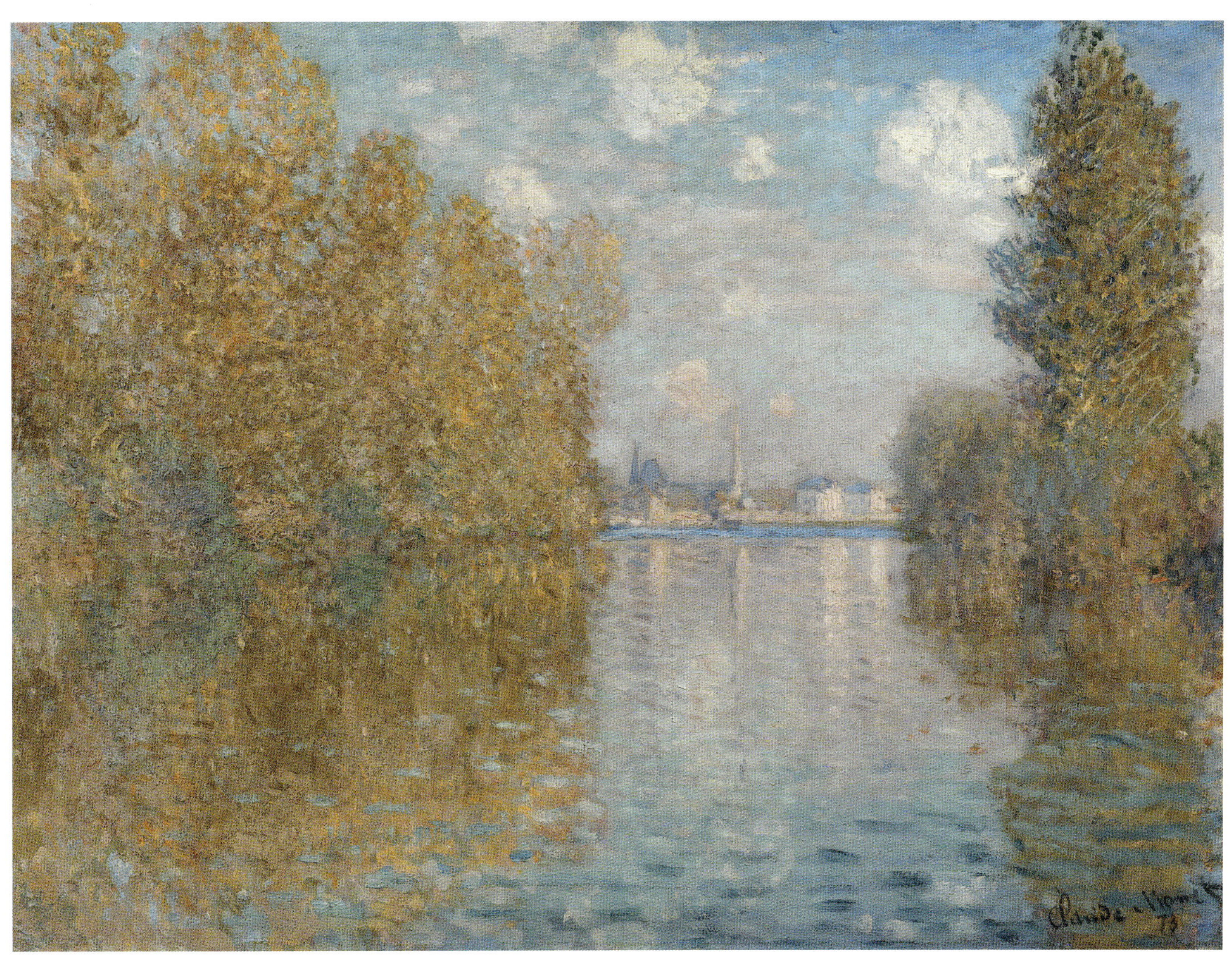

Claude Monet
Antibes, 1888

Oil on canvas, 65.5 × 92.4 cm
The Samuel Courtauld Trust, The Courtauld Gallery, London
P.1948.SC.276

Monet spent the period from mid-January to May 1888 painting the town of Antibes, in the south of France, and its environs. Here he has set up his easel on the Cap d'Antibes, facing south-west across the Golfe Juan towards the Montagnes de l'Estérel, which line the horizon in this picture, linking sea and sky. After decades of capturing the transitory effects of the cool light of northern Europe, the intensity of the Mediterranean sunshine, and its swiftly changing light effects, set him a new challenge. Monet responded by heightening and harmonising his colour palette.

From Antibes Monet wrote to his partner Alice Hoschedé: 'What I bring back from here will be sweetness itself, white, pink and blue, all enveloped in this magical air.' He applied those colours in complementary warm and cool tones across the whole canvas to balance the composition. Monet's final touches to this work intensified the reds and oranges on the distant mountains and the tree, before adding a bold red signature.

The maritime pine twisted and silhouetted in the foreground, and the composition at large, reflects Monet's interest in *ukiyo-e* prints from Japan. The painter had collected these since the 1860s, as a craze for Japanese products swept France. Katsushika Hokusai had depicted Mount Fuji through the pines in his second volume of *One Hundred Views of Mount Fuji* (1835). Despite the overall impression of a specific moment of light, Monet's composition is carefully planned.

The ancient Côte d'Azur town of Antibes was a thriving tourist resort. The artist made his way south by train like many other travellers, but upon arrival avoided their company. Monet's views of Antibes are unpopulated. In this vista the city of Cannes is excluded, just out of sight on the right side of the bay. Antibes' popularity with tourists served Monet well, and his paintings of this picturesque destination attracted buyers. Monet exhibited this and nine other views of Antibes at a branch of the Boussod & Valadon gallery run by Theo van Gogh, Vincent's brother. Two years later, Monet would commit fully to the practice of painting the same motif in different light effects and then exhibiting the series together.   RMcK

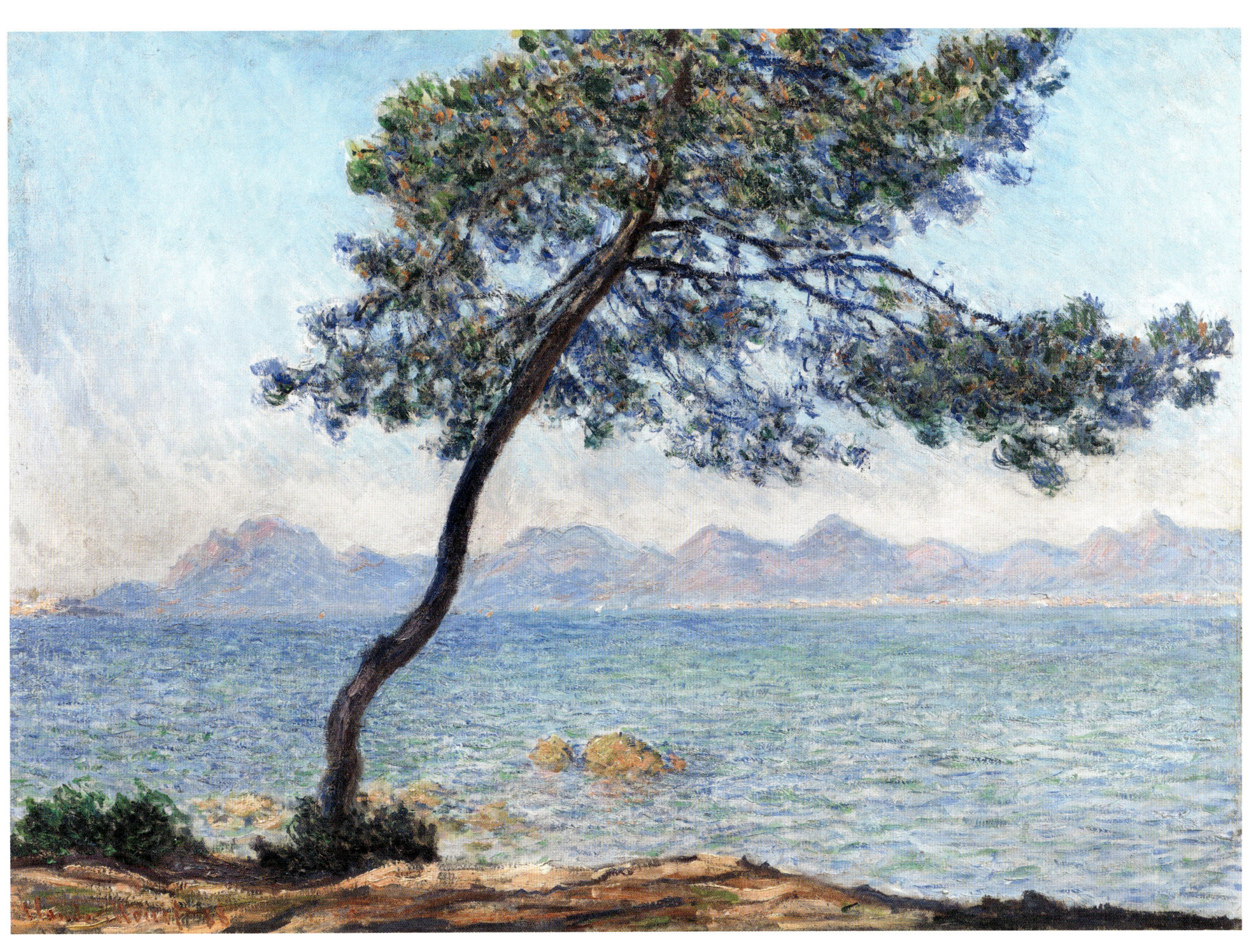

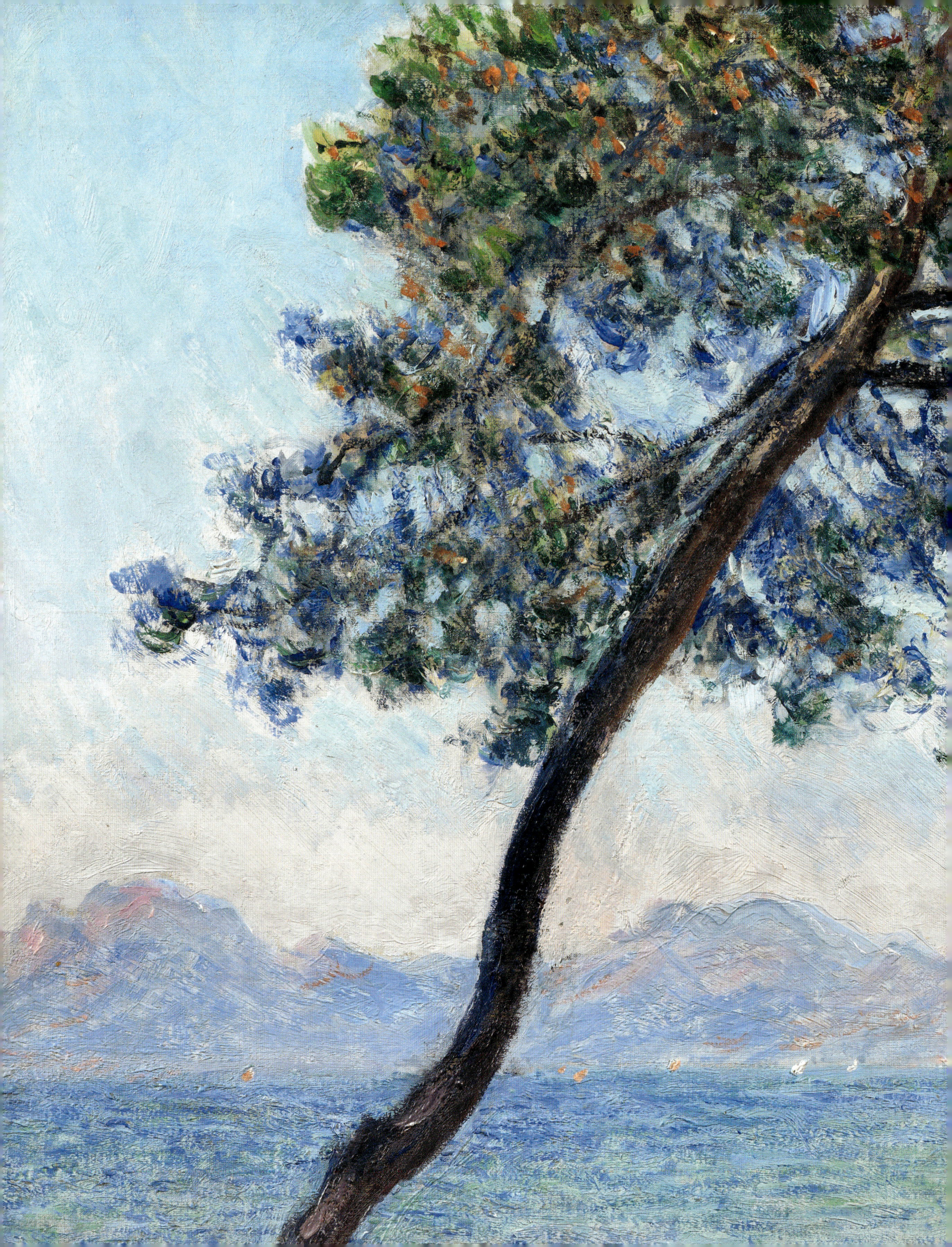

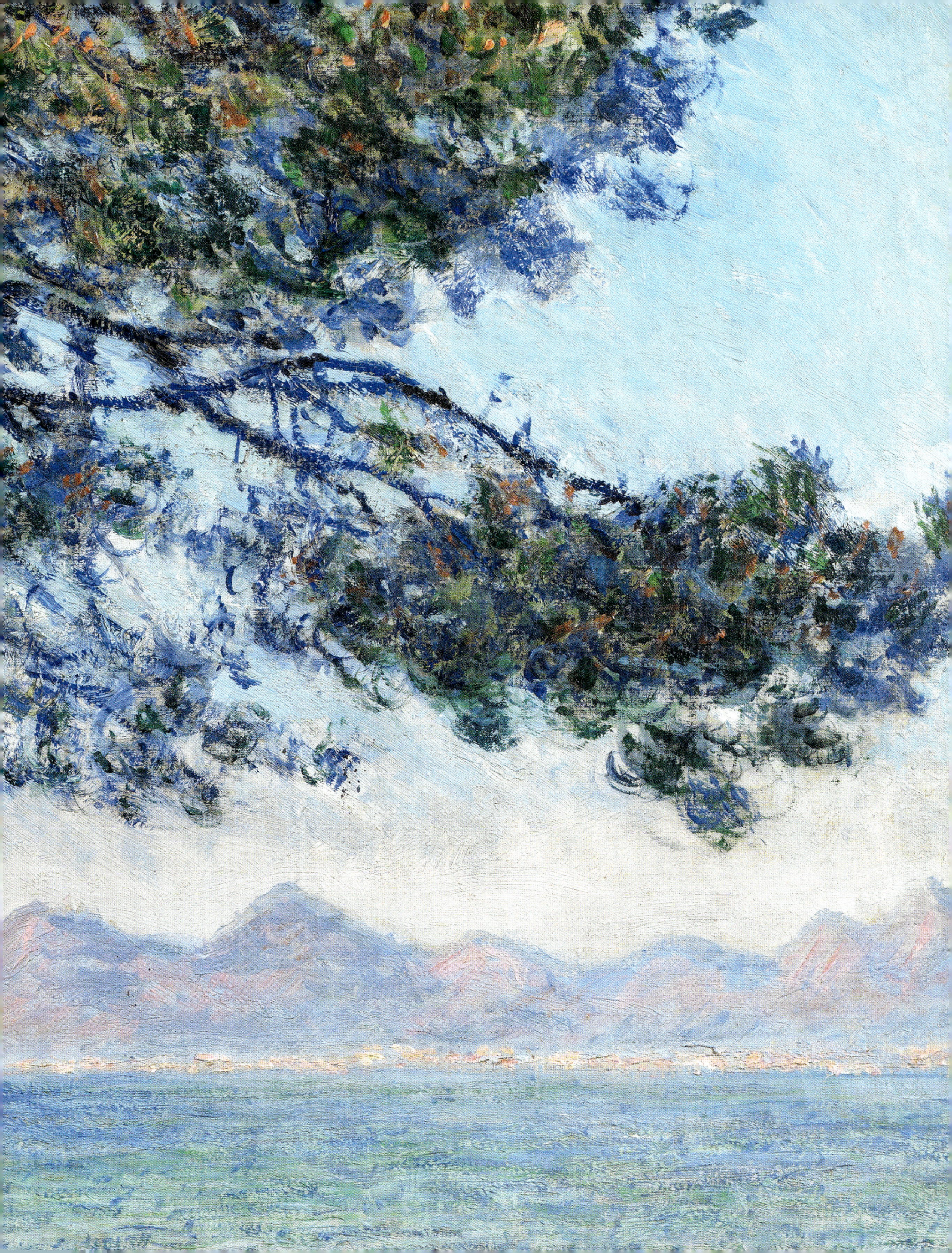

Camille Pissarro (1830–1903)
Place Lafayette, Rouen, 1883

Oil on canvas, 46.3 × 55.7 cm
The Samuel Courtauld Trust, The Courtauld Gallery, London
P.1932.SC.319

In 1883, on the advice of his friend Monet, Pissarro travelled to the city of Rouen in search of new subjects. During his seven-week stay he made 17 paintings, plus drawings and watercolours. He eschewed the medieval centre, although the famous cathedral does appear in the background of three views. Instead Pissarro depicted Rouen as an important commercial port and industrial centre. *Place Lafayette, Rouen* is the most populated of these scenes. Unlike the majority of the others, it seems to have been painted from a high vantage point, possibly his hotel room in the Place de la République, rather than in the street, where he struggled to work in peace.

The river Seine, which cuts a shallow diagonal strip across the canvas, is lined with barges. Across the water is the Ile Lacroix, with its smoking factory chimneys nestled between trees. The church sat atop the hills is also modern: the Gothic Revival Basilique Notre-Dame de Bon-Secours was completed in 1844. Its spire echoes the upward thrust of the boats' masts, the chimneys and the streetlights in the foreground.

The *place* itself is animated by figures, some with horses and carts moving goods along the wharf. A building casts a blue shadow over much of the thoroughfare. Its form and colour demonstrate Pissarro's quest for balanced and unified compositions. The edge of the shadow seems to follow the line of the quay wall. Its blue colour chimes with the river in the middle ground and the hills beyond; the far right of the canvas is marked by a blue line, perhaps a drainpipe, adding to the chorus of verticals.

Pissarro's application of colour in small spots in the foreground pre-empts his adoption of pointillism. The sweeping *balayé* brushstrokes in the sky are comparable to those of Seurat in his *Bathers at Asnières* (p. 121); Pissarro met the 26-year-old Seurat two years after this Rouen trip. A friend of both the older and younger generations of artists showing their work at the Impressionist exhibitions, Pissarro – especially in paintings such as this – bridges Impressionism and Post-Impressionism.

Pissarro's 1883 Rouen paintings also anticipate another development in his art: that of repeatedly painting the same motif in series. When Pissarro returned to Rouen in the years following 1895, he was more deliberate about producing series. This practice became the norm for his urban paintings, including *The Boulevard Montmartre at Night* (p. 109).   RMCK

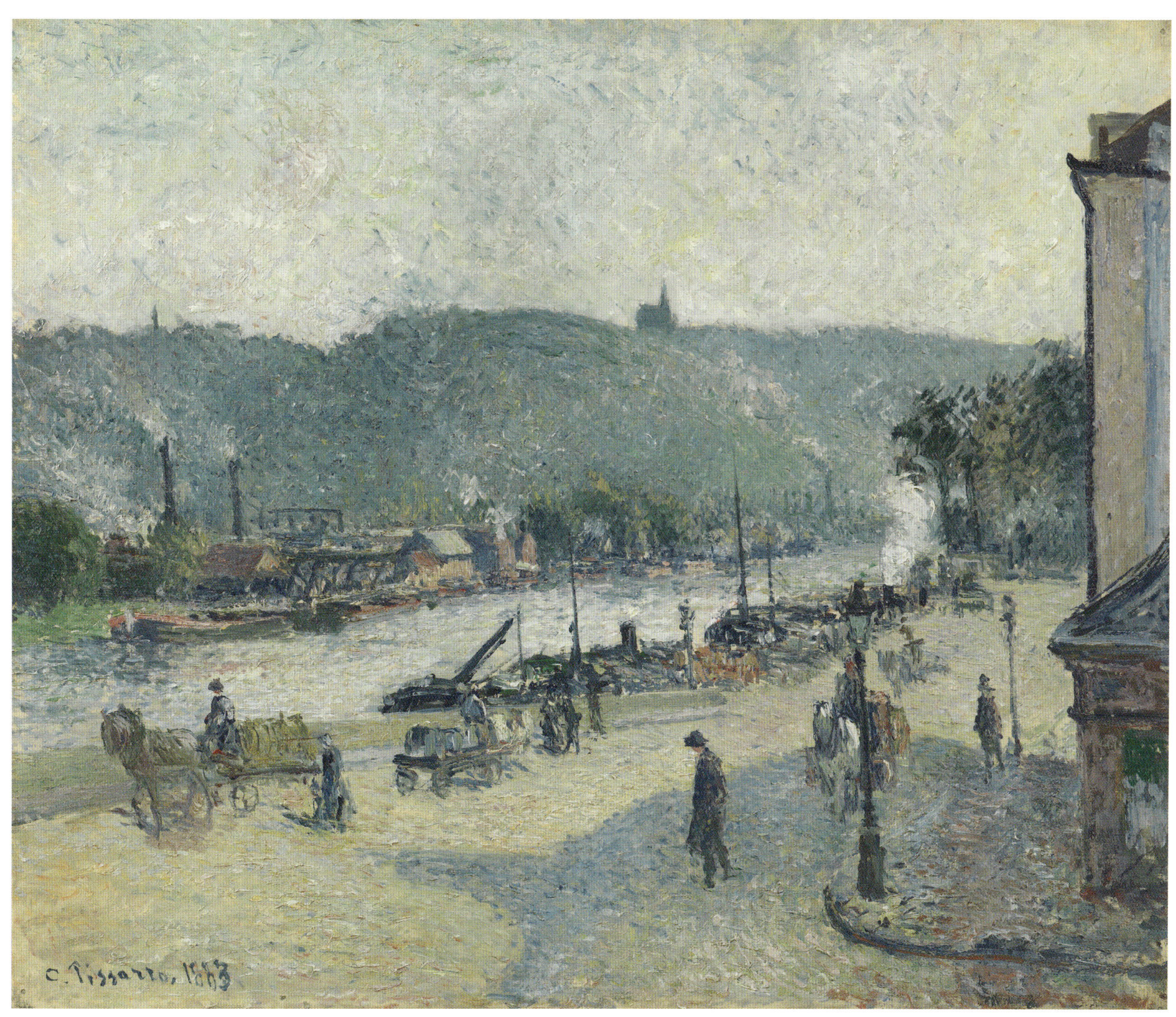

Camille Pissarro
The Boulevard Montmartre at Night, 1897

Oil on canvas, 53.3 × 64.8 cm
The National Gallery, London. Bought, Courtauld Fund, 1925
NG4119

While most of the Impressionists had moved away from depicting the city that so fascinated them in the 1860s and 1870s, Pissarro returned to Paris in the final years of the nineteenth century to attempt to capture the capital's modernity as a counterpoint to the rural subjects for which he had become best known. The ageing artist, whose eyes now watered when he attempted to paint outside, rented a room at the Grand Hôtel de Russie and, with the success of Monet's series paintings in mind, set out to paint this view of the Boulevard Montmartre at different times of the day and in varying weather conditions. 'I have begun my series of boulevards', Pissarro wrote to his son Georges in 1897, 'I have an extraordinary motif that is going to need interpreting in every possible light.' Pissarro painted 14 different versions of this view: on a crisp winter morning, an afternoon in the snow, on a late summer afternoon, at twilight, the trees budding with spring leaves and, on only one occasion, at night.

Here, Pissarro portrays the glimmering effects of light on the wet pavement following a downpour with a virtuosic range of rapid brushstrokes, animating the whole composition. The rain has stopped and the Parisian crowds, merely suggested by short dabs of dark paint on the pavements, are strolling through the streets and perusing the lit shop windows. Pissarro delighted in capturing the different forms of artificial light illuminating the boulevard. Cutting into the centre of the composition at the bottom of the picture is the white orb of an electric street light. They had only recently been introduced to the streets of Paris and Pissarro took particular care in rendering its cold light with strokes of thick white paint and the blue aura surrounding it, as well as the other lamp posts receding into the distance. By contrast, the pavement glimmers with reflections of the warm glow of the shop windows, the displays bathed in gaslight suggested by rapid fluid strokes of orange and red, sometimes mixed straight onto the brush. The cabs lining the boulevard waiting for the spectators about to leave the show at the Théâtre des Variétés have yellow oil-burning lamps. These various sources of light illuminate the façades of the buildings, while further up still, light pollution rises from the horizon obliterating the night sky, an ultimate manifestation of modernity.   JD

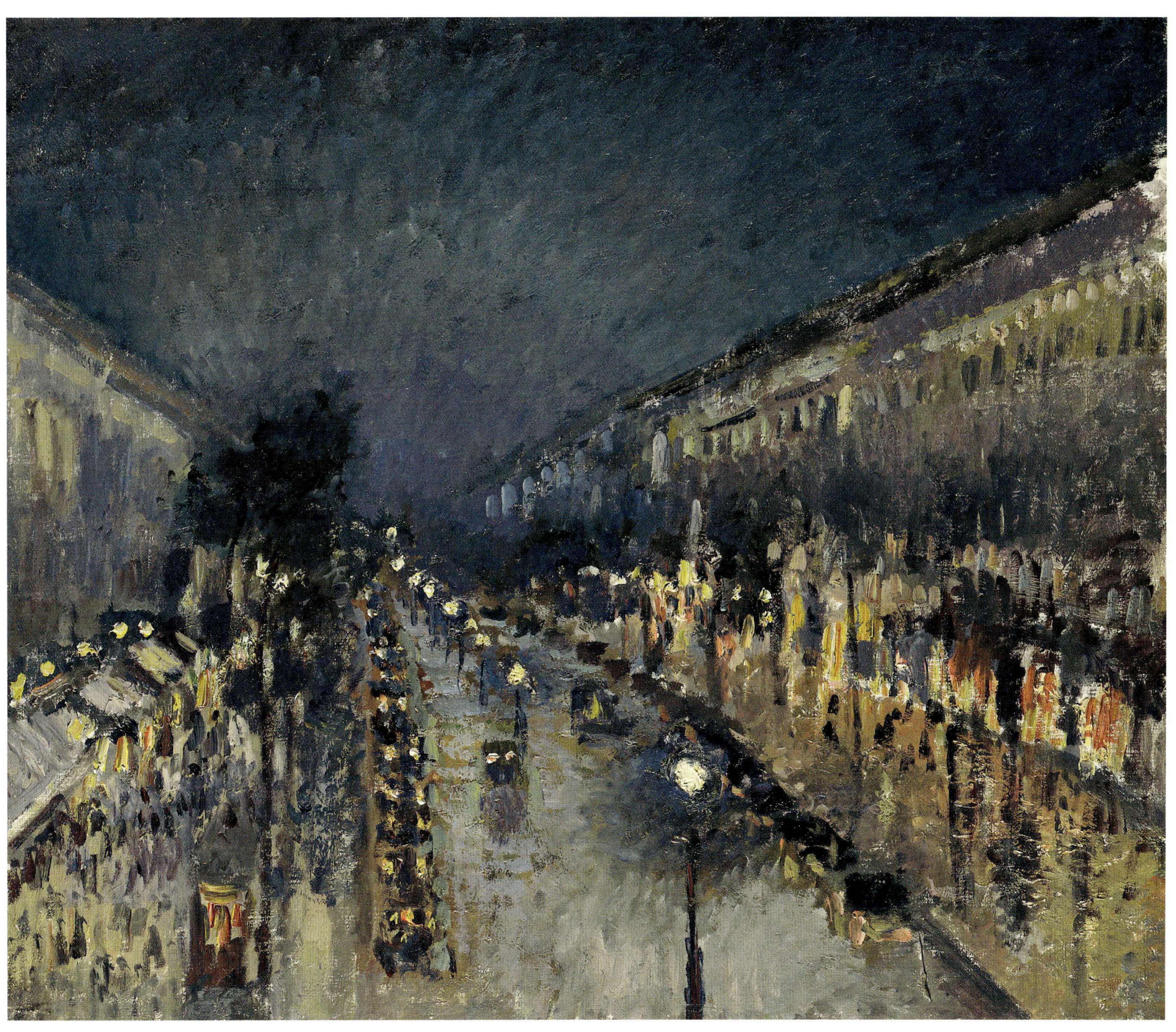

Pierre-Auguste Renoir (1841–1919)
La Loge (Theatre Box), 1874

Oil on canvas, 80 × 63.5 cm
The Samuel Courtauld Trust, The Courtauld Gallery, London
P.1948.SC.338

A beautiful young woman in a striking black-and-white striped dress draws admiring gazes to her box at the theatre. Fresh flowers in the pink tonality of her cheeks adorn her bodice and hair. She knows she is being observed and has lowered her gilded opera glasses so as not to impede our view. Nor do her own eyes seem to focus on anything; she is an object of pure and passive delectation. It is no accident that her face is the most highly finished detail of the painting, the rest more summarily and scintillatingly rendered. Behind, her male companion lifts his opera glasses to scan the house in search of further pleasures. Whatever might be taking place on stage seems superfluous to the proceedings.

This is Renoir's earliest and most elaborate depiction of theatre audiences and the glances that dart around the auditorium as the Parisian *beau monde* appraises and admires itself. A few years later, in 1876–7, came *At the Theatre* (p. 115), which the Courtauld Fund acquired for the nation in 1923, two years before Samuel Courtauld purchased this canvas for his private collection. Renoir was not alone in exploring the motif; Degas and Cassatt did so as well, and cartoonists had a field day with the vain spectacle and the often-ambiguous social status of the women, respectable wives and daughters, or *cocottes*. In this case we know the names of the protagonists – Nini Lopez, a model from Montmartre, and Renoir's brother Edmond – and undoubtedly they posed in Renoir's studio.

The picture was included in the First Impressionist Exhibition, which opened on 15 April 1874 in the studio of the photographer Nadar, and was one of seven Renoir submissions to that legendary display. Critics singled it out for praise then, and it has since come to be regarded as a quintessential masterpiece of early Impressionism, capturing the ephemeral pleasures of modern life with quick brushstrokes and a luminous palette. It was sent for exhibition in London as early as November 1874, but found no buyer, and was back again for Paul Durand-Ruel's Grafton Galleries exhibition of Impressionist masterpieces in 1905, again without luck. Courtauld acquired it from Durand-Ruel in Paris.   CR

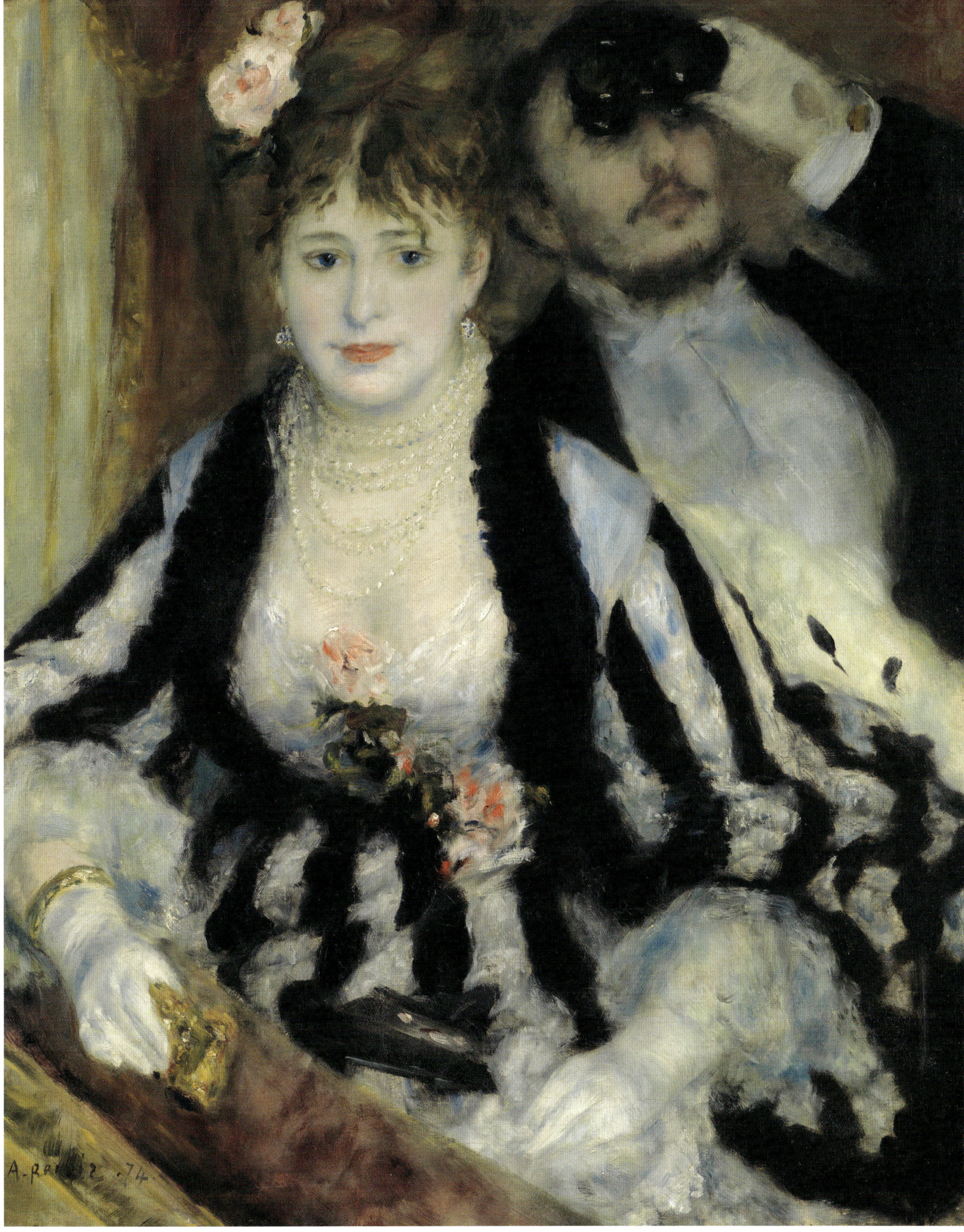
A. Renoir. 74.

Pierre-Auguste Renoir
The Skiff (La Yole), 1875

Oil on canvas, 71 × 92 cm
The National Gallery, London. Bought, 1982
NG6478

In a quintessential Impressionist painting of light and leisure, formerly in Samuel Courtauld's private collection, Renoir depicts two women boating on the Seine in the outskirts of Paris. The skiff (or *yole* in French) they idly row gives this painting its title. The colour and form of the long narrow boat lends structure to an image that feels like it could easily dissolve under the dazzling sunlight that reflects across the surface of the river.

The vermilion orange boat is particularly vivid against the cobalt blue water. Renoir was drawing on contemporary colour theory, primarily that of French chemist Michel Eugène Chevreul in 1839, to affect the perception of colours. Renoir placed hues from opposite sides of the colour wheel, known as complementary colours, next to each other to mutually enhance their intensity. The way the water and sunshine dissolve the clarity of line between the boat and the water means that the orange bleeds into the blue, not as a murky mixture of the two, but as a shimmering interlacing of colours.

Like Monet in *Autumn Effect at Argenteuil* (p. 101), Renoir used short horizontal brushstrokes known as *taches* (spots) to give the effect of light on water. He also dragged drier paint across the surface to give subtle touches of colour that give a feeling of depth to the water. Elsewhere the artist allowed his colours to mix on the canvas to create more subtle reflections.

Boating on the Seine was a common leisure activity. Some art historians have patronisingly noted that the women are staying close to the shore, as implied by the greenery in the foreground. Yet their position on the water, closer to the near bank and almost parallel to the far, is essential to the composition. The horizontal lines of the boat and the bank structure the image, aided by the clearly drawn building and railway bridge on the far bank.

The exact location of the scene is unknown. It may have been the leisurely area of Chatou, but Renoir is not concerned to show us a particular spot, even if he did paint it *in situ*. The speeding train in the background, its puffing steam merging into the sky, reminds the viewer of the proximity to Paris, the modern industrial city that these women are escaping.   RMcK

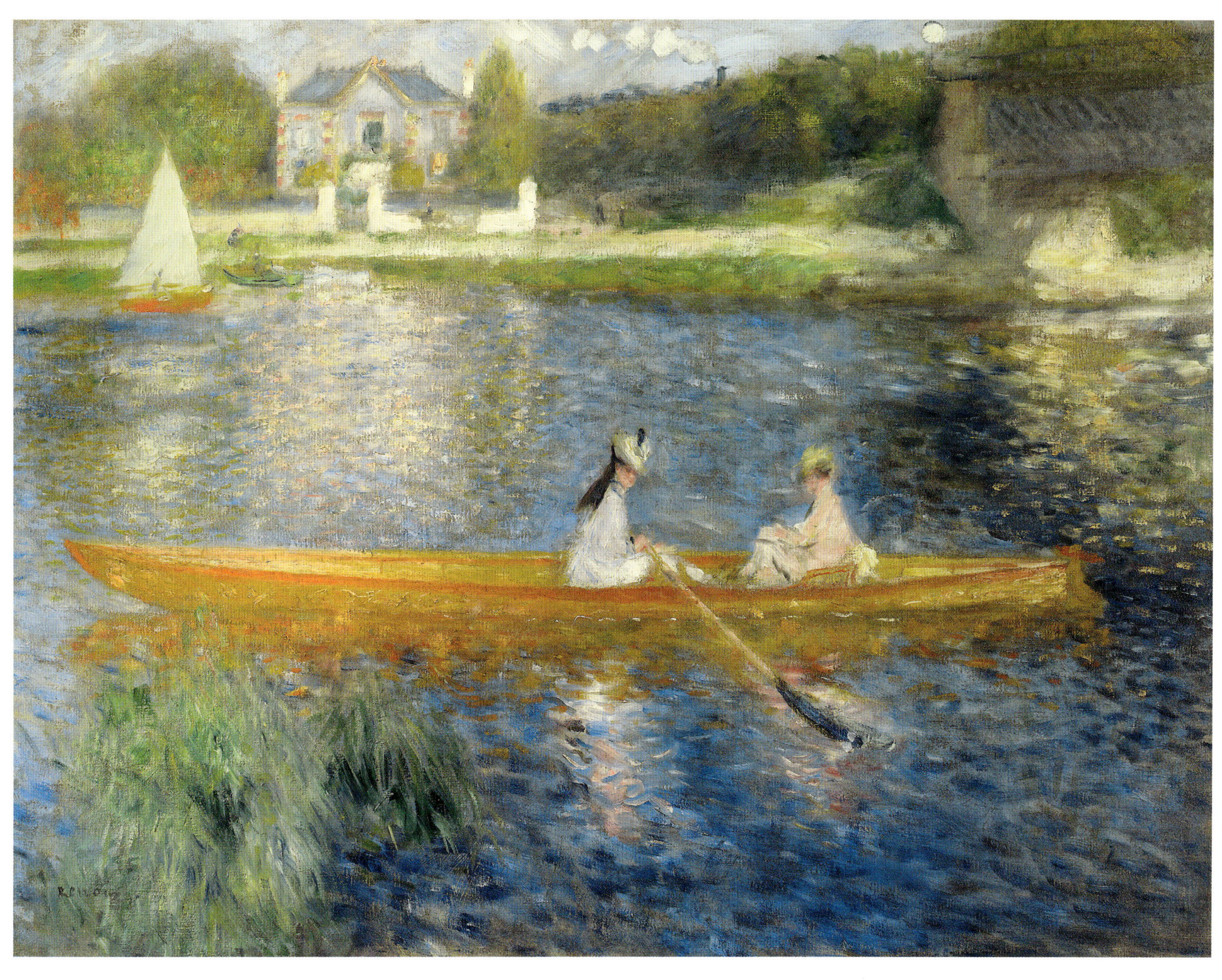

Pierre-Auguste Renoir
At the Theatre (La Première Sortie), 1876–7

Oil on canvas, 65 × 49.5 cm
The National Gallery, London. Bought, Courtauld Fund, 1923
NG3859

A young woman clutching a posy of flowers leans forward expectantly in her theatre box. Her profile, clearly outlined against the architecture, emphasises her youth, as does the presence of a female companion. She is quite unlike the woman in Renoir's earlier *La Loge* (p. 111). She does not turn to acknowledge the artist or viewer, who also must be seated in the box; instead she and her companion gaze outwards. It is unclear if they are looking towards the stage or the rest of the audience, some of whom are seen on the left of the picture.

Renoir uses harmonious colour to ensure that the stark difference in scale between the figures in the foreground and background does not unbalance the picture. The blue tones of the young woman's outfit repeat across the canvas. Renoir had originally painted two more large figures on the left-hand side before redesigning the composition to the current format, which would prove to be influential. A few years later the American Impressionist Mary Cassatt adopted this intimate format in her depictions of women observing, and being observed, at the theatre (for example, *In the Loge*, 1878, Museum of Fine Arts, Boston, The Hayden Collection – Charles Henry Hayden Fund).

In Renoir's picture, lively brushwork also ensures that the focus is balanced between the background and foreground. In addition, it conveys the animation of the audience, whose unruly behaviour suggests an alternative location for this scene. Turning in their seats, it could be that the spectacle is in the more relaxed environment of a café-concert, yet from the perspective of the hesitant young woman, the atmosphere is formal. Her fashionable outfit dates this picture to the period 1876 to 1877.

The painting has also been known as *The Café-Concert*. The performers and audiences in both venues were popular with the Impressionists and other artists seeking scenes of modern life. The subtitle *La Première Sortie* was adopted later, possibly to emphasise the sentimental narrative of the young woman's first formal outing and thus to appeal to the British art market. This title may have been used to distinguish this picture from *La Loge*, bought by Samuel Courtauld for his private collection two years later.   RMcK

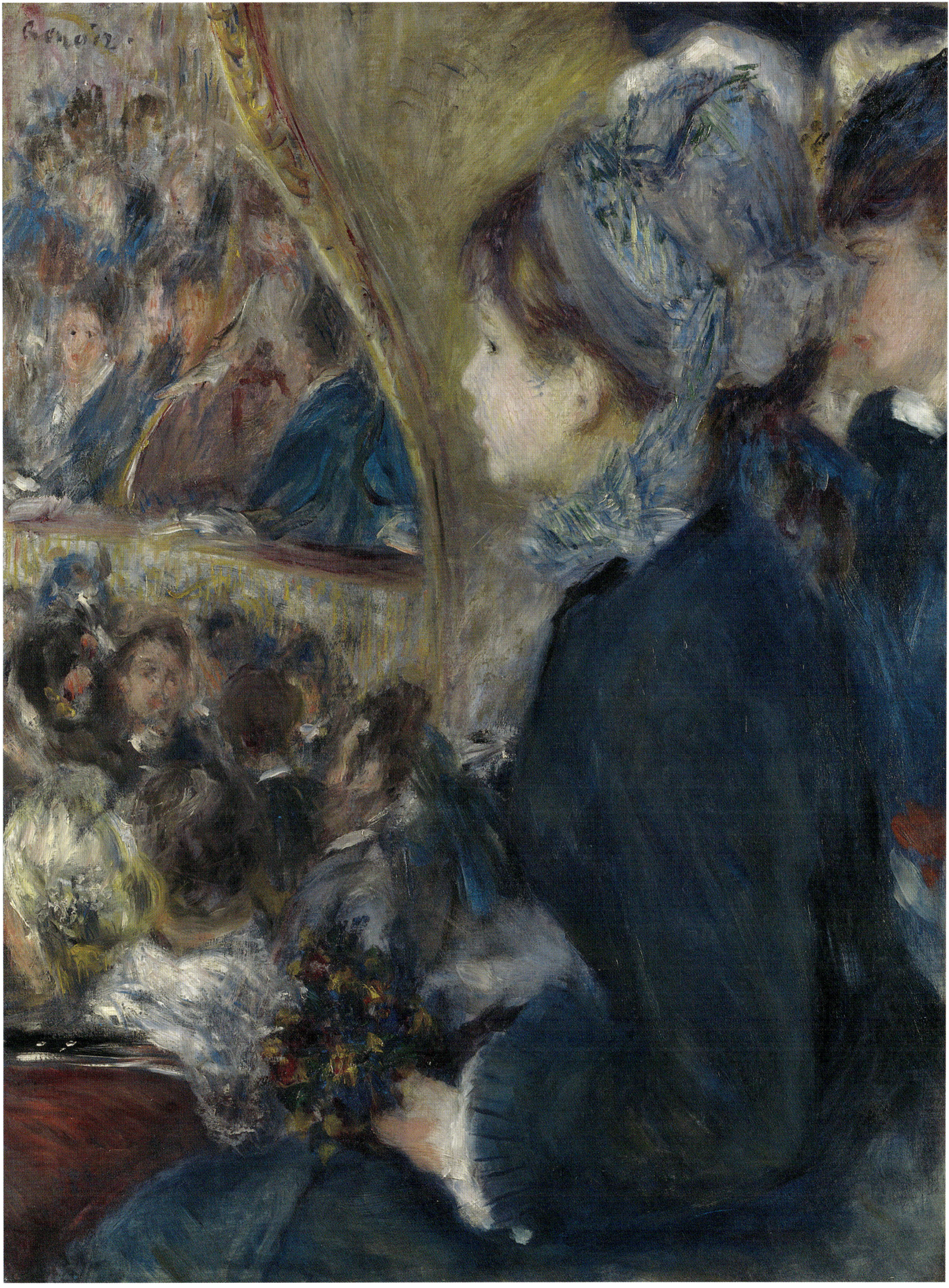

Pierre-Auguste Renoir
Portrait of Ambroise Vollard, 1908

Oil on canvas, 81.6 × 65.2 cm
The Samuel Courtauld Trust, The Courtauld Gallery, London
P.1932.SC.340

Renoir was already famous and prosperous by the time he met Vollard in 1895, and was in a successful, long-standing business relationship with his dealer Paul Durand-Ruel. Nonetheless, the ageing and increasingly irascible Impressionist, who often ridiculed Vollard to his face, saw the advantage in an alliance with a brash, adventurous and accommodating acolyte. Over the next several years, Vollard would be one of Renoir's principal dealers.

One of the few demands Vollard made of his artists was that they paint his portrait. According to the sitter, Cézanne's required 115 sessions before it was 'abandoned' (Musée du Petit-Palais, Paris). Picasso's was one of his early Cubist masterpieces (Pushkin Museum, Moscow). Renoir depicted Vollard no fewer than five times. In one portrait of 1917 (Nippon Television, Tokyo), the obese and dishevelled dealer wears a toreador's trim and glittering suit of lights, souvenir of a recent visit to Barcelona. In another he dons a bandit's bandana (Musée du Petit-Palais, Paris). Along with the business acumen they shared, role-playing and fantasy were part of Vollard's relationship with Renoir. This portrait was painted when he visited the artist at Cagnes in the south of France, where Renoir was building a house and living in rented accommodation. It, too, creates a character for Vollard to perform.

A Renaissance painting tradition, practised by Titian and Bronzino among others, shows the connoisseur caught up in rapt admiration of works of art. Renoir updates the tradition. Here, Vollard holds, indeed seems to caress with his chubby fingers, a plaster by Aristide Maillol, his *Crouching Woman* of about 1900. Also on the tabletop are two blue-and-white ceramics, a faience bowl and what may be a Ming Chinese water dropper in human form. Maillol was admired by both artist and dealer, and Vollard especially loved Chinese art. Renoir executed the portrait quickly, using thin paint that washes across the canvas with exuberance. Subtle red tonalities and deft touches of black animate the surface. Horses dance merrily across the tablecloth. It is a kindly image of refined, deeply felt discrimination.

Promised to the Musée du Petit-Palais in Paris, instead in 1927 Vollard sold the painting to Samuel Courtauld for 800,000 francs. Ten years later he wrote to Courtauld that he understood the painting would go to the National Gallery one day; the idea filled him, he said, with 'beaucoup de plaisir'. The portrait, however, had been part of the Courtauld Gift of 1932.   CR

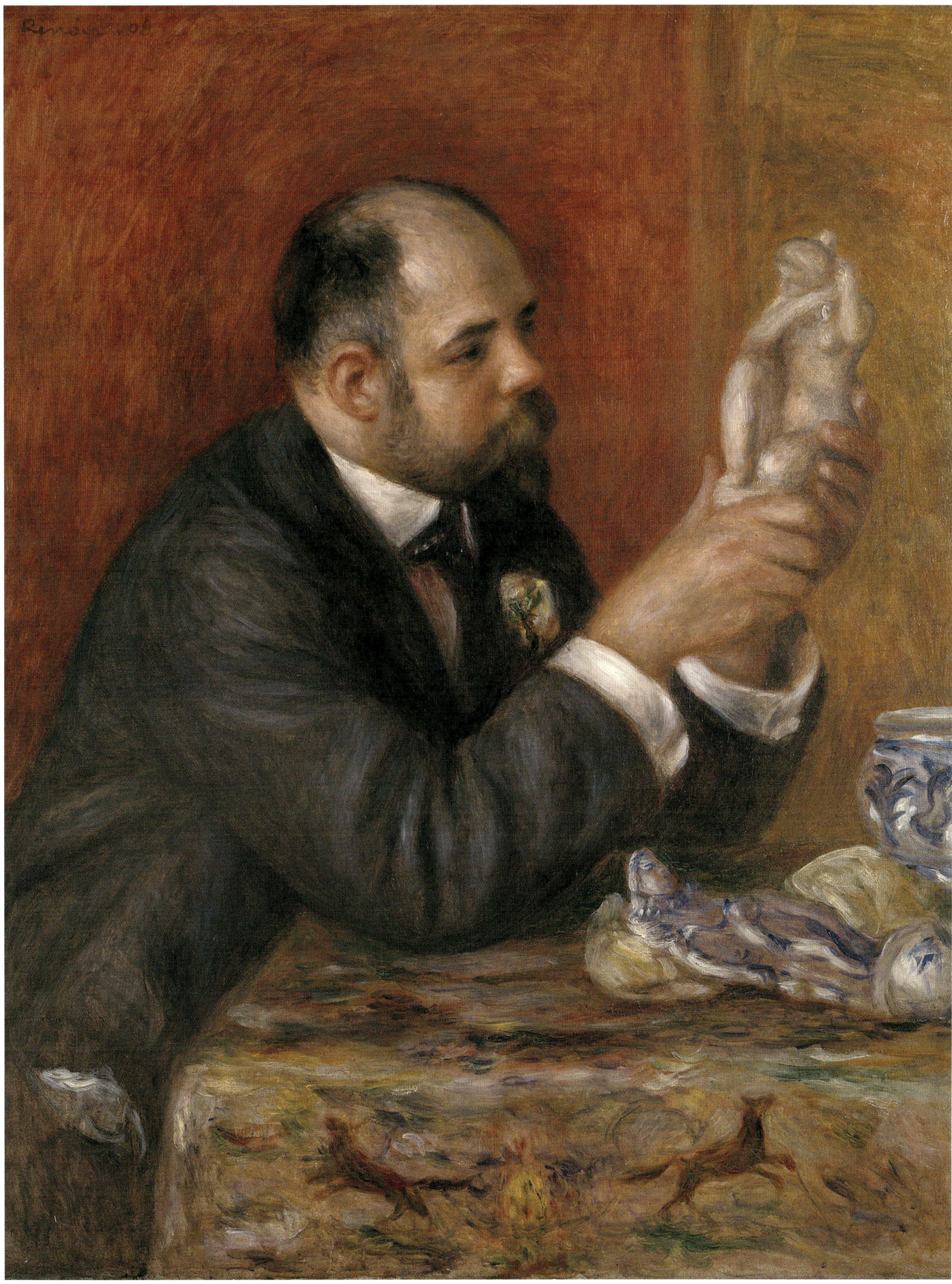

Renoir 08

Pierre-Auguste Renoir
Woman Tying Her Shoe, about 1918

Oil on canvas, 50.5 × 56.5 cm
The Samuel Courtauld Trust, The Courtauld Gallery, London
P.1932.SC.341

Renoir's late art is a taste of the early twentieth century, passionately shared by Picasso and Matisse among others, which has been all but lost a century on. Major recent exhibitions and the diligent explications of scholars fail to elicit much public enthusiasm for works that for many seem overblown, feeble in execution, and in their obsession with the voluptuous female form lost in self-absorbed rituals of undressing, bathing, dressing, somehow culturally inappropriate. Memoirs like his son Jean's *Renoir, mon père* (original French edition 1962) paint a picture of an old man, brush strapped to wrist, endlessly uttering pearls of Gallic peasant wisdom as he limns fleshy buttocks. They do little to sustain the artist's reputation as a fearless leader of the avant-garde, which during his long lifetime was never in question.

Here, a seated blonde woman in a white slip – we do not know the model – leans over to tie a shoelace. The dress she will don is tossed casually on the bed beside her. It is a simple act from everyday life executed without need of reflection. It holds no secrets. It is in Renoir's reckoning uniquely 'female' and 'natural'. The picture is rendered in skeins of pastel colour, thinly applied, animated by strokes of brilliant white paint.

The entire surface is similarly alive with rapid, glinting touches of colour. Forms dissolve into one another. Renoir here is an aged master of his increasingly free and improvisatory craft.

Samuel Courtauld began his collection of French art with this very work, probably dating from the final year of Renoir's life, which he acquired in 1922 along with a landscape of 1921 by the not-quite-forgotten Jean-Hippolyte Marchand. The joint purchase suggests that Courtauld briefly set out to be a collector of contemporary art rather than historic Modernism. Moreover, John House has pointed to 'fascinating parallels' between Courtauld and the legendary Philadelphia collector Dr Albert C. Barnes, who during these same years was assembling the world's largest collection of late Renoir paintings, particularly buxom female figures. This is not one such parallel as *Woman Tying Her Shoe* was Courtauld's sole, tentative footstep down that rosy path.   CR

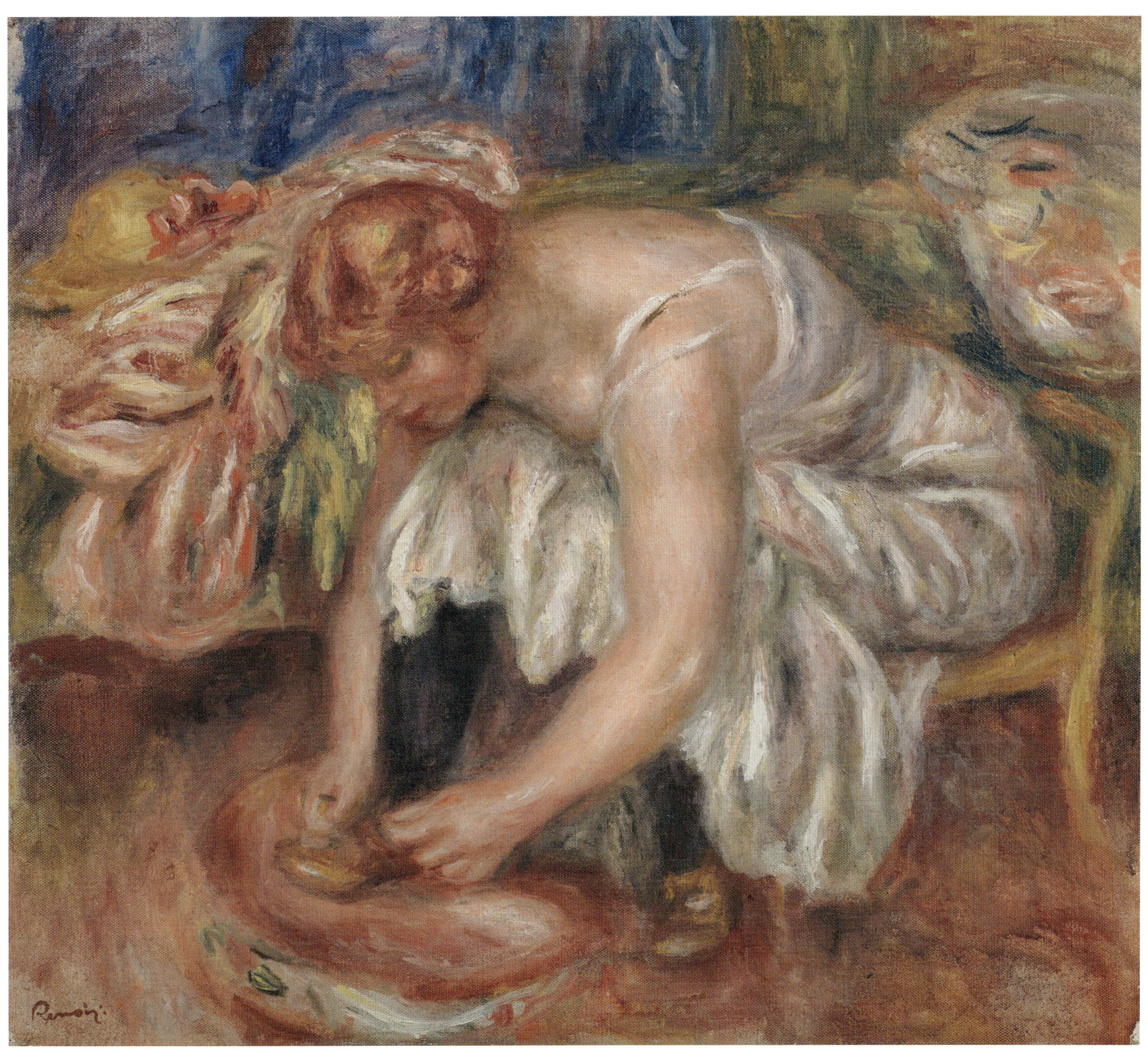

Renoir

Georges Seurat (1859–1891)
Bathers at Asnières, 1884

Oil on canvas, 201 × 300 cm
The National Gallery, London. Bought, Courtauld Fund, 1924
NG3908

Seurat's first large-scale painting shows industrial workers resting on the banks of the Seine at Asnières, north-west of Paris. Although geographically close to the leisured landscapes of Monet and Renoir (pp. 101, 113), and drawing on the same colour theories, Seurat's painting subverts the Impressionist norms of the previous decade with his monumental scale, classical poses and dedication to meticulous preparation over spontaneity. Yet his grand treatment of working-class people alienated the official art world, which rejected this work from the Paris Salon of 1884.

Seurat had a traditional academic artistic training at the Ecole des Beaux-Arts in Paris. There he learned to draw from classical sculptures and studied the paintings in the Musée du Louvre. This knowledge is reflected in the bathers' poses. The boy in the water on the far right with his hands to his mouth evokes the Greek god Triton blowing his conch shell. The man with a straw hat on the far left, whose arms rest on his knees, echoes a pose used by the French neoclassical painter Hippolyte Flandrin. The landscape is also classicising in structure, yet distinctly modern in content, with the factories and bridge at Clichy along the horizon.

Seurat's modern inclinations are also evident in the way he applied colour. He would go on to create pointillism, a technique that amplified the Impressionist use of complementary colours and short brushstrokes to a scientific degree. In this picture, the water is rendered with horizontal strokes, a more refined version of those used by Monet and Renoir, while the grass is a criss-cross of strokes of different colours evoking its texture. Seurat's use of lilacs among grass-green demonstrates his interest in the colour theory of Michel Eugène Chevreul, and others. Chevreul's work on the optics of tapestries inspired Seurat's weaving of contrasting colours through his compositions. As Seurat developed his technique, he would use finer points of pure colour that would blend on the retina. He reworked parts of *Bathers* accordingly. The red hat of the boy in the water is dotted with yellow in the highlights and blue in the shadows to give form as well as luminosity.

Seurat refined his pointillist technique in his next major work, showing a nearby site on the Seine of more elevated social standing: *A Sunday Afternoon on La Grande Jatte* (1884–6, Art Institute of Chicago). RMcK

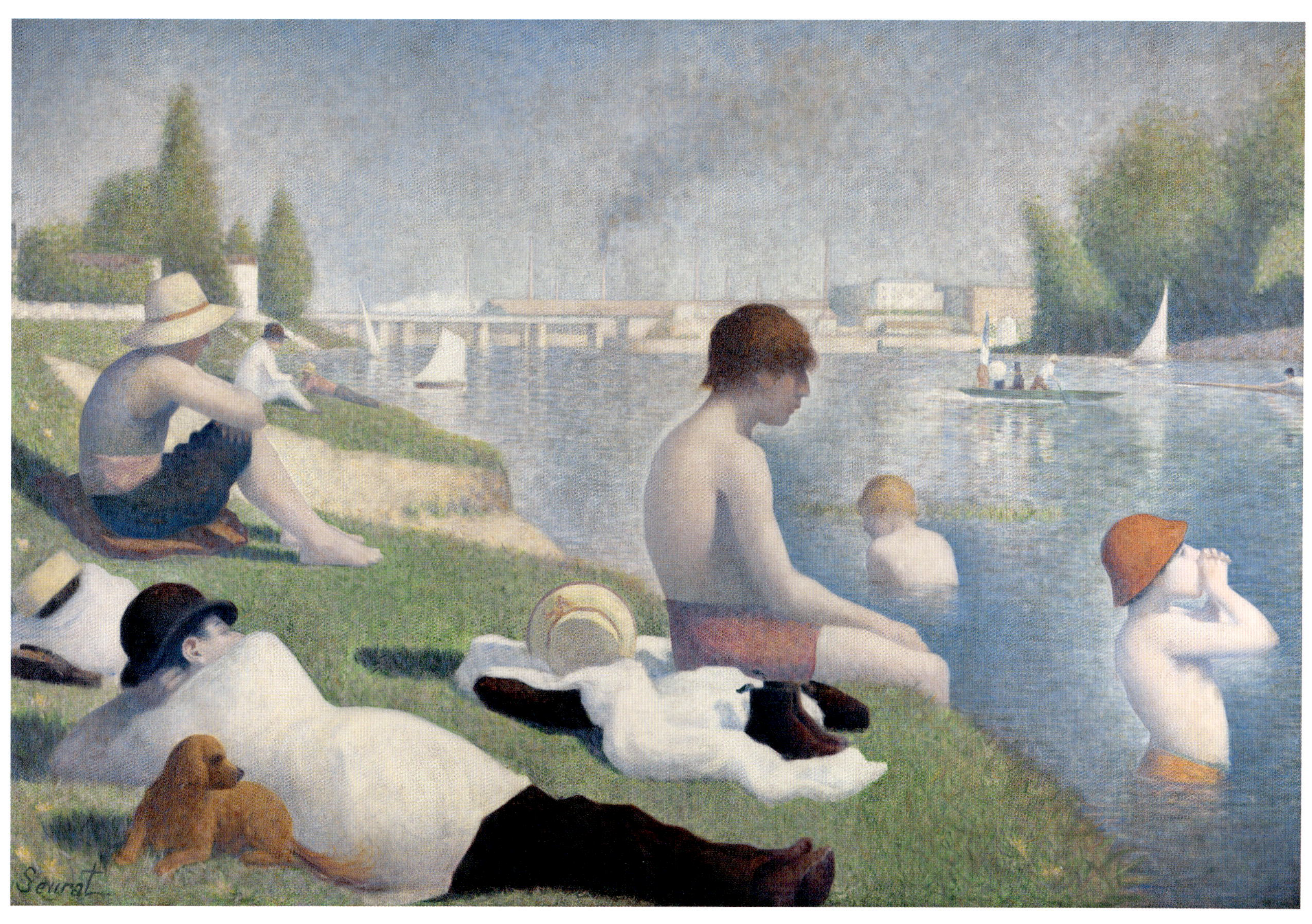

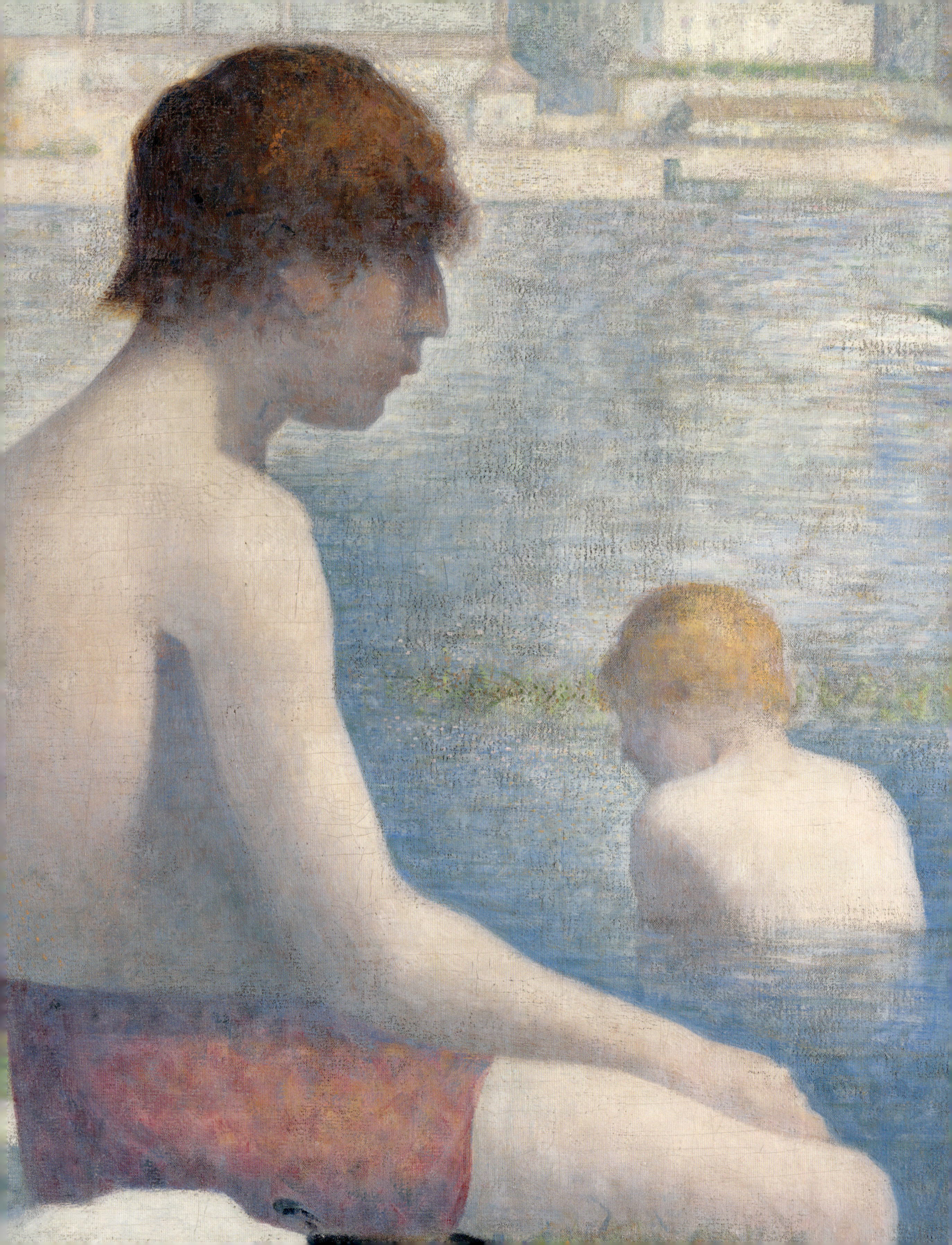

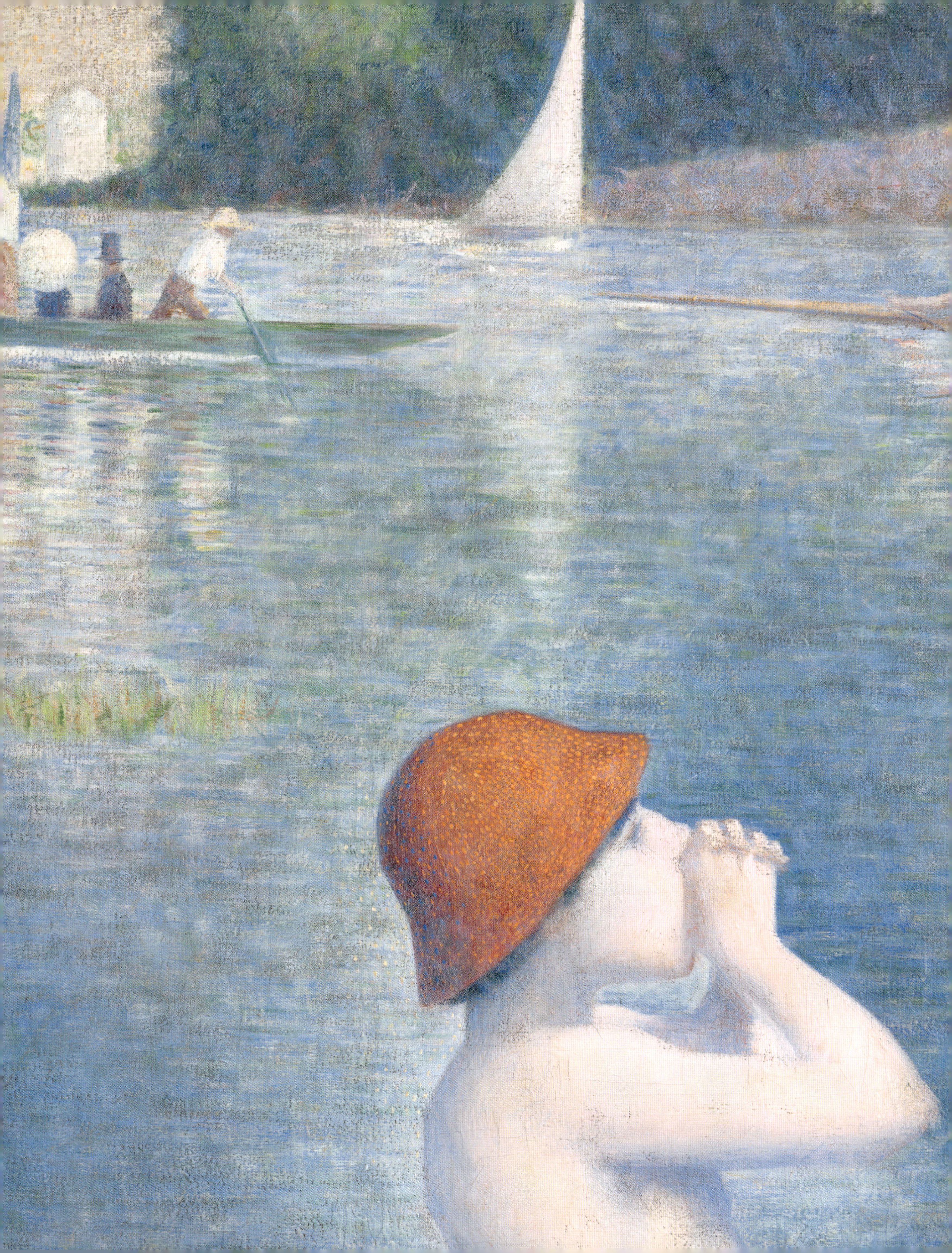

Georges Seurat
Bridge at Courbevoie, 1886–7

Oil on canvas, 46.4 × 55.3 cm
The Samuel Courtauld Trust, The Courtauld Gallery, London
P.1948.SC.394

Seurat brings angular order to the riverside landscape of the western outskirts of Paris. This location is a little nearer the city than Monet's *Autumn Effect at Argenteuil* (p. 101), and close to the site of Seurat's own *Bathers at Asnières* (p. 121). In the years since *Bathers*, Seurat had fully developed his pointillist technique, refining his application of small uniform brushstrokes. This is one of the first landscapes conceived with this technique in mind. The artist made a conté crayon study *in situ* and then began painting in a small format that allowed him to take the canvas to the site, to capture the light effects as his Impressionist predecessors had done.

In the painting, as in the drawing, geometric simplicity rules the landscape. The river Seine and the Bineau Bridge bisect the canvas horizontally. The island of La Grande Jatte slopes across the composition, striped by sunlight in shades of olive-green. A chimney in the industrial suburb of Courbevoie punctures the sky, its strong verticality echoed in the nondescript mass at the right-hand edge of the canvas and the masts of the boats that are reflected in the river. Although seemingly perpendicular, these masts tilt slightly to the left, invoking the gentle movement of the water. The leafless tree on the right and the mass of foliage at the top left act as foils to the minimal geometry of the surrounding elements.

It is the same island populated with bourgeoisie in Seurat's large-scale painting *A Sunday on La Grande Jatte* (1884–6, Art Institute of Chicago). That scene was painted behind the viewpoint of this picture, to our right. Dressed in heavier, darker clothing than the figures in the larger picture, the two figures on the bank in this picture are similarly dehumanised.

The quiet stillness of the scene also permeates the colours. Among the white of the water and sky touches of warm and cool tones add variation and create the reflections and the wisps of smoke and clouds in the sky. In the summer of 1887, Van Gogh painted the same bridge with a more intuitive approach to structure, but with an application of vibrant colour in horizontal strokes demonstrating his own variation of Seurat's pointillism (Van Gogh Museum, Amsterdam).   RMcK

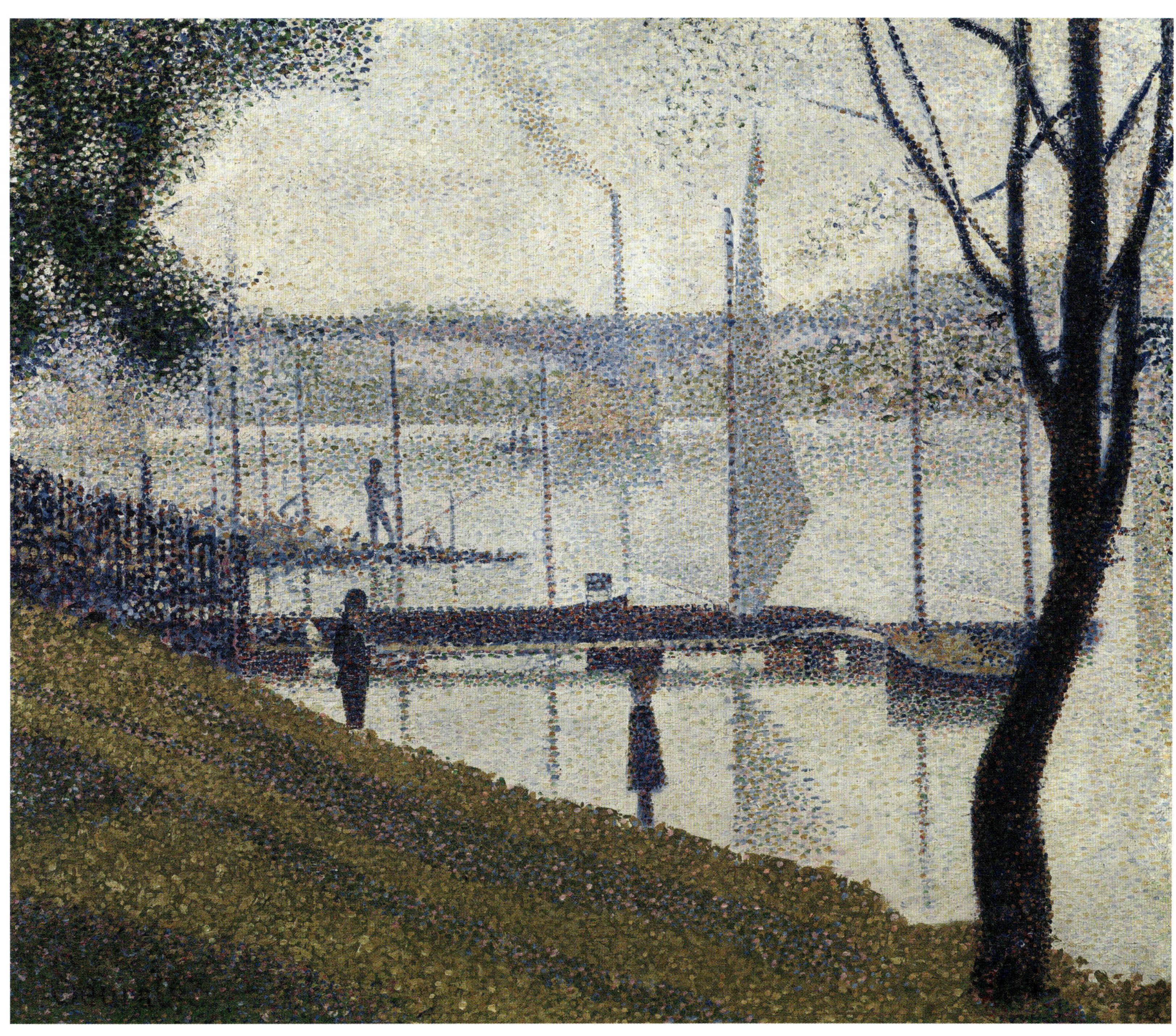

Georges Seurat
Young Woman Powdering Herself, about 1888–90

Oil on canvas, 95.5 × 79.5 cm
The Samuel Courtauld Trust, The Courtauld Gallery, London
P.1932.SC.396

In a modern interpretation of the art-historical tradition of depicting the goddess Venus at her toilette, Seurat presents a young woman looking into a mirror and raising a powder puff to her face. The artist had long abandoned the contrived naturalism of *Bathers at Asnières* (p. 121); this work sits with the more stylised pointillist paintings *Le Chahut* (1889–90, Kröller-Müller Museum, Otterlo) and *Le Cirque* (1890, Musée d'Orsay, Paris). The woman's act has connotations of vanity and artifice, which are reflected in the construction of the picture, complete with a painted border that curves gently across the top.

Seurat's painting plays with the illusion of space by making the background boldly flat and the figure emphatically three-dimensional. The young woman's voluptuous body is attentively modelled, the artist using blue tones in his characteristic pointillist technique to shade her corset. By contrast, the turquoise and coral wallpaper behind her – with a motif like a stylised version of the bow atop her mirror – runs parallel to the picture plane. As in *Bathers* (p. 121) and the sky of *The Channel of Gravelines* (p. 129), Seurat lightens the background where it meets a body in shadow, and darkens the shade where adjacent to light forms.

The emphasis on the woman's physical presence is increased by the scale. She overpowers the diminutive mirror and elegant curved table in front of her. This modern Venus is coiffed and corseted like a café-concert performer. Unbeknown to viewers in 1890, but well established today, the young woman is the artist's mistress Madeleine Knobloch, who worked as an artist's model in Paris. This is the only painting by Seurat related to his closely guarded personal life.

In recent years, technical imaging has confirmed the anecdote that Seurat had originally included a self portrait in this picture. In the mirror at the top left, the artist depicted himself in the act of painting. Told by a close friend that the effect was somewhat comical, Seurat painted it out, replacing the self portrait with the flowers now visible. A visual echo between the two tables (one more ornate than the other), and between the pink tone of the bow on the mirror and the flowers, serves to further emphasise the artifice of the picture. The wilfully three-dimensional mirror sitting awkwardly against the flat wallpaper is a microcosm of the painting's uneasy *mise-en-scène*. RMcK

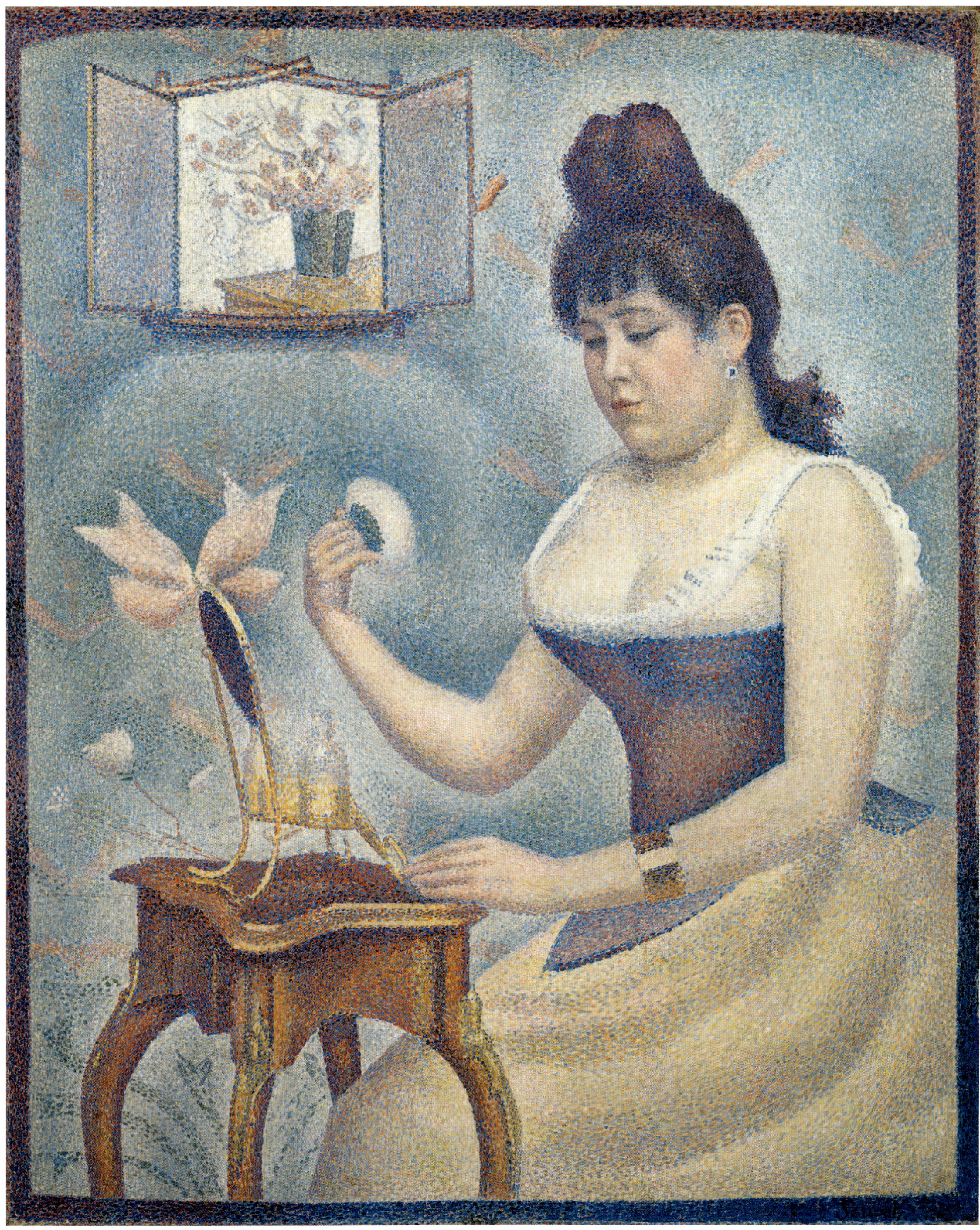

Georges Seurat
The Channel of Gravelines, Grand Fort-Philippe, 1890

Oil on canvas, 65 × 81 cm
The National Gallery, London. Bought with the aid of a grant from the
Heritage Lottery Fund, 1995
NG6554

This is one of four major marine paintings
Seurat made in 1890 near the town of Gravelines.
Situated between Calais and Dunkirk on France's
northern coast, the small port at the mouth of
the river Aa offered Seurat a sparse landscape that
appealed to his interest in nature and artifice.
As in *Bridge at Courbevoie* (p. 125) Seurat stylises the
landscape to the point of linear clarity, but on this
occasion there is no preliminary study. He uses
his pointillist technique to bathe the scene in the
luminous morning light of the channel coastline.

The picture is structured around the cool blue
strip of water that cuts cleanly across the entire
canvas, sloping gently upwards towards the right.
On the channelised river sits a small boat, with
masts that, together with two moorings on the
nearside bank, draw the eye up to the ordered
forms of the buildings lining the far side. Some
figures are just visible, but there is little suggestion
of narrative. In the foreground, the composition
is even sparser: a white trail leads the eye through
the sand, aided by the patch of grass on the left, a
green hypotenuse typical of Seurat's compositions.

Fresh blue sky and pale blond sand dominate
the colour palette as well as the composition.
Seurat carefully modulates the tones in the foreground to evoke wet sand. In the sky he increases
the luminosity by intensifying the blue tone where
it meets a light-coloured structure, a technique
also seen in the background of *Young Woman
Powdering Herself* (p. 127).

The Gravelines picture features a painted
border, an element used by Seurat to create a
transition between the image itself and the frame.
Predominantly indigo towards the bottom of the
canvas, it subtly shifts in tone to contrast with
the adjacent area of the image: for example, red
dots appear near the green at the bottom left, and
orange predominates at the top above the blue sky.

This work was acquired by Samuel Courtauld
for his private collection in 1926. It entered the
collection of Heinz Berggruen in 1986 and was
bought by the National Gallery in 1995, joining
Seurat's *Bathers at Asnières* (p. 121), which had
been purchased for the nation by Courtauld in
1923.   RMcK

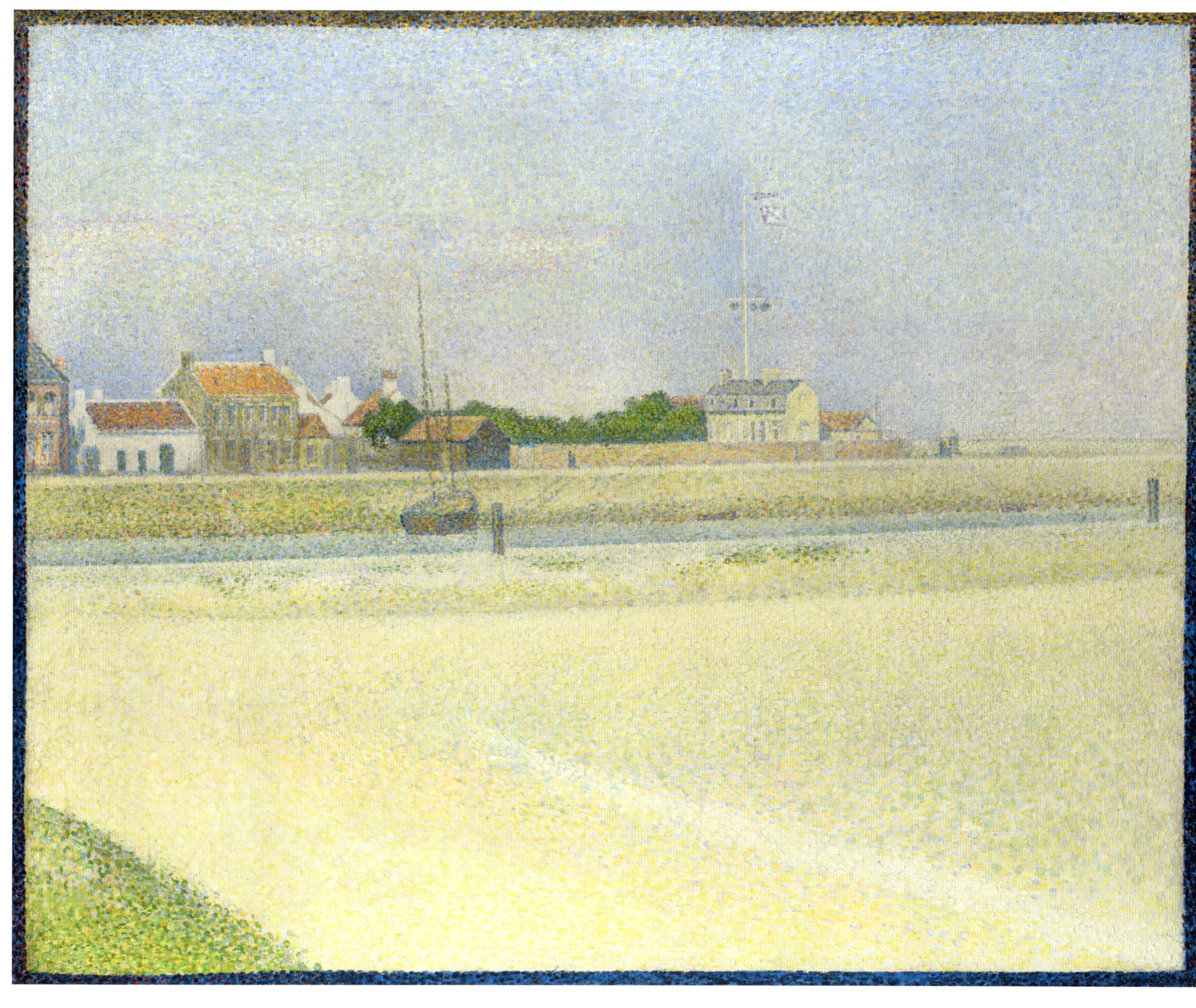

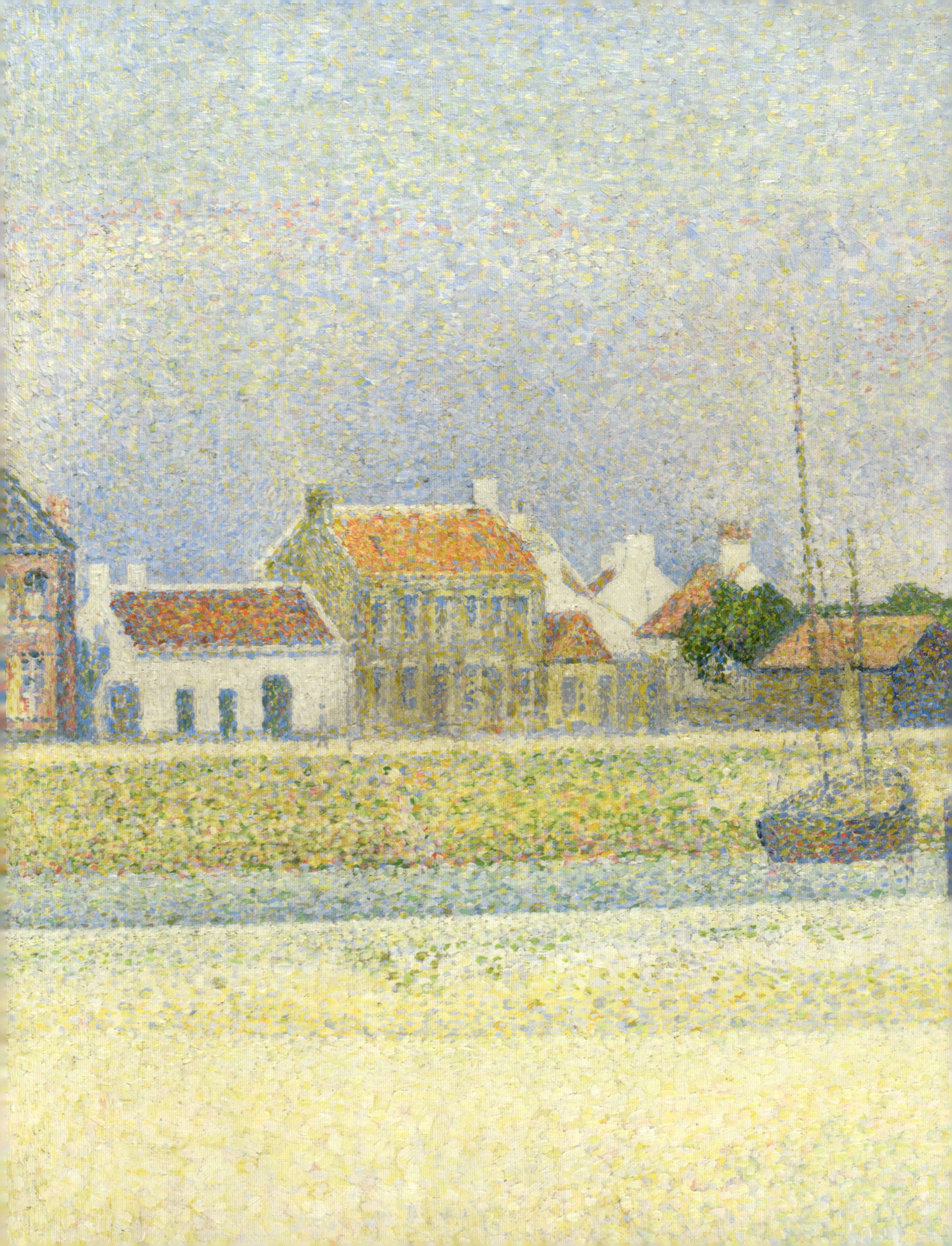

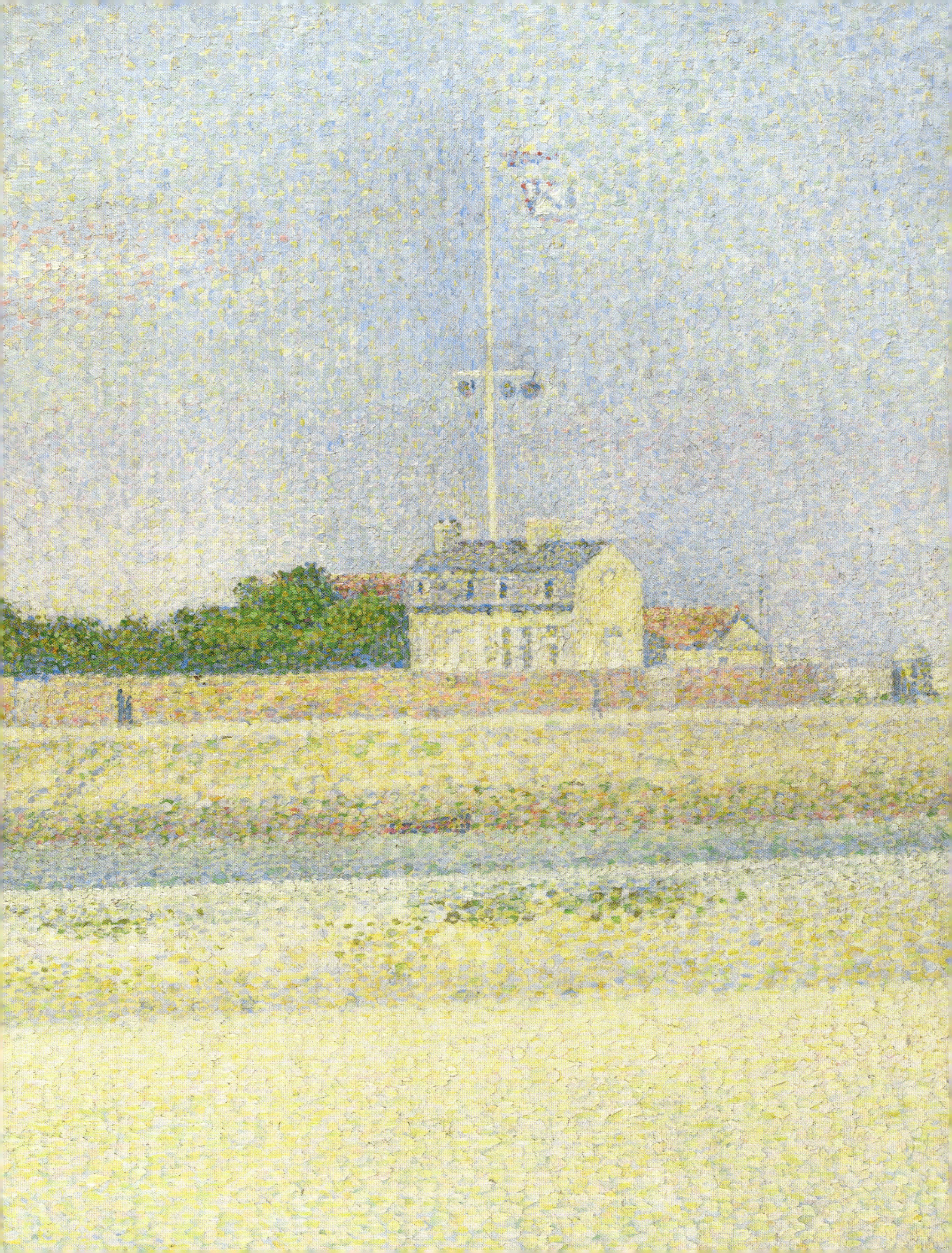

Henri de Toulouse-Lautrec (1864–1901)
Woman Seated in a Garden, 1891

Oil on millboard, 66.7 × 52.8 cm
The National Gallery, London. Bought, Courtauld Fund, 1926
NG4186

A young woman with an inscrutable expression sits in a tranquil, if unkempt, garden. She is thought to be a dancer called Gabrielle, surname unknown, a model favoured by Toulouse-Lautrec. The garden is probably that of the retired photographer Père Forest, the artist's neighbour in Montmartre, an area of northern Paris known for its bohemian residents and nightlife.

This is one of numerous half-length plein-air portraits of female friends, shop assistants and prostitutes produced by the artist. In these, Toulouse-Lautrec came closest to the Impressionists' attempts to capture natural light effects. Arriving in Paris from Albi in southern France to train as an artist in 1882, the year of the Seventh Impressionist Exhibition and the last year of Manet's life, the young Toulouse-Lautrec adopted Impressionism's revolutionary zeal and techniques.

Nearly a decade later he makes his loose and sketchy brushwork clearly visible. His technique emphasises his skill in drawing forms – like Daumier (see pp. 63, 65), Toulouse-Lautrec was a prolific printmaker – and allows the neutral colour of the millboard to show through. The paint colours are likewise muted, bar the bright white of the woman's blouse. Her face is subtly rendered in flesh tones, with a blue outline that adds shadow to the edge of her features, extending to delineate the garden around her.

Unlike some Impressionists, Toulouse-Lautrec insisted on the primacy of the figure over the landscape. In this picture, the garden is dominated by the sitter's imposing presence. Gabrielle's extended left hand curls uneasily around the arm of the chair, demarcating her personal space. Her strong profile recalls Renaissance portraiture like Baldovinetti's *Portrait of a Lady* (about 1465, The National Gallery, London), which Toulouse-Lautrec is known to have admired.

The women from Toulouse-Lautrec's garden studies sometimes reappear within more populous scenes of Montmartre's nightlife. Gabrielle's profile, from the opposite side, is recognisable in his later brothel scene *Rue des Moulins* (1894, National Gallery of Art, Washington, DC). In contrast to that intimate portrait of a prostitute undergoing a medical inspection, here she is demurely dressed, her blouse buttoned up to her chin. The timeless quality of this portrait belies the permeation of the artist's social and artistic milieu.   RMcK

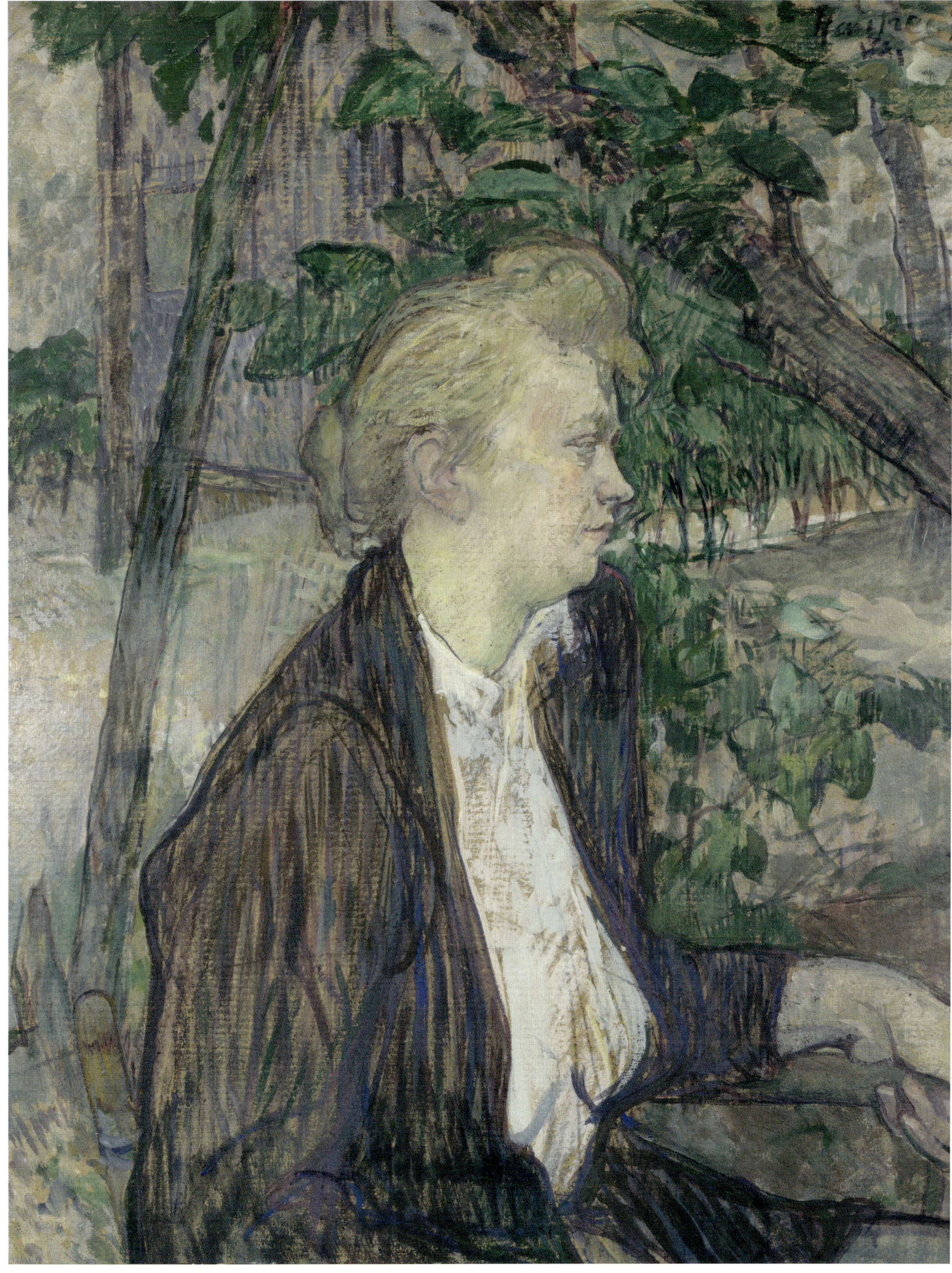

Henri de Toulouse-Lautrec
Jane Avril in the Entrance to the Moulin Rouge, about 1892

Oil and pastel on millboard, laid on panel, 102 × 55.1 cm
The Samuel Courtauld Trust, The Courtauld Gallery, London
P.1932.SC.465

Neither performing nor posing, the dancer Jane Avril (1868–1943) stands at the entrance to the famous nightclub, the Moulin Rouge. The friend and favoured model of Toulouse-Lautrec is contemplative, her body stilled and elongated by the vertical brushstrokes that dominate her coat and the surrounding walls. The nocturnal blue at top right, punctuated by the warm glow of a carriage light, suggests she is arriving to perform. The coat and hat hanging in the entryway prefigure the removal of her own fur-collared coat. Toulouse-Lautrec used doorways as backgrounds for portraits of male friends, but Avril's position at the threshold between her private and public personas is more striking.

Born Jeanne Beaudon, she adopted the name Jane Avril when she began performing at the Moulin Rouge. Avril fostered her public image through paintings and posters made primarily by Toulouse-Lautrec, which showed her flaming red hair and distinctive physiognomy in a variety of guises. His first poster portraying her, an advertisement for the Divan Japonais cabaret (1892), enhanced both their reputations. In that poster, although not on stage, she is clearly performing, exuding a self-assurance quite different to the young woman in Renoir's similarly composed *At the Theatre* (p. 115).

In this picture, by contrast, Avril's stillness and withdrawn expression are at odds with her reputation as an exuberant and erratic dancer; her nickname 'La Mélinite' refers to a powerful explosive. Avril choreographed her own performances and produced often elaborate, and always corset-less, costumes that complemented her off-stage dress sense.

Toulouse-Lautrec often paid special attention to Avril's extravagant millinery. Here the addition of white pastel animates the frothy hat decoration; it closely resembles the feathered hat the artist borrowed from her to wear at the 'Women's Ball' held by the satirical magazine *Le Courrier français* in 1892. The bright yellow handbag hanging from her arm is perhaps the same as in the Divan Japonais poster.

In the present work, the strokes of oil paint and pastel in a combination of subdued and vibrant shades might appear idiosyncratic. Yet as a skilled printmaker Toulouse-Lautrec deftly uses colour and line to establish space and texture, and to ensure this composed image of Avril teems with energy.   RMcK

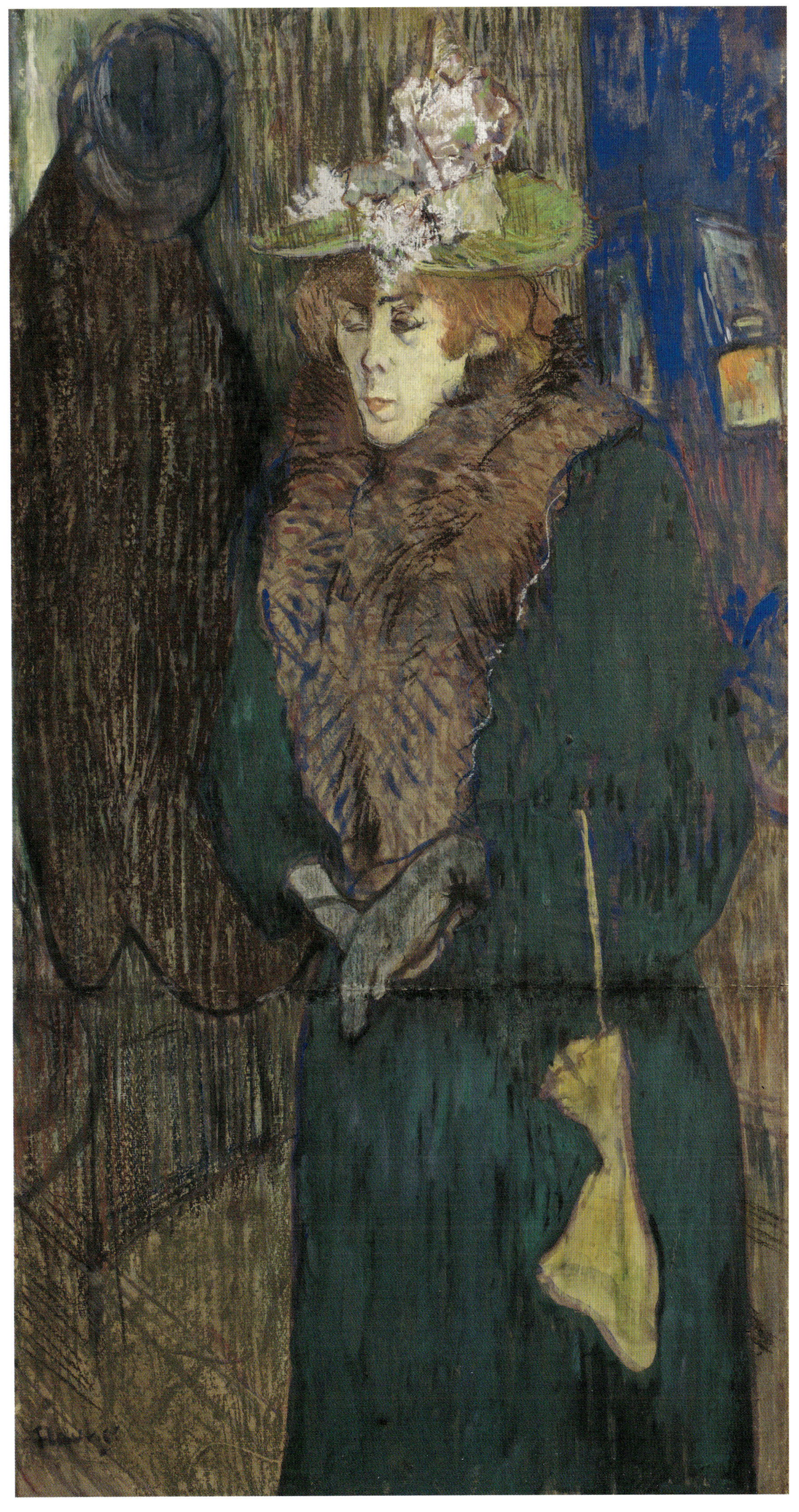

Vincent van Gogh (1853–1890)
A Wheatfield, with Cypresses, 1889

Oil on canvas, 72.1 × 90.9 cm
The National Gallery, London. Bought, Courtauld Fund, 1923
NG3861

In the summer of 1889, when working at Saint-Rémy, southern France, Van Gogh began to paint cypresses. These dark-green elongated trees, which the artist compared to Egyptian obelisks, were populous in the region of Provence, where Van Gogh had lived for the past year. He wrote to his brother Theo on 25 June, 'The cypresses are always occupying my thoughts, I should like to make something of them like the canvases of the sunflowers, because it astonished me that they have not yet been done as I see them.'

As in his *Sunflowers* series of the previous year, Van Gogh produced multiple versions of the same composition. The version of *A Wheatfield, with Cypresses* in the Metropolitan Museum of Art, New York, was made *in situ*, while this painting and a smaller version now in a private collection were produced in the studio. Repeating the composition, Van Gogh was able to make the National Gallery version more decorative and schematic. The paint is not so thickly applied, but Van Gogh still uses his characteristic bold swirling brushstrokes to evoke the expressive forms of the trees within the Provençal landscape. The cypresses and sheaves of wheat blow in a breeze also apparent in the cloud formations in the sky.

The dynamic lines of Van Gogh's stylised landscape show his interest in Japanese *ukiyo-e* prints like Katsushika Hokusai's *Under the Wave off Kanagawa* (about 1831). Japanese prints had been circulating in France since the mid-nineteenth century and had found popularity with Impressionist painters, especially Monet. Van Gogh's bright palette stemmed from his meeting modern painters in Paris in 1886, including Degas, Gauguin and Seurat. Van Gogh's brother Theo, to whom he sent this painting, was an art dealer in Paris and would send his brother the tubes of emerald green, chrome yellow, cobalt blue and zinc white used to create *A Wheatfield, with Cypresses*.

This painting dates from a productive 12-month period in Van Gogh's short career. Having voluntarily entered an asylum at Saint-Rémy in May 1889, over the following year he painted around 150 works in its environs. The motif of the cypresses reappears in one of his most famous works, *Starry Night* (1889, Museum of Modern Art, New York), which was painted the same summer.   RMcK

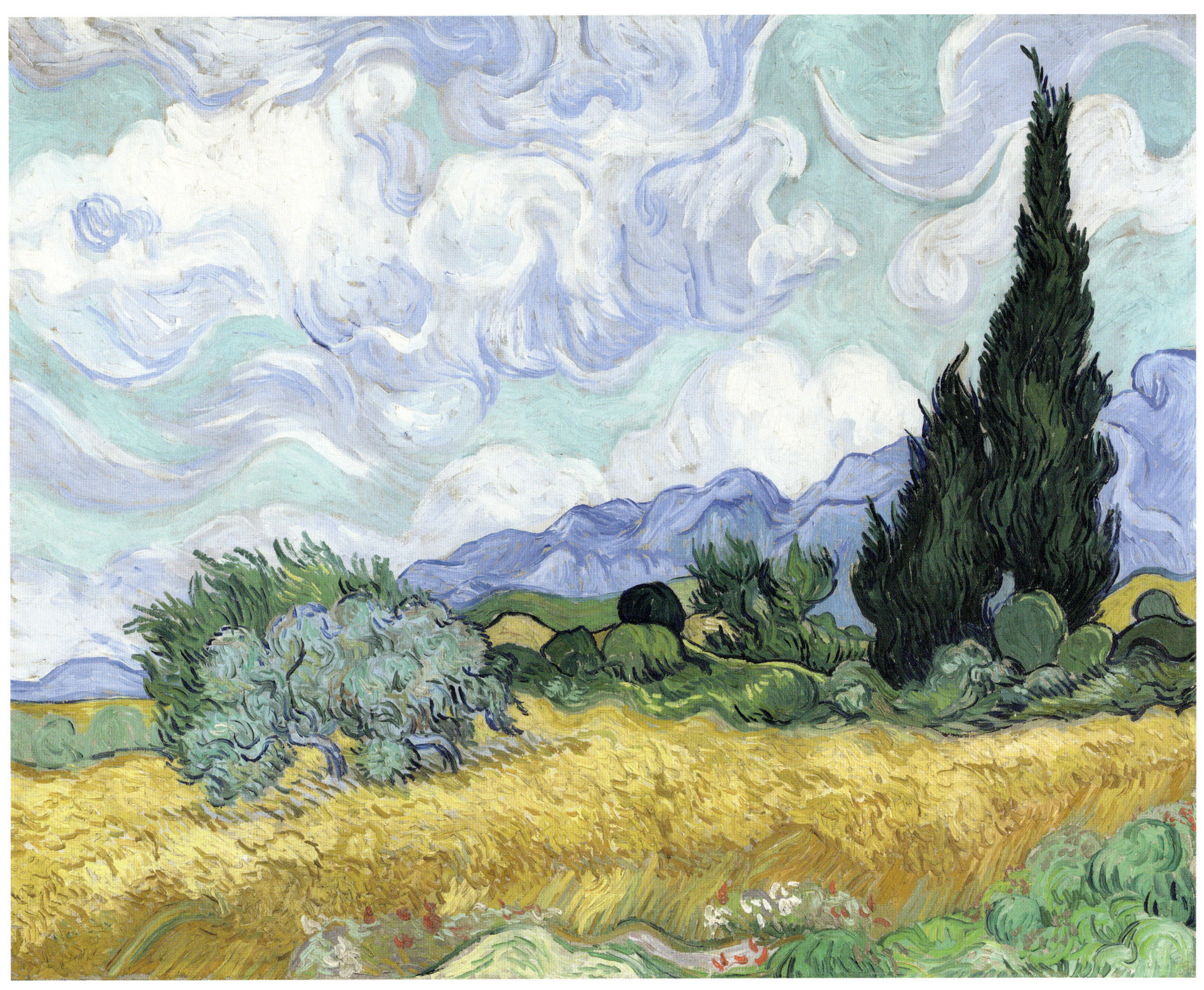

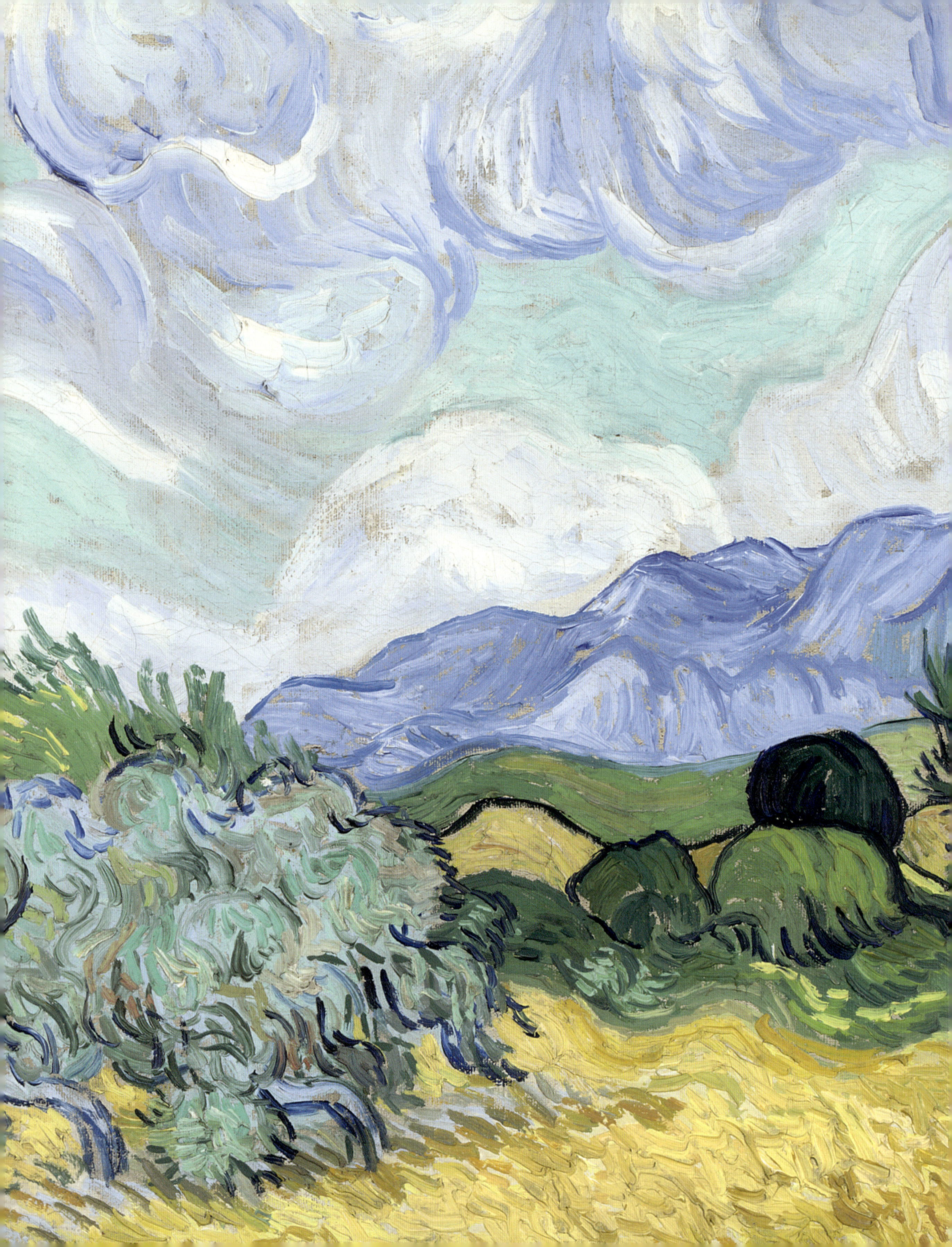

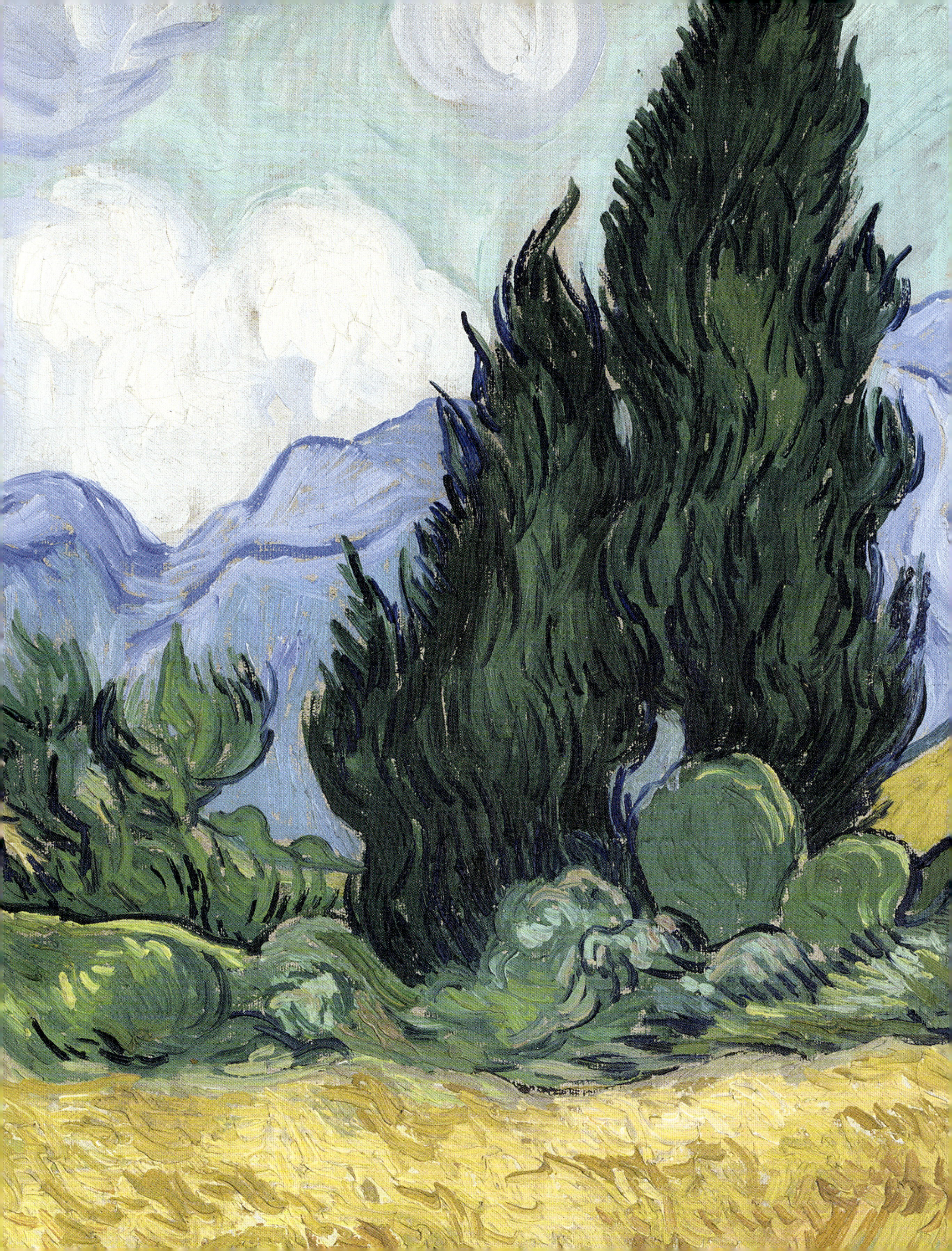

Acknowledgements

This exhibition has been made possible thanks to the exceptional generosity of
the Trustees of the Samuel Courtauld Trust, who have lent 26 paintings. I am deeply
grateful to our colleagues at the Courtauld Gallery, Ernst Vegelin van Claerbergen,
Director, and curators Barnaby Wright and Karen Serres, who supported the
project with enthusiasm from its outset, granting me the privilege of studying the
outstanding collection of Impressionist and Post-Impressionist works assembled
by Samuel Courtauld and now in their care. This study is crucially indebted to their
and the late Professor John House's scholarship, showcased in his unsurpassed
exhibition *Impressionism for England*, organised with John Murdoch almost 25
years ago, and in remarkable exhibitions held at the Courtauld Gallery in the last
two decades. I would particularly like to thank Professor Deborah Swallow, Director
of the Courtauld Institute, for her advocacy of this exhibition.

This exhibition and catalogue were initiated by Gabriele Finaldi, Director of the
National Gallery, to whom I am grateful for his support and trust. For their constant
encouragement I would like to thank Jane Knowles and Caroline Campbell. This
exhibition has benefited from the latter's extensive knowledge of the Courtauld
collection, as its former Curator of Paintings, and I am thankful to her for the
luminous, insightful essay she has contributed to this book. Caroline Campbell
assisted me in every stage of the development of this exhibition, as did Christopher
Riopelle, who provided vital help and advice, also writing entries. I would like
to thank him, as well as Sarah Herring, Rosalind McKever and Julien Domercq,
for their contributions. This publication benefited from the attentive care of
Sophie Kullmann, Jan Green, Suzanne Bosman and Jane Hyne. As the Project Editor
Sophie worked tirelessly, with rigour and creativity, to turn our texts into this book;
Mark Thomson can be credited for its beautiful design. I thank them warmly.

My gratitude goes to Howard Batho for his assistance and constant support.
The exhibition also owes a debt to Judith Cernogora, trainee curator at the Institut
National du Patrimoine in Paris, who spent a 'stage' at the National Gallery during

a vital period of the project's development. I am no less thankful to my colleagues at the National Gallery Research Centre: Richard Wragg, Jonathan Franklin and Alex Leigh, who facilitated my work in the National Gallery Archives and helped me with various aspects of the project; I am particularly indebted to Alan Crookham, Head of the Research Centre, who generously shared his expertise and insight – my essay in this book has greatly benefited from his comments. My gratitude also goes to the staff at the Tate Archives, who provided invaluable help, and to the archives at the Centre de Documentation du Musée d'Orsay, where I would like to thank Isabelle Gaëtan in particular.

I am grateful to our colleagues at the Tate, Maria Balshaw, Frances Morris, Matthew Gale and Caroline Corbeau-Parsons, who supported this exhibition by contributing loans and expertise, and would like to extend my sincere thanks to those who assisted this project in a variety of ways: Graeme Barraclough, Giovanna Bertazzoni, Julia Blanks, Belén Cao, Iona Eastman, Nancy Ireson, Chris Oberon, Lois Oliver, Belinda Phillpot, Dimitri Salmon and Joanna Weston. I am grateful to Luc, Edgar and Gabriel for their patience.

Anne Robbins

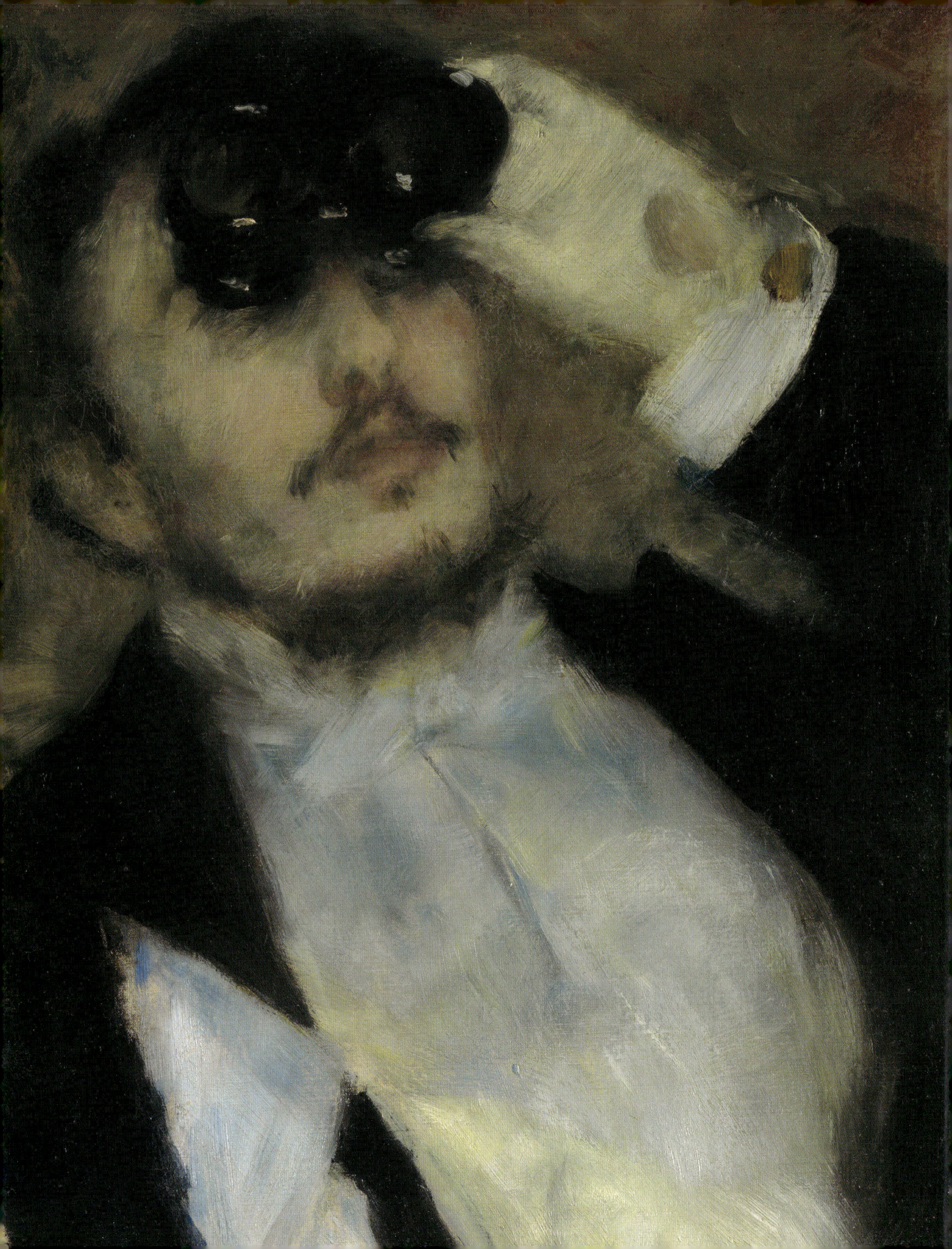

Selected Bibliography

For the essential bibliographical information on each of the Courtauld pictures, please see each painting's entry on the Courtauld Gallery collection website.

Bardell 2012
Michael Bardell, *Whither the Tired Mechanic Could Resort*, Braintree 2012

Blunt 1954
Anthony Blunt, 'Samuel Courtauld as a Collector and Benefactor', in Cooper 1954A, pp. 1–8

Braham 2003
Helen Braham, *A Century of Silver: The Courtauld Family of Silversmiths 1710–1780*, London 2003

Coleman 1969–80
D. C. Coleman, *Courtaulds: An Economic and Social history*, 3 vols, Oxford 1969–80

Cooper 1948
Douglas Cooper, 'The Courtauld Collection at the Tate Gallery', *Burlington Magazine*, vol. 90, no. 543, June 1948, pp. 170–3

Cooper 1954A
Douglas Cooper, *The Courtauld Collection*, London 1954

Cooper 1954B
Douglas Cooper, 'Catalogue of the Courtauld Collection', *Burlington Magazine*, vol. 96, no. 612, March 1954, pp. 119–122

Courtauld 1949
Samuel Courtauld, 'Art Education', in *Ideals and Industry. War-Time Papers*, Cambridge 1949

Crawford 1999
Elizabeth Crawford, 'The Courtauld Family', in *The Women's Suffrage Movement: A Reference Guide, 1866–1928*, London 1999, pp. 142–3

House 1994
John House, 'Modern French Art for the Nation: Samuel Courtauld's Collection and Patronage in Context', in London 1994, pp. 9–33

Korn 1996
Madeleine Korn, 'The Courtauld Gift – missing papers traced', *Burlington Magazine*, 138, April 1996, p. 256

Korn 2004
Madeleine Korn, 'Exhibitions of Modern French Art and their Influence on Collectors in Britain 1870–1918: the Davies sisters in context', *Journal of the History of Collections*, vol. 16, no. 2, 2004, pp. 191–218

London 1994
John House and John Murdoch, *Impressionism for England*, exh. cat., Courtauld Institute Galleries, London 1994

Murdoch 1994
John Murdoch, 'The Courtauld Family and its Money', in London 1994, pp. 47–55

Oliver 2004
Lois Oliver, *Boris Anrep: The National Gallery Mosaics*, London 2004

Salmon 2018
Dimitri Salmon, *Le Saint Joseph Charpentier de Georges de La Tour: un don au Louvre de Percy Moore Turner*, Ghent 2018

Sieveking 1957
Lance Sieveking, *The Eye of the Beholder*, London 1957

Spalding 1998
Frances Spalding, *The Tate: A History*, London 1998

Stephenson 1994
Andrew Stephenson, '"An Anatomy of Taste". Samuel Courtauld and Debates about Art Patronage and Modernism in Britain in the Inter-war Years', in London 1994, pp. 34–46

Tatlock 1926
Robert Tatlock, 'The Courtauld Trust', *Burlington Magazine*, vol. 48, no. 275, February 1926, pp. 57–65

Turner 2018
Sarah A. M. Turner, *Percy Moore Turner: Connoisseur, Impresario and Art Dealer*, London 2018

Weber (1904–5) 1932
Max Weber, *The Protestant Work Ethic and the Spirit of Capitalism (Die protestantische Ethik und der Geist des Kapitalismus)*, first published as a two-part article in 1904–5 (*Archiv für Sozialwissenschaft und Sozialpolitik*); first published in English in 1932

Wright 2008
Barnaby Wright, *The Courtauld Cézannes*, exh. cat., Courtauld Institute Galleries, London 2008

1923
August
Edouard Manet, *Corner of a Café-Concert*,
probably 1878–80, The National Gallery,
NG3858
Pierre-Auguste Renoir, *At the Theatre
(La Première Sortie)*, 1876–7, The National
Gallery, NG3859

October
Vincent van Gogh, *A Wheatfield, with Cypresses*,
1889, The National Gallery, NG3861

1924
January
Hilaire-Germain-Edgar Degas, *Young Spartans
Exercising*, about 1860, The National Gallery,
NG3860

February
Vincent van Gogh, *Sunflowers*, 1888,
The National Gallery, NG3863
Vincent van Gogh, *Van Gogh's Chair*, 1888,
The National Gallery, NG3862

March
Georges Seurat, *Bathers at Asnières*, 1884,
The National Gallery, NG3908

July
Claude Monet, *The Beach at Trouville*, 1870,
The National Gallery, NG3951

1925
October
Hilaire-Germain-Edgar Degas, *Miss La La at
the Cirque Fernando*, 1879, The National Gallery,
NG4121
Alfred Sisley, *Pont de Moret*, The National
Gallery, formerly NG4120, sold in 1927
to acquire Claude Monet, *The Water-Lily
Pond*, 1899, The National Gallery, NG4240.
Whereabouts of the Sisley currently
unknown.

November
Camille Pissarro, *The Boulevard Montmartre
at Night*, 1897, The National Gallery, NG4119

December
Pierre-Auguste Renoir, *Young Woman Bathing
(Nu dans l'Eau)*, about 1888, The National
Gallery, formerly NG4137, sold by the Tate in
1944, now at Pola Museum of Art, Hakone
Paul Cézanne, *Self Portrait*, about 1880–1,
The National Gallery, NG4135
Maurice Utrillo, *La Place du Tertre*, about 1910,
The National Gallery, formerly NG4139,
transferred to Tate, N04139
Pierre Bonnard, *The Table*, 1925, The National
Gallery, formerly NG4134, transferred to Tate,
N04134
Alfred Sisley, *The Watering Place at Marly-le-Roi*,
probably 1875, The National Gallery, NG4138

1926
January
Paul Cézanne, *Hillside in Provence*, about
1890–2, The National Gallery, NG4136

March
Hilaire-Germain-Edgar Degas, *Portrait
of Elena Carafa*, about 1875, The National
Gallery, NG4167

May
Henri de Toulouse-Lautrec, *Woman Seated in
a Garden*, 1891, The National Gallery, NG4186
Vincent van Gogh, *Long Grass with Butterflies*,
1890, The National Gallery, NG4169

June
Hilaire-Germain-Edgar Degas, *Ballet Dancers*,
about 1880–1900, The National Gallery,
NG4168

1927
March
Claude Monet, *The Water-Lily Pond*, 1899,
The National Gallery, NG4240 (acquired in
part-exchange for Alfred Sisley, *Pont de Moret*,
The National Gallery, formerly NG4120,
acquired in October 1925).

Bought through partial aid from the Courtauld
Fund [with the remainder of the money]:

1932
Camille Pissarro, *The Louvre under Snow*, 1902,
The National Gallery, NG4671

1939
André Dunoyer de Segonzac, *La Route de
Grimaud (The Road from Grimaud)*, 1937, pen
and ink and watercolour on paper, Tate,
N05043, partly bought from the Courtauld
Fund

Acquired by the Tate with the proceeds of
the sale of Renoir's *Young Woman Bathing*,
The National Gallery, formerly NG4137 (sold
in 1944):

1949
Pablo Picasso, *Seated Female Nude (Femme nue
assise)*, 1909–10, Tate, N05904
Henri Matisse, *Notre-Dame*, about 1900, Tate,
N05905

1954
Pierre-Auguste Renoir, *Moulin Huet Bay,
Guernsey*, about 1883, The National Gallery,
NG6204

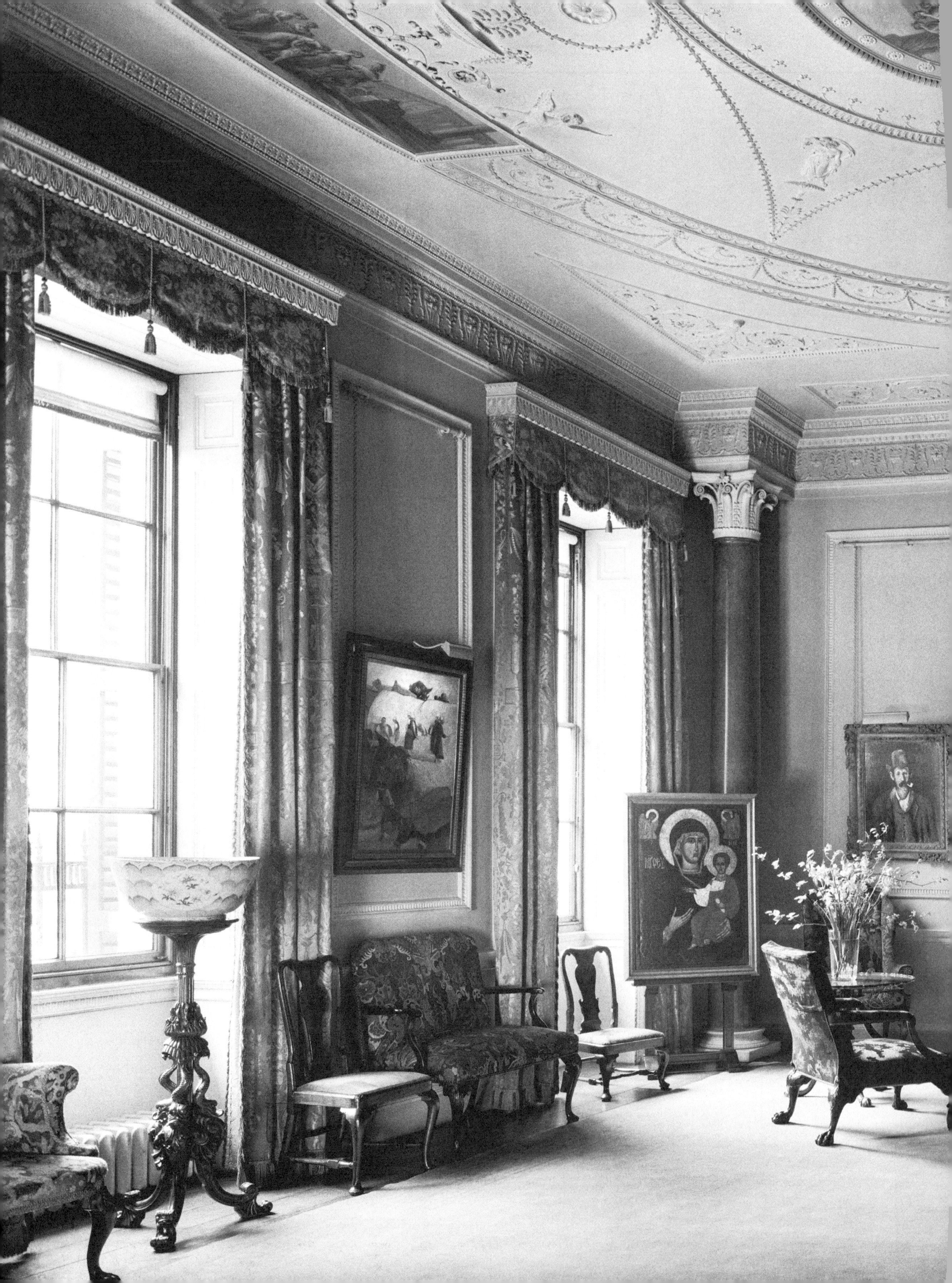